Chart
Garza Family

D1244594

t wife, Gertrudis Becerra)
s Becerra)

a Garza (last male heir to occupy Rancho
Bontan   Alamito lands)

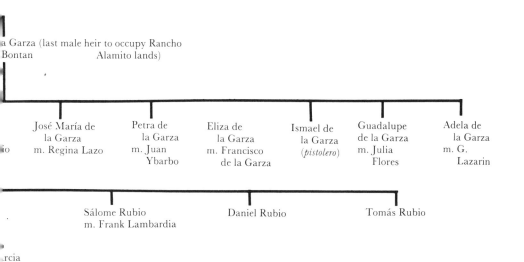

| José María de la Garza m. Regina Lazo | Petra de la Garza m. Juan Ybarbo | Eliza de la Garza m. Francisco de la Garza | Ismael de la Garza (*pistolero*) | Guadalupe de la Garza m. Julia Flores | Adela de la Garza m. G. Lazarin |

Sálome Rubio
m. Frank Lambardia

Daniel Rubio

Tomás Rubio

rcia

eleven children including . . .

Abel Rubio (author)

Stolen Heritage

Stolen Heritage

A Mexican-American's
Rediscovery of His Family's
Lost Land Grant

Abel G. Rubio

Edited and with foreword by
Thomas H. Kreneck

EAKIN PRESS
Austin, Texas

FIRST EDITION

Copyright © 1986
By Abel G. Rubio

Published in the United States of America
By Eakin Press, P.O. Box 23066, Austin, Texas 78735

ALL RIGHTS RESERVED. No part of this book may be repro-
duced in any form without written permission from the publisher,
except for brief passages included in a review appearing in a news-
paper or magazine.

ISBN 0-89015-548-8

Library of Congress Cataloging-in-Publication Data

Rubio, Abel G., 1929–
    Stolen Heritage

    1. Mexicans — Texas. 2. Becerra family. 3. Land grants — Texas. 4. Garza
family. I. Title.
F395.M5R8 1986 929.2'0973 85-32070
ISBN 0-89015-548-8

To the memory of two of my cherished ancestors, great-grandfather Antonio de la Garza, Refugio County, Texas, cattleman of the 1860s and 1870s, and his beloved wife, my great-grandmother, Ponposa Bontan, for being ultimately responsible for my seeing the light of day; and for having been so grievously wronged.

Contents

Foreword

I have often wished that the Mexicans, or some one who had their confidence, could have gone among them and got their stories of the raids and counter raids [in South Texas]. I am sure that these stories would take on a different color and tone.

> Walter Prescott Webb,
> January 1963, two months
> before his death

In the development of the United States from the late eighteenth century until the early twentieth century with its urbanization, sophistication of labor and industry, and rise of the professions, land ownership was fundamental to personal wealth, status, and power. Owning or controlling land was an essential factor in determining an individual's place in society. Moreover, it was central to the vision of opportunity and expectation. The desire for land ownership primarily motivated frontier westward expansion, the core of the American experience. Much of American character and its world view has been configured by the continual quest for land from the Cumberland Gap to the Pacific Ocean. When, in 1890, the Bureau of the Census officially declared that a frontier no longer existed within the continental United States, the news created a mental crisis that was discussed in the highest intellectual circles of the nation. Even the most urban-dwelling American still defines his position in society partly in terms of land possession, mainly in the form of home ownership.

Nothing was more important to an individual's place in Texas society during the nineteenth century than land, either for agricultural pursuits or for speculation. It formed the basis of most individual empires and underscored personal security for a family and its descendants.

vii

Central to the vision of opportunity which brought the first non-Hispanic settlers to Texas in the early 1820s was the promise of owning land. The Spanish and then the Mexican governments' promises of land to the individual, through *empresarios,* swelled the population of Texas from the original Old Three Hundred of Stephen F. Austin to over 30,000 by the eve of the Texas Revolution. Texas in the 1820s and 1830s was a large and virtually unoccupied territory. Most Texas lands were open, and the settlers had much to choose from. Only the Indian stood in the way of settlement, and this barrier, formidable though it was, receded decade by decade until only an obscure handful of red men remained on Texas soil. The majority were either exterminated or removed to regions outside the borders. Chief Bowles and his Cherokees and their affiliate tribes along the Angelina and Neches Rivers in East Texas serve as perhaps the most startling example of land dispossession in early Texas history. Bowles and his people claimed thousands of acres of rich farming ground. During the Texas Republic, however, these Indians were systematically and brutally driven from their homes north across the Red River by government forces so that the region could be utilized by mainstream Texan society.

Although the Indians gave way to the new order of things, there were other people occupying coveted land in Texas prior to Anglo usurpation. A century of Hispanic claim to *Tejas* left a residue of settlement in places as far east as Nacogdoches and as far west as El Paso del Norte. Most of the several thousand Hispanics in Texas, who can be referred to as *Tejanos,* lived in the southern and southwestern regions. Their northeastern border included the line from Refugio to Goliad and San Antonio. In these villages and their outlying regions, there existed an indigenous *ranchero* culture that had done its share to neutralize its predecessors, the Indians. There was little in Texas to lure the Hispanic north of the Rio Grande in those years, and the population remained relatively small though secure on land grants from the Spanish and Mexican governments.

The *Tejano* population was veritably inundated by Anglo immigration after 1821. By the end of the Texas Republic, if not earlier, the *Tejanos,* as a group, had lost the economic, social, and political prominence they had once possessed. By the end of the nineteenth century, ownership of the land, even in South Texas, changed from Spanish surnames to the non-Hispanic newcomers. Land was the object of desire in the territory south and southwest of the Refugio-Goliad-San Antonio line just as it was in the rest of United States development.

While the vast majority of the present Hispanic population in Texas originated with the Mexican Revolution of 1910 and the resultant immigration northward, there is still a relatively small but viable group of residents who can claim direct descent from this pre-1820 *Tejano* population. They can rightfully claim to be the first non-Indian culture in the state. Especially strong among these *Tejano* descendants is the traditional view of land dispossession of the nineteenth-century Texas Mexicans — a view that, in its generalities, remains in the standard histories on the subject. That view holds that with the inundation of Texas by non-Hispanic immigrants, especially from the United States and numbering around 100,000 people by 1846, life was never again the same for the *Tejanos*. After the region changed hands in 1836 and again in 1846 with annexation by the United States, the *rancheros Tejanos* began to lose their lands from San Antonio to Port Isabel. The *Tejanos* witnessed a change to Anglo laws, language, administrative system, and values, all of which were alien to them. Soon after the American army under General Zachary Taylor came to the Rio Grande area in 1846 to fight a war with Mexico, non-Hispanic merchants and cattle barons penetrated the region. Through business practices, both legal and unscrupulous, legal maneuvering, shifty lawyers, discrimination, and physical intimidation and violence, the land changed ownership in South Texas. The *Tejanos* were dispossessed of their landed heritage. The Treaty of Guadalupe Hidalgo, ending the Mexican War in 1848 and supposedly structured to protect their rights, actually signaled their demise as a people of property and standing. While today many non-Hispanic families in Texas were handed a legacy by forebears who in the nineteenth century accumulated land and wealth from the virgin territory, the twentieth-century descendants of the original *Tejanos* were left bitter memories from having been stripped of their property, now in this century to struggle for survival with the recent Mexican immigrants often as part of an underclass in Texan society. Their position in America was largely determined by the loss of their ancestral land. So strong is this traditional belief that several thousand of these descendants banded together as the *reclamantes* to file suit reclaiming their titles to lost properties.

Such is the generality of *Tejano* land dispossession. It is based on a condition and the end results. But generalities must be based on specific cases. Who specifically was unjustly deprived of their property, and what exactly was the process by which this dispossession took place? What were the precise steps, honest, dishonest, or unscrupulous, taken by which individuals against what families over which specific pieces of land? The historian who seeks the truth, no matter how elusive it may be, or how great his sympathies are, must call for more than generalities. That is the importance of this book by Abel Rubio.

Abel Rubio, a direct descendant of Manuel Becerra, one of the more prominent of those early *Tejanos*, has provided us with a case study of South Texas land dispossession. Rubio examines the ownership of a piece of South Texas property from its original federal Mexican land grant in 1832 to Manuel Becerra, to the 1870s when Becerra's grandchildren, members of the historic de la Garza family, were driven from what they had retained of that acreage. The grant, without question, involved at least 8,856 acres in present Refugio County, and this book deals precisely with how it became alienated from its Mexican owners during one of the most violent periods of South Texas history. It is the story of how this 8,856 acres of land changed ownership from the *Tejano* to the non-Hispanic after the American Civil War during the years of economic penetration of the region by the newcomers. His conclusions about land dispossession in this specific case are startling and thought-provoking. Finally driven from the last 2,214 acres that the grandchildren occupied, the family would inherit poverty instead of landed wealth.

The case of the dispossession of the Becerra descendants during the 1870s offers an informed Mexican-American perspective of those turbulent years. Historians have noted that after 1865, there was much violence against *Tejanos* — a reflection of the community feuds, agrarian discontent, vigilantism, and general outlawry of the Reconstruction period. The numerous shootings and lynchings of Mexicans in South Texas were often in retaliation for alleged outrages against Anglo residents, but were carried out indiscriminately and with the vengeance of a race war. Certainly, there was little consideration for due process of law. The late 1860s and 1870s was an era of lynch law that has prompted historian Arnoldo De Leon to conclude that it is impossible to determine the exact number of *Tejanos* who were victimized.

Within this context of terror during the mid-1870s, Abel Rubio's story of his ancestors in Refugio County takes on broader meaning. Between 1874 and 1877, when his family's troubles were most severe, the Refugio County region was experiencing virulent persecution of its *Tejano* residents. Vigilante groups from Refugio, Goliad, and Nueces counties scoured the countryside and brutalized Mexican herdsmen and farmers. Rubio's ancestors clearly were victims of such outrages. His explanation of how local Refugio County non-Hispanics came to possess the Becerra grant, however, adds an important dimension to the history of this period and suggests an underlying economic motivation for the expulsion of Tejanos.

My association as editor for this volume began on a June day in 1980, when I telephoned Abel to respond to his request for help at the Houston Metropolitan Research Center of the Houston Public Library. He told me that he was seeking professional assistance in editing a manuscript he was in the process of writing. He explained that he was not a historian, but a retired Marine who now worked as an accountant.

In my work as a public historian for over four years, I have encountered at least 200 laymen who claimed that they were "writing books" about the history of their families. None of the people, I should add, ever completed their projects; the difficulty of such a task always outstripped their ability and enthusiasm. Abel was the sole exception. He began to send me chapters for review.

Abel was researching and writing his book with a determination that I had rarely seen equaled even in the history graduate programs I had attended. His inner motivation and sincerity were the first things I began to understand. He went about his task with the determination of a Marine (which he was with distinction for twenty years) and with the meticulousness of an accountant (which he is today). As his vocations also suggest, Abel was no "radical," but a stalwart, law-abiding citizen who did not start out to find fault with the system or its past.

His determination sprang from an obsession — his obsession to find out and reveal exactly what had happened to his family's ancestral land grant in South Texas. He was a man who had made a profound discovery that began to torment his life. He came more and more to believe that he had uncovered an injustice against his family, and he was bound to reveal that injustice to the world.

As I labored over the chapters of his manuscript, I discovered that Abel knew the facts of the Becerra land grant as thoroughly as was humanly possible. I posed him no question regarding vagueness or apparent discrepancies in the text that he could not clarify with the evidence he had amassed. He held speculation to a minimum. When he did conjecture, it seemed based on sound reasoning and interpretation of the data. I came to have faith in his powers of analysis not because of his personality but because of the soundness of his argument.

He necessarily places great emphasis on the details which trace the ownership of the acreage. These facts, obscured by the passage of more than a hundred years since they occurred, form a complex story. Indeed, the narrative at times may seem convoluted to the reader because the author has written his book in a most interesting manner which chronologically follows the course of his own discovery and research since 1972. It is written in the first person and likewise reveals his personal, introspective journey.

Often his research left him at loose ends; his suspicions led him to more original documents and soul-searching, which again piqued his curiosity and led him to further research. His search was seldom a neat package as he uncovered family legend and documentary records to unravel the story of the lost land. Regardless of its complexity, this work draws coherent, penetrating conclusions. The supporting evidence of his central thesis is intricate because it is a case study which seeks to go beyond sweeping generalizations about *Tejano* lands.

Abel garnered much of his evidence from documentary materials such as county records, maps, standard histories, and printed primary sources. With the written records fundamental to his research, he gathered rich oral tradition from elder family members who had heard the stories again and again from their elders, Mexican-Americans who had lived through harsh times on the Texas frontier. He wisely sorted through this family oral history to separate fact from error to ascertain that essential kernel of truth from oral reminiscence, which is always a difficult but rewarding task.

He has thus done, in one particular case, what Walter Prescott Webb, the dean of Texas historians, wished for over twenty years ago; that is, that a sympathetic listener go among the Mexican-Americans and get their side of the story about the troubled years when the Hispanic and non-Hispanic people in Texas met and conflicted.

Although Abel's discovery and research might raise particular legal questions, my concern is that of Webb's — to understand the past. My desire, as a Texas historian, is to understand what Rubio illumines about South Texas history between 1832 and 1900, especially the methods of property accumulation as well as what implications this information has on the present broader condition of Texas Mexicans. Land dispossession was indeed a central experience for *Tejanos* in those years with dire consequences for them in the twentieth century. Was the example of the heirs of Manuel Becerra the actuality of the many? Only future research can tell us for sure; however, Abel Rubio has provided us with a point of departure.

As a Texas historian who seeks the subjective reality of the elusive past, I considered it my professional obligation to perform the duties of editor of this manuscript. It should be made clear, however, that this book is entirely that of Abel Rubio. The book contains his statement, his ideas, not mine. The service I rendered was largely of form not substance. I am convinced, however, that his *research* is pure, but of course the ultimate conclusions drawn are entirely Rubio's.

Centering around the status of a tract of South Texas property, this book, often introspective, spans the generations of Mexican-American existence as they are reflected in a man's mind and extended family. These people were not gentle "salt of the earth" immigrant Mexican people, but salty, old-time Texans born of the ranching tradition with its hard and violent elements. These people, like their non-Hispanic contemporaries on the frontier, were always rugged and often ill-tempered. Such were Manuel Becerra and his descendants, the de la Garza, Rubio, Martinez, and Bontan families. Among the generations of these important families mentioned in the text, the reader will note an interconnectedness with Texas history from the late eighteenth century until the present.

Rubio's work is a study in Mexican-American rediscovery.

The discovery of a missing piece of ancestral land by Abel Rubio and his relatives led him to rediscover their kinship back over 150 years and their relationship with their region's past. In the process of such rediscovery, Rubio and others in the family became possessed by a righteous indignation — an indignation not of "sore losers" but of people dispossessed of something that was theirs. As they attained this self-discovery, they came together in a common struggle to claim their lost heritage. Rubio outlines this family organization, the Manuel Becerra Family Association, at great length.

As historical case study and expression of Hispanic literature, Rubio's volume is also a cry for continuing reassessment and justice, an important element of the collective consciousness of Mexican-Americans in Texas, perhaps nationwide. On a visceral level is their belief that they were dispossessed of their portion of this nation's bounty by having what was initially theirs taken away. This feeling transcends the idea that they were simply targets of prejudice and forms of resentment at the pit of the conscious mind that only accentuates the 150 years of continual discrimination in Anglo-American society.

The rejoinder, given by the insensitive, to this feeling of dispossession, might include "Well, so were the Indians." The native Americans, however, are simply not analogous to the Mexican-Americans as the latter is an urban, aware, dynamic, involved, and integral part of our society — as well as a segment that is *growing*. Their increasing importance in the United States and their view of land dispossession in the nineteenth-century Southwest necessitates recognition by the larger society if America is to undergo inevitable change and continue tranquilly to exist. Admission is the first step toward atonement, and American society must bring subliminal suspicions to the surface to remain healthy. Because land has always been so important to Americans, all Americans, we must continue to discuss the nature and history of its ownership. Abel Rubio has made a valuable contribution to that dialogue.

THOMAS H. KRENECK, Ph.D.
Houston, Texas

Acknowledgments

Among the fine people who assisted me during the research, and who gave of their time unhesitantly, are Lanell Aston, Records Section, General Land Office, for helping me with the old maps of Refugio County; Virginia Taylor, archivist/historian, Spanish Collection, General Land Office, for copies of the Spanish documents; Ruth B. Pickle of the State Comptroller's Office, Microfilm Department, for the tax rolls of Refugio County; Benito Martinez, for his general aid and comfort; and María Carmona, for her splendid assistance in arranging the index.

Special thanks are due to Jack Jackson, artist/historian, for his fine artistic works; to Lucille Fagan Snider, for assisting in locating the old cemeteries in Refugio County; to Sálome Rubio de Lambardia, for relating to me our fascinating family history; to Tomás Rubio, for our family history and excellent stories involving his grandfather Antonio de la Garza; to Daniel Rubio, for telling me of the de la Garza gunfight at La Bahía; to Romana de la Garza, for family genealogy; to Rafael de la Garza, for family history and tales of old-time Mexican *vaqueros;* and to Don Plácido Martinez, for providing the tragic story of his mother Paula Lozano (who lived on a remote *rancho* in Refugio County in 1877) and no less tragic, more information on the dispossession of Antonio de la Garza and his sister, Trinidad de la Garza, and the final wresting away of our ancestor's land grant.

Becky Caplen, a business teacher at San Jacinto College in Deer Park, Texas, edited the original manuscript for proper English grammar. She began this Herculean task in February 1979. She has typed all the revised manuscripts since that time. Her task was made more difficult because Mrs. Caplen had to perform her editing work from the handwritten first manuscript. She did an admirable job from beginning to end, and I am very grateful to her.

Dr. Thomas H. Kreneck, historian at the Houston Metropolitan Research Center, Houston, Texas, first saw only half of the original manuscript in June 1980. He was keenly impressed with these first six chapters, and knowing that I was not a journalist or a historian, immediately advised that I continue preparing the manuscript as I had started. He advised that I not deviate from the present course. By the time the entire manuscript was typed, Dr. Kreneck was deeply interested in the project. He edited and arranged it into book form. Professor Kreneck felt then and even more so now that the story of our family should be brought to the American public. He has remained constantly by my side offering advice and encouragement, particularly when I experienced depressing moods and suffered mental anguish in completing such a complex project. Dr. Kreneck is not only a Texan historian but is a champion of the underdog, in this case a Mexican-American family whose ancestors explored and settled in the Texas wilderness over 200 years ago. I am deeply grateful to him for spending hundreds upon hundreds of hours reorganizing this work prepared by an amateur researcher/historian and bringing it into proper perspective.

Introduction

This volume came into existence by a quirk of fate and my own intense curiosity to discover the unrecorded history of a family and the land they settled and occupied during the nineteenth century. It is a history of my people which focuses around a lost Mexican land grant that came into the possession of my family over 150 years ago. This land grant, issued in 1832 by the Mexican government to Manuel Becerra, my direct ancestor, in what is now South Texas, comprised 8,856 acres (though some records indicate that it may have included nearly 11,000 acres).

Manuel Becerra's descendants in the twentieth century possess none of this ancestral property, even though much of it was never conveyed to anyone outside the family. My discovery of this lost land grant and my search to determine its history and status drew me, and my extended family, into an almost fanatical endeavor that has lasted over a decade. I have tried to make this book a record of how I methodically and relentlessly pursued this lost land as well as the often unrecorded and neglected Mexican heritage in Texas. Although I never seriously considered giving up in my quest over the years, looking back, there were times when it may have been the prudent thing to do.

Spanish and Mexican land grants are uniquely fascinating. The Spaniards who first came to the New World, and later the Mexicans, devised a land distribution system unparalleled in the history of North America. It was established to entice hardy colonists to settle in inhospitable regions. The originators of this program of granting land could not have known that their system would one day become, in the present-day United States Southwest, the object of bloody contests of wills between the Mexicans and the Anglo-Americans who came in from the northeast. The Mexican government proved even more generous than the Spanish in granting lands to foreigners. Much has been written about these land grants. Some people have tended to romanticize them. Such unfortunate romanticization is a myth because the truth is that those lands, granted so long ago by the Spanish and Mexican governments, often ran red with the blood of the original Mexican grantees or their descendants, as I was to discover in the case of the Becerra grant. It seems as if those land grant documents, now just old, yellowish manuscripts with curious writing, were "instruments of the devil," for the result was often violence and bloodshed.

Perhaps my research and this book could establish a precedent for others to locate lost land grants in their family. I am especially concerned about sharing my knowledge as a guide for other descendants of original grantees who may have had the misfortune of losing their ancestral lands to land-grabbers and speculators. I believe that the diligent researcher can uncover deception, murder, and other vile practices that were resorted to over 100 years ago to deprive people of their lands. Researchers must, however, be unyielding in their efforts. They must be persistent and have a strong belief in the family honor for a successful investigation. Prayers and personal sacrifice also play a role in such an endeavor.

This narrative is not a standard history of Texas because it was never intended as such. But how can one write about an old-time frontier Texas family without involving the entire region and its society? The early Mexican families that are included in this work were a rare breed of people — spirited, hard-core Texans from the rowels of their spurs to the crowns of their *sombreros*. They withstood the onslaught of Indian tribes and other perils of the wilds north of the Rio Grande. Their most difficult challenge came, however, with the opening of immigration to Texas by Stephen F. Austin. For my family that was the beginning of the end.

This study is based on documentary sources and countless interviews and notes taken during those interviews with elderly family members, one of whom was ninety-three years of age. I found that their stories were surprisingly precise when they could be compared to the written record.

This volume is primarily a history of the early Texan Don Manuel Becerra and his descendants. Becerra was born in La Bahía in 1765 and lived almost to the mid-nineteenth century. He was an explorer in Texas, an Indian fighter, colonizer, large *ranch-*

ero, statesman with the local native American tribes, and a public man in La Bahía and Refugio, Texas, during both the Spanish and Mexican regimes. He was endowed with courage and an unbreakable spirit which were prerequisites for survival in a remote frontier. Becerra was one of the first native-born Texas Mexicans to gain firsthand knowledge of the character of the Anglo-American settlers in that region when he served as guide for Stephen F. Austin and his companions. As a portent of things to come, Becerra reported to his superiors that these newcomers were "not what they purport to be," and he felt they would be of more harm than benefit to Mexico.

This book likewise deals with the de la Garza family of La Bahía and Refugio. They were contemporaries of Becerra, but they were, if possible, even more rawhide tough. They were noble and gallant frontiersmen who held their lands against all comers in the early and mid-1800s. The head of this clan, Don Carlos de la Garza, and his brothers were deeply involved in the turbulent times of the Texas Revolution. The family itself was split in its loyalty — a faction supported the Texas rebels while another part remained loyal to Mexico. Tragically, this division among the family could only have come from Mexico's long neglect of these Mexican frontiersmen. Left unprotected on the frontier by their government and surrounded by savage tribes, some members of the de la Garza family had no recourse but to turn their backs on their own family and government. But their story is inseparable from that of Manuel Becerra because of family ties and the land grant.

By the 1870s the de la Garza brothers and Becerra were long dead, but their sons and grandsons carried on their tradition. As their parents, the later generation led turbulent lives of violence and hardship. Theirs too is a story that is powerful and tragic, poignant and nostalgic. Peace never came easy for this Texas Mexican family.

This book chronicles the lives of family members who were farmers, soldiers, peace officers, ranchers, and, the most colorful of all, *vaqueros*. They all played a part in the story of the lost lands. These people were witnesses to hangings, cold-blooded murders, and intimidation of their own kinsmen, my ancestors, in the stormiest days of Texas history, especially for the Mexican Texan.

As my search for the lost Becerra land grant developed, I evidenced a change of attitude. The discovery of murders, persecution, prejudice, and brutal injustices against my ancestors deeply affected me. All these crimes were committed for the acquisition of a mere piece of land by non-Hispanics in the Refugio County region of Texas. I made it my mission to uncover the facts and drag the names of the offenders into the light of day as best as could be done. That task was an insatiable obsession. Often the facts eluded me, but I persevered until I believe I have uncovered and arranged the story in understandable form. The story is nothing less than the rape of a Mexican land grant.

The land-grabber in nineteenth-century Texas was powerful and ruthless, cunning as a weasel, and often a supposedly respected member of the region where he lived. His respectability was only an illusion. To me, he was in fact *el diablo,* the devil. Few knew of the land-grabber's activities except the people who were his prey deep in the woods, away from town and other people. His victims most times never had a chance to tell their story. Some of the victims did not survive these depredations. The land-grabber resorted to fraud, murder, intimidation, persecution, and manipulation of the law. The unfortunate souls who fell victim to these unscrupulous villains were in most instances unsuspecting Mexican-Americans. This, I believe, was certainly the case at least with my ancestors because Becerra's grandchildren, Antonio de la Garza and his sister, bore the brunt of the land-grabbers' wrath in the 1870s and were driven from their land. My ancestors probably never realized how neatly they were swindled out of their property; but over 100 years later I uncovered as many of the evil details as is probably possible. These facts I will submit to you the reader for your judgment.

The Becerra-de la Garza descendants banded together into a formal association in the mid-1970s with the object of reclaiming their lost land grant. This book reveals that process and the numerous trials and tribulations our family has experienced in that effort. As the reader will see, wresting the land away from those people who currently occupy the land (descendants of the one who came into possession of the property in 1875) has become an almost insurmountable challenge — one fraught with difficulties at every turn. In this regard, this book is about the continuing saga of our family which began in Texas long before the Anglo-American came to the area. Destiny struck cruel blows at our family in the 1800s, but destiny also decreed that we contemporary descendants methodically quest for our lost lands. In an attempt to fulfill that destiny, I want this book to establish a link between our generations past and present. In doing so, I learned a great deal about our history and even more about myself. It is impossible to explore one without understanding the other.

[1]

The Search Begins

The scene before my eyes was like a horrible nightmare. An eleven-year-old at the time, I stood petrified and unable to comprehend the terrifying sight. It must have been true, though, for the seven caskets arranged in a semicircle contained the remains of my father, Guillermo Rubio; my mother, Estefanita Lopez Garcia; three sisters, Sofia, Elena, and Teresita; and two of my brothers, Rosendo and two-year-old Ramón, whose little coffin lay between those of my father and mother.

This unforgettable day was the afternoon of June 15, 1942, at the Artero Memorial Funeral Home in Victoria, Texas. The tragedy occurred about midnight of June 14 at the Port Lavaca causeway. It was one of the worst automobile accidents in Texas history involving a single family. Three drunken Anglos caused the accident and left the scene, later surrendering to the sheriff of Port Lavaca. The only children who survived were those who fortunately were at home or elsewhere — Sálome, Guadalupe, Guillermo, Daniel, Josephine, and myself. The day was hot and the humidity was nearly 100 percent; the sweet odor from so many flowers about the room was nauseating. In spitè of the heat, I felt a cold sweat, and the hair on the back of my neck seemed to rise. Then I remembered

1

our dogs at the farm. When they were scared, their hair stood straight up, including the strands on their tails, with the possible exception being my tiny hairless Mexican dog who was nearly devoid of all hair. For that reason I called him Pelón. The thought of Pelón was the only thing that gave me comfort at the funeral home.

There was a huge throng of people inside and outside. Many were standing and smoking close to the nearby railroad tracks. They were relatives and friends alike, as well as strangers who had come to pay respects.

It seemed as if I remained rooted to the same place for an eternity. Finally, I moved closer to view my loved ones beginning with Father. The tears began to flow, although very slowly at first. After seeing Father and moving as if in a trance, I paused by the tiny casket of the chubby baby boy, Ramón. My first instinct was to reach out and touch his little face and hands.

Dreading every second, I came to Mother's casket. Salty tears began to flow like water. I lovingly and tenderly touched her face and for the first time noticed that she had gray hair. For a long moment I remained by her casket and remembered how loving she had been to us.

By the time I arrived at the seventh casket containing my youngest sister, Teresita, my knees felt as weak as the rubber on my slingshot. The ordeal had been terrifying, and I hurried from this death scene feeling somewhat ashamed to have people see me crying, for I considered myself *macho*.

The women's wailing was frightening. I remembered that the grown folk used to say the sorrowful screams and wailing of a woman resembled those of a *pantera* (panther) in a dark night.

I felt cold beads of perspiration on my forehead and upper lip, and my body was covered with goose pimples. I sought out Uncle Tomás Rubio and his wife, Juanita Gonzales, for comfort and safety. They abundantly gave me, their orphaned nephew, the love and affection I sought. Women kinfolk embraced me and offered encouragement. I noticed that their eyes appeared puffy and red from crying, the free-flowing tears thoroughly ruining their mascara. My young mind told me that these women resembled *brujas en la noche* (witches in the night), and a confrontation face to face with any of them in a dark night would end in total disaster for me. Swiftly removing myself from this throng, I headed toward the nearby railroad tracks and trees, for I wished to be alone. Then I saw an uncle tipping a huge whiskey bottle and, after taking a long pull, passing it on to one of his cohorts. The man grabbed the bottle and began to take the longest drink, in competition with his *amigo*. When all the liquid spirits had been expertly drained from the bottle, one of them threw the empty bottle near where I was standing. Then they lit up their cigarettes and belched the whiskey they had consumed. All seemed keenly disappointed that there was no more whiskey to be had, at least for the moment. They appeared to be wavering from side to side as they walked, and I marveled that the contents of the bottle made these men stumble like plow horses on the farm.

Rosary was said early in the evening with the priest chanting masses for my departed loved ones. The priest simply stated that God had called this branch of the Rubio family. Standing in a corner, sullen and bitter, I wondered why God had called on the young and innocent.

Aunt María Ybarbo fixed a bed for me and my brother, Guadalupe, in one of the upstairs rooms. Several times during the night I awoke to the sad and lonely whistle of the passing trains. To this day I can vividly recall the first night at the Artero Funeral Home, and each time I hear the whistle of a train I always remember the night of June 15, 1942.

The mile-long funeral procession from Victoria to La Bahía was a spectacle in itself because instead of the usual one hearse there were four. Before crossing the bridge on the San Antonio River, I caught a glimpse of Presidio La Bahía, though I didn't know its name at the time, and then heard the bells begin tolling. These were the saddest sounds I had heard in my youthful life. The priests in their long, black robes began the Mass in the beautiful Chapel of Our Lady of Loreto.

The elder priest said that Guillermo Rubio, who had been baptized there in 1888, and his wife and children had returned to the place of beginning. I would have never believed that one day this ancient Spanish fortress would become the point of my own beginning again. I, nonetheless, was observant of all that was going on. Undoubtedly, the man who performed one of the most painful tasks during these days was Uncle Tomás Rubio. The awesome job of digging the seven graves fell on his broad shoulders. The sweat-drained Rubio wept as he dug the tiny grave for his two-year-old nephew, Ramón, whose place of rest was between my mother and father.

The final earthly journey for my loved ones was but a short one from Our Lady of Loreto to the Rubio cemetery directly behind the old *presidio* some 400 yards away. There were seven graves awaiting seven mortal remains, and my instinct was to view the little grave of Ramón. While the priest was chanting the final Mass for the departed, I could clearly hear a great many sobs from the womenfolk, some weeping uncontrollably. It seemed as if their moans of anguish became shrieks, and again I thought of the *pantera*.

When the service ended, and upon a nod from the priest, I reached down and took a handful of soil as was the custom. As I walked by my father's grave, I released some of it upon his casket. Pausing a long moment by the tiny casket of Ramón, I released more dirt than perhaps I should have. By far, the most painful and terrifying moment came when I paused by my mother's grave; for by then my eyes were full of tears. The torment and sorrow were great because this was the moment of truth which I somehow endured. By the time I reached the seventh grave there was just a little dirt in my hand; and due to the tears obstructing my sight, I did not know whether I cast those final particles upon the casket of my sister, Elena.

With a final glance at the seven caskets, I moved far away down the dirt road to grieve beside a line of trees. I could see the rustlings of the leaves and hear the mournful sounds created by the wind. Turning to the right, I caught glimpses through the moving branches of the massive stone chapel with the cross. In this hour of grief, I was strangely fascinated with the building and its cross. When I rejoined the procession, I kept staring until we crossed the San Antonio River. As we drove up a slight rise on the road to town, I looked back through the rear window of the car and saw the cross. High above the cross I noticed many large clouds partially obscuring the sun and moving rapidly by the force of the winds. The sun's rays that penetrated to earth seemed truly the arms of God reaching from the heavens.

Some thirty years later, while residing with my family in California, I received notice that my brother-in-law, Antonio Flores, had died on September 30, 1971, in Houston.

I immediately made preparations so that I could be with my sister, Josephine Rubio, and her children in Texas. Josephine, the daughter of Guillermo Rubio and Estefanita Lopez Garcia, was born in Goliad on April 4, 1918. Her husband, Antonio, was born on June 16, 1903, in Fannin, the oldest son of Eugino Flores and Euginia Longoria, both of whom I had known since my earliest youth. During the early stages of my life, Antonio and Josephine were responsible for my proper guidance and I generally considered them my parents. Without their guidance my life might well have turned out to have been a wayward one. Poor though they were, these two never once turned their faces away from me, and I shall always be grateful to them.

The night before my departure for California I met with my cousin, Guadalupe (Core) Rubio, and his wife Olga. It was good to see my first cousin again after so many years. Quite late in the evening, Core told me about some documents he had in his possession, which he had received from one of our relatives, Romana de la Garza, of Beeville. The old documents pertained to a Mexican land grant once owned by one of our direct ancestors. Very vaguely I recalled hearing about some land the family owned in Goliad County which only amounted to three acres.

Core assured me in a somber tone that this was an entirely different matter. He carefully explained that the old documents now in his possession represented a land grant given to our sixth-generation grandfather, Don Manuel Becerra, in 1832. The land grant was from the Mexican government, although he was unaware of its nature or the acreage involved. We knew, though, that land grants involved large tracts of land.

I was surprised on hearing about this new discovery in our family, but the ancient pieces of paper were a thing from out of the past and were promptly forgotten. The following day I took a plane to California. What Core told me, I suspected, was a tall tale, for I had not seen any documents to substantiate his statements. Few Mexicans in Texas or anywhere else in the Southwest owned even portions of land grants; these grants were solidly under the control of Anglo-Americans. To attempt to wrest away any portion of land from Anglo-Americans and particularly by Mexicans was foolhardy. This would be like a bold but stupid field mouse walking into the powerful jaws of a black-maned African lion. I felt that such false illusions should best be forgotten, and the quicker the better.

But I could not forget the name, Manuel Becerra. What would be the consequences to the family if this were indeed a real Mexican land grant which might actually have been passed down to the other ancestors from the original grantee, Manuel Becerra? If this purported land grant was genuine in its entirety, why then had not the family made a serious attempt to reclaim it in years past? To begin a search now would be an awesome task, including responsibility for the individual who led the way. The costs, always inevitable, could very well reach astronomical proportions. The vast majority of the Becerra descendants were very poor; many or most having lived in abject poverty in the past, sustaining the family on a day-to-day basis to survive. The elder members lived on fixed incomes, and the costs already described could not be afforded.

With the passage of weeks I began with increasing frequency to think about the land grant. I was quite curious by the middle of March 1972 and contacted Core Rubio, expressing a desire to see the documents for myself. He eagerly agreed to have all the documents available in case I decided to make the trip to Texas. Although I had no knowledge of Spanish and Mexican land grants, a strange curiosity motivated my thinking. Such grants were indeed a thing of the past and in most cases nothing more than a historian's paradise. But the Becerra grant bothered me. Finally, I made the decision to return to Texas. On March 28, 1972, the search for my heritage had begun.

After I arrived in Houston, Core brought forth the documents. For the first time in my life I viewed the papers pertaining to my heritage, a Mexican land grant of 1832. These historical documents appeared fragile and truly ancient. With great care and awe I touched them. Core had not been telling me a tale as I had thought some months before.

The great seal of the Republic of Mexico was plainly visible, with the eagle and the serpent catching my attention as well as the words, *Coahuila y Tejas 1832–33*. Don Manuel Becerra had read these words in Spanish then signed his name with a flourish, never

realizing that 140 years later one of his descendants would make a journey of 1,500 miles just to see what he had signed.

We tried vainly to interpret the Spanish on the documents, though our efforts proved fruitless. In this respect, Core and I were soundly defeated. However, we could understand some surveyors' reports because they were written in English. Our mother tongue had done us a bad turn or so it appeared, for we were unable to read the ancient, formal Spanish. Be that as it may, these documents were very valuable. Of that we were certain.

The first report was written at Villa de Goliad on May 14, 1832. The approving parties to this transaction were J. Antonio Vasquez and Juan José Hernandez, probably the town officials of Villa de Goliad. The second report had signatures, but we could learn nothing from them. There were three other documents which were reports dated for the years 1874, 1875, and 1876, that appeared to be connected with the estate of Francisco de la Garza, who had died in 1870 in Refugio. Antonio de la Garza was shown on all the reports as the heir or administrator of his father's estate. The reports, which described the condition of the estate of Francisco de la Garza, were apparently inventories showing property owned by Antonio. These were signed by R. P. Clarkson, clerk of the probate court of Refugio County for the period 1874–76. A man named Clarkson was in the habit of signing for Antonio de la Garza. If Antonio could not read or write, there should have been witnesses present to verify the inventories; but this seemed to have been disregarded. Antonio de la Garza was appointed administrator of his father's estate on April 25, 1870, by E. P. Upton, county judge.[1]

The inventory dated February 11, 1874, seemed unbelievable. Of livestock owned by Antonio, there were found dead 100 head of cattle and fourteen horses on the de la Garza range land. It was possible that the ranchers of Refugio suffered severe losses of livestock that year due to cattle disease. I did not purport to be an authority on livestock diseases, but I concluded that if it was from disease, it had to have been one which destroyed not only cattle but also horses. Possibilities raced through my mind.

Research of probate court records or county histories should reveal any epidemic of livestock-killing disease for 1873–74. If, however, such a search failed to disclose any information, then one must conclude with reasonable certainty that the animals were purposely destroyed. But what manner of person or persons would have deliberately destroyed cattle and horses, and what would have been the motives? These certainly would have been no friends of the young de la Garza. In 1874–75, the report stated, Antonio sold his cattle for ten dollars each. Although horses sold for at least forty dollars in those years, the assessed value or market for horses was eleven dollars and sixty cents per animal.

Quickly I calculated that Antonio de la Garza suffered a severe loss in early 1874, which amounted to $1,162.40 — a terrible and disastrous setback for a cattle rancher in Refugio.[2] This was assuming that he sold the horses at the assessed value. On March 17, 1875, Antonio was still selling his cows for ten dollars each. Apparently, nothing significant occurred that year; however, the inventory for November 2, 1876, definitely showed that he disposed of his entire estate with the exception of the land and the horses. The two men who purchased the 250 head of cattle were R. P. Clarkson, probably the probate clerk of Refugio County, and H. Scott. The total amount paid for the cattle was $1,300. They gave him $500 cash and a note for $800 payable within twelve months from the date of the sale, which appears to have been September 18, 1876.[3]

The documents reflected an interesting situation. In 1874–75, Antonio was selling his cattle for ten dollars each, but by September 18, 1876, he disposed of his cattle at five dollars and twenty cents each, a tremendous decrease of four dollars and eighty cents per cow. Either the cattle market in Refugio County decreased drastically or Antonio was in a hurry to sell to the first buyers who came along — in this case, Clarkson and Scott.

The reports for February 11, 1874, and the cattle sale of September 18, 1876, clearly showed that something most unusual occurred in Refugio in those years. After concluding the visual inspection of the reports, Core and I agreed that something must have happened on the de la Garza range lands. Based·on the information disclosed by the reports of 1874–76, I believed that my great-grandfather, Antonio de la Garza, had fallen on hard times and was in serious trouble in Refugio. In our minds, the shadow of evil was cast on the de la Garza past. Poor great-grandfather had no more cattle after September 18, 1876. I felt an immediate compassion and closeness to the old gentleman in the documents.

The inventory of November 2, 1876, indicated that he owned one-quarter league of land, the equivalent of 1,107 acres. The report did not show what disposition, if any, was made of the land. This land was located somewhere near Copano and Alamito creeks in Refugio County, according to the surveyors' report included in the documents dated March 12 and 13 of 1849. The resurvey was made for the heir of Manuel Becerra and was signed by the district surveyor of Refugio County, David Snively. The names of John de la Garza and James Reed appeared on this report, apparently the chain carriers or assistants to Snively.

Core told me that the town of Refugio was situated southeast of Goliad, near a large body of water known as Copano Bay. He noted that within Refugio County were numerous small streams or creeks and that they all flowed into Copano Bay. The documents I saw were exact duplicates of the originals, but Core said that a relative who lived in Goliad would be able to give us the address of a relative in California who had the originals.

We arrived in Goliad on March 30, 1972, and talked with my uncles, Jesús and Tomás Rubio. Uncle Jesús, Core's father, said that his relative might not cooperate with us, but he gave us the name of another woman from Victoria who might be able to help. Uncle Jesús was absolutely correct in his assumption about the relative in Goliad, Genoveva de la Garza. Genoveva was the last surviving daughter of my great aunt, Eliza de la Garza, a longtime resident of Goliad. When we appeared at her door, I got the impression that she was deliberately ignoring us and refused to answer any of our questions. This was our first disappointment — but not the last.

Jesús and Tomás Rubio claimed their grandfather, Antonio, often told them that he owned over 8,000 acres of land in Refugio County. The inventory reports showed that he had only 1,107 acres, but I did not dispute my great-grandfather's claim to more acreage, especially since the original Becerra grant comprised two leagues or 8,856 acres as shown on the David Snively survey report of 1849. Neither Jesús nor Tomás Rubio knew anything concerning the inventories of 1874–76, yet what they began to tell us coincided perfectly with those inventories — a most remarkable coincidence indeed. They also told us that Antonio suffered abject poverty in

his old age and lived with the memories of his once vast herds and acreage.

With our curiosity piqued, Core and I went to see the de la Garza cemetery, which was located directly behind Presidio La Bahía. All of the de la Garza kinfolk were interred in this cemetery. My grandmother, Francisca de la Garza, was born at a place the family called Rancho Alamito near Copano and Alamito creeks in Refugio County on March 3, 1869. We had quickly made the connection between that *rancho* and the land in the 1849 Snively survey. The Goliad County census of July 27, 1870, showed her as being one year old at the time, though it is not known what Antonio, her father, was doing in Goliad then. The census clearly indicated he was there. It is possible that he remained there a few months after attending to the funeral and estate of his father, Francisco de la Garza, who died on March 3, 1870. Antonio appeared again in Refugio County in early 1872.[4]

Francisca de la Garza had expired in Goliad on August 21, 1935. As I stood by my grandmother's grave I thought of many things concerning her. I wondered what she was like when she was a young girl. Was she small and frail looking? Or perhaps lovely and delicate? Her eldest son Guillermo (my father) was born on January 10, 1888, in Goliad County. Grandmother was about seventeen years old when she and Juan Rubio were married on January 29, 1887.

Grandfather, a deputy sheriff of Goliad County for many years, was born in 1860 in San Antonio (Bexar County). Juan Rubio was twenty-seven years old when he claimed Francisca de la Garza for his wife, according to their eldest daughter, Sálome Rubio de Lambardia. She said that her father died on February 24, 1903, in Goliad. Señora Rubio de Lambardia was born in Goliad County on April 18, 1889, and despite her age, she was very alert and keen of mind when I first interviewed her after my search began.

Thirty-three years after the passing of Grandfather Rubio, Grandmother Francisca was laid to rest near him and their son, Juan Rubio, Jr. I deeply regret not having the opportunity to have known her, though I vaguely remember seeing her at her funeral when I was about six years old. Afterward, when I asked my mother why my grandmother had died, she replied that she had died because of a disease she had in her stomach, which I later learned was cancer.

Directly across the road from the Presidio La Bahía church stood the forlorn cabin Antonio de la Garza moved from Refugio County to Goliad County in the mid–1870s. The oldest members of our family told me he used oxen to accomplish this Herculean task at night. The house was weather-beaten and had deteriorated to some extent, but it still had a remarkable appearance. Francisco de la Garza probably owned the cabin; and perhaps he and his son, Antonio, built it. Regretfully, there was no way to determine its age, but our family tradition was that Grandmother Francisca and her brother, José, were born in the cabin while Antonio was still residing in Refugio County. Their other children were likewise born in the same cabin, but in Goliad County. The old cabin was at least 105 years old. Cabins such as this which were still standing were a rarity and a mute reminder of the Texas frontier era. Relatives of ours, the Garcia brothers, purchased the cabin from Genoveva de la Garza, the last known person to have occupied it.

Antonio de la Garza may have left Refugio County after the cattle sale of September 18, 1876, or after the inventory of November 2, 1876; but he was indeed a cattle rancher as was his father, Francisco. No prudent cattle rancher would sell his entire herd without purchasing additional cattle if it were his sole livelihood. We had no records that indicated Antonio had purchased additional cattle in Refugio and Goliad, and my uncles claimed that he never did.

Jesús and Tomás Rubio vigorously asserted to Core and me that their grandfather had told them many things about his past. Principally, he told them that he had never disposed of his land in Refugio County, but that evil things had befallen him while living in that place. The inventory of November 2, 1876, showed no disposition had been made.

As I stood there, near the foot of my grandmother's grave on March 30, 1972, I resolved to rediscover my heritage. The old cabin, the old family cemetery plot, and the even more ancient documents that Core had revealed to me mingled with my uncle's words — all these helped to insure that I would not rest until I had the answer to the very basic questions that had begun to form in my

mind about the lost lands of Manuel Becerra and his grandson, Antonio de la Gárza.

Core urged me to help unite the rest of the Becerra family in this effort. He did not have much persuading to do. From that day, Core and I would begin to bring together the huge Becerra family who were scattered to the four winds.

Attempting to unify such a large family was a formidable task in itself; however, we felt confident that this could be done, especially if we had the assistance of uncles Jesús, Tomás, and Daniel Rubio. I was greatly elated when I found out that these three men had a powerful influence within the Becerra family. Some of the others like Alfredo and his wife, Romana de la Garza, quickly rallied to the cause.

I was dismayed to learn that there was rivalry and suspicion among some members of the Becerra family. Some felt that others knew more about the missing land grant than the majority. Still others felt that there were some "underhanded things going on." This was an ominous sign of events yet to come, and I would find myself squarely in the middle of a family feud. By then it was too late for me to retreat, regardless of the pressure from irate kinfolk. One thing was certain, though; the lost land was still in Refugio County and no doubt being occupied by someone reaping the fruits of my great-grandfather's labor.

Under the circumstances, we began to discuss the possibilities of approching a reputable law firm to analyze thoroughly the Becerra documents and obtain legal advice on the problem with which we were confronted.

Would it be worth the trouble and expense — especially the expense — to find out what really happened to the Becerra grant whose last holder of record was Antonio de la Garza? Again we agreed that it was well worth a try.

We arrived in Victoria and went directly to see the woman whom Uncle Jesús Rubio had mentioned. She proved to be kind and helpful, and in due time we had the address of the relative in California who supposedly had the original Becerra documents. Before my departure for California, there was a small family gathering in Houston. Nearly all present agreed that I should approach a California law firm and obtain legal advice. A small fund was collected so that I could pay the attorney. Thus was the inauspicious beginning of the Manuel Becerra land grant investigation from which there would be no turning back.

Alvin L. Harris was selected to represent the Becerra heirs from Texas. Core Rubio had sent me copies of the old documents, including a list of the de la Garza heirs. My appointment with Harris was during the first week of May 1972.

In attempting to determine the reasons why the Becerra grant was resurveyed on March 12 and 13 of 1849, I scrutinized the report thoroughly and arrived at two possible conclusions for the resurvey. First, the word "resurvey" clearly indicated that the land was previously surveyed by Mexican land surveyors or surveyors from the Republic of Texas. Secondly, the Treaty of Guadalupe Hidalgo between the United States and the Republic of Mexico was signed on February 2, 1848. Texas was no longer an independent republic but was an American state, hence the Becerra land had to be resurveyed according to American law. The most significant aspect of the Treaty of Guadalupe Hidalgo was the final acquisition by the United States of the state of Texas (from whence the original problems began between the United States and Mexico) and the Mexican provinces of New Mexico, Arizona, California, Nevada, and Utah for the sum of $15 million. It appeared that the leaders of the Mexican government made a vigorous and sincere effort to assert the rights of the native Mexican inhabitants who were included in the sale of the above mentioned provinces.

The treaty provided that native Mexicans had the choice of returning to their motherland (but what motherland, one may ask; where they were had been their motherland for years) or remaining to become American citizens and be looked upon as foreigners by the Anglo-Americans who quickly classified them as aliens. Native Mexicans who chose to remain on their native soil suffered unfortunate consequences. They endured hardships and prejudice, but they stubbornly clung to their ancient acreages of land, or what remained of their land grants. However, not for long. In due time the Mexicans, now known as Mexican-Americans (after February 2, 1848), lost the land their forefathers had once owned. Much of this was probably due to the complicated American laws of which they knew very little. Such laws were enacted and passed by the various states for the benefit of the newcomers, certainly not for the benefit of the Mexicans. My ancestors were some of the earliest Spanish-

Mexican settlers in Texas, but apparently in the end these ancestors lost out just like the other Mexican settlers. Core and I wanted
to discover *exactly* what happened to the lost land owned by Antonio de la Garza in Refugio County.

   Attorney Alvin L. Harris was a big man and his appearance
might have led the unwary to believe that he could have been of
Mexican extraction. His disposition was amiable and witty; in spite
of his size I got the distinct impression that he moved fast when the
occasion demanded. He was impressed and asked many questions,
including the reasons why the family wanted the land and documents investigated. I explained everything the various members of
the family suspected and described my most recent trip to Texas to
see the documents for myself. I told Harris that of 8,856 acres once
belonging to Don Manuel Becerra, none were presently owned by
his heirs.
   Harris expressed a strong interest in our cause from the beginning. After a thorough and careful examination of all the documents, he suggested a title search of the records in Refugio County.
He agreed to approach a title research company in Los Angeles for
an estimate of the costs. I became hesitant about these documents
being examined by any Texas agency, particularly those from Victoria, Goliad, and Refugio counties. Harris assured me that these
agencies were all bonded and trustworthy. In spite of Harris's as-
surances, I still had my suspicions of the trustworthiness of these
Texas agencies. I was deeply concerned with the agency in Refugio
County because our original family problems started there, where
the land was located.
   Harris was particularly interested in knowing the family's history in Texas. According to family tradition, Don Manuel Becerra
had been employed by Stephen F. Austin in the year 1821. Some
years later, Becerra had been employed by one José Jesús Vidaurri
of Coahuila, Mexico; but at this time I did not know the year or
years of his employment with Vidaurri. One of the de la Garza colonists had married one of Becerra's daughters, and it was through
this marriage that we became direct descendants of Manuel Becerra. I believed that it was the colonist Francisco de la Garza who
married the Becerra girl, but I was not absolutely certain of this
fact. Juan Rubio, my grandfather, married the daughter of Antonio
de la Garza, and Antonio was the son of Francisco de la Garza.

I told Harris that my knowledge of the family ancestry was limited, but I would find out more about them. Thus began my relentless and almost fanatical genealogical research of the de la Garzas. Harris quickly sent the family documents to the Los Angeles Title Company, with a cover letter requesting an estimate of the costs of a title search. Just as I feared, that company subsequently mailed the documents to the Refugio Mission Title Abstract Company.

Shortly after my return from Texas, I became deeply involved in studying the early history of Mexico and Texas. Of utmost importance to me at this time was any information concerning land grant distribution by the Mexican government to the early Texas settlers, both native Mexicans and Anglo-Americans. Through my research I gathered an abundance of historical material relating to early Texas history. I was thoroughly amazed that all the names on the maps of the era were those of American *empresarios* who received large land grants from the Mexican government, while only one name appeared to be of Spanish-Mexican extraction. This man was Don Martin de Leon from Victoria County.

The Mexican government issued grants of land to the Texas settlers through the *empresario* system (similar to a contractor) by prescription and limitation. The settler was under commitment to make improvements on his land for a period of six years. At the end of this time period or before, the *empresario* had the authority to issue good title to the settler provided he had made the improvements called for in the contract.[5]

Unquestionably, the best and most desirous type of land grant was that which was known as a first-class land grant. These grants were generally issued to officials of the Mexican government for their service and loyalty, or to petitioners, mostly native Mexicans, who desired this type of land grant. The final authority to approve these federal land grants was the governor of Coahuila y Tejas, whose headquarters were in Monclova, Coahuila, Mexico. Final title was issued by the Mexican land commissioner in the district where the grantee resided.[6]

The first-class land grant required the initial approval of the local villa or town government called the *ayuntamiento;* afterward, the approved petition was forwarded to the central government for its review and final approval. The final approval was given only if the petitioner had complied scrupulously with all the requirements, including the sending of the required funds, as well as complying with the colonization laws of the state. The governor of the provinces of Coahuila and Texas was the highest ranking civil authority to approve all land grants. This included those petitioned for by the Texas *empresarios*.[7] Sometimes the petitioner waited months and even years before receiving the approved grant from the governor. The most significant aspect of the first-class grant was its apparent precedence over those issued by the *empresarios*. This first-class federal grant was to take on extreme importance in my own family research.

During the days I was waiting for a reply from the Refugio Mission Title Company, my thoughts were unpleasant because, frankly, I questioned the reliability and impartiality of that organization to perform a search into an old Mexican land grant whose heirs were of Mexican-American extraction. My suspicions were well founded. The Becerra family were of the opinion that Refugio was one of the most anti-Mexican towns in Texas; hence, they had no faith in any Refugio abstract agency. I expressed my dissatisfaction to Harris, to which he replied that all abstract companies were generally impartial. I suggested he did not know the history of Texas and particularly of Refugio as my family and I did. The Becerra family legend had been that something dreadful happened to Antonio de la Garza in Refugio County in the early and middle 1870s. Early on in my search, my uncles told Core and me that one of the largest landowners in the county was involved in the eventual downfall of Antonio, and hence he retreated to Goliad County in the 1870s.

My mind kept returning to the inventory for 1874 which showed all of the dead livestock on the de la Garza range in Refugio County. My dissatisfaction with the Refugio abstract agency handling the search of the de la Garza heirs' land records had a long background.

I became frustrated, and a sense of failure and helpless anxiety played a grim role in my everyday life. I was beginning to feel an awesome responsibility, and this was only the beginning of a long quest. I had maintained constant communication with Core, who informed me that emotions were running high with many of the Becerra family descendants over their suspicions about Refugio.

In May 1972, Harris received the long awaited reply from the Refugio agency. Things did not look good. We met at his office and both of us scrutinized the contents of the letter. I told Harris again that we had the evidence that Antonio de la Garza had possibly 8,856 acres of land in that county. Perhaps some people in Refugio County did not want us around — and with good reason.

[2]

Mounting Suspicions

Hobart Huson, president of the Refugio Mission Title Abstract Company, had written the disheartening and, what I considered, useless letter. He explained that the Becerra grant was issued by prescription and limitation, but he failed to report the type or class of grant it was.

Huson was a well-qualified authority able to tell the difference between the two classes of grants already mentioned.[1] As we learned in time, he had very good reason for not revealing any information regarding a title search of the Becerra grant. He advised Harris to contact the archives in Mexico City. This process, he said, would be a difficult and costly undertaking. Huson reminded Harris that title searches of the Spanish-Mexican land grant variety were at most long-shot ventures with very few payoffs. Additionally, he informed us that the Becerra grant was going to be 140 years old on May 14, 1972. We were well aware of that already.

The Refugio Mission Title Abstract Company did not perform the abstract requested by Harris. At no time did they mention the costs of the title search. Harris only received an abundance of free advice that he had not requested. The contents of the letter seemed an attempt to discourage us from continuing the investigation.

21

Harris and I discussed at length all our possibilities. If he contacted other abstract companies from California through the mail and they repeated the procedure of the Los Angeles Title Company, we would be confronted with the Refugio agency again. As a result of further possible contact with that agency, we discarded this procedure as unwise. I suggested that we approach the First American Title Company from Santa Ana, California, and have one of its agents do the research in Texas. Harris believed that the cost would be prohibitive.

The situation appeared hopeless, and we were only beginning. Harris then offered to do the search of the family records in Refugio himself, but the full approval of the Becerra heirs would be needed. I quickly contacted Manuel Garcia at Goliad, and soon the family gave approval to Harris to investigate the Becerra grant himself.

In the meantime, there was a flurry of activity within the Becerra family in Goliad. Manuel Garcia was elected committee chairman, thus becoming the first leader of the Manuel Becerra heirs. The family raised the necessary finances for Harris's trip, which would be the real beginning of the search and the first time ever for such an undertaking. Everyone was optimistic that Harris would soon find out what had happened to the Antonio de la Garza land in Refugio County.

On June 5, 1972, Harris departed for Texas. These days I was restless because I desperately hoped that Harris would find information advantageous to the family. I equally considered the possibility that he might find unfavorable information regarding the lost land. While Harris was in Refugio, I continued my own research of my ancestors' history as well as that pertaining to Mexico and Texas, especially Texas, since this was my forefathers' domicile in the wilderness many years before the arrival of the North Americans.

I became deeply involved in research of Texas history. By far the most fascinating material I found was that produced by noted historian Hubert Howe Bancroft. Bancroft was a master historian of early Spanish and Mexican history. In his two-volume *History of the North Mexican States and Texas,* he vividly described the colonization of Texas by North Americans and the eventual separation of Texas from Mexico. Finally, he sadly described the war between the United States and Mexico. In my opinion, this war was perpetrated principally by arrogant Anglo-Texan agitators. This is not to say that all of them were such, but being a native-born Texan (a true native Texas Mexican is one who is a direct descendant of the original Spanish-Mexican colonists who did not retreat across the Rio Grande after the Texas rebellion of 1836) I have firsthand knowledge of their arrogance and attitude which still prevails to this day. During the Texas Revolution, few native Mexicans remained, as many had retreated swiftly across the border into Mexico. Only the most hardy Mexican colonists remained, but unfortunately these were far too few.

I became intensely interested in the history written by Bancroft because of the remote possibility of finding Manuel Becerra in one of these volumes, since Becerra was with Stephen F. Austin in Texas in 1821. This was not to be, but I did find reference to *Libro Becerro or Becerra*, a book supposedly located in district court records in Refugio.[2]

Before Harris's return from Texas, I acquired several volumes written by Texas historians. By this time I was most zealously pursuing Texas history and in so doing was rudely awakened with concern for the state's history; thus, my attitude began to change.

For example, *The Texas Rangers*, by Walter Prescott Webb, was somewhat interesting but thoroughly prejudiced toward Mexicans. According to Webb, "When the Mexican women saw the huge bearded Texas Rangers approaching, they screamed in fear and fainted, while the Mexican men or peons fled in terror." Webb's imagination was truly unique. The reader formed a mental image of the giant Texas Rangers riding giant horses towering mightily above the mesquite trees of South Texas. In their wake they left terrified and fainting Mexican women and equally terrified peons scurrying for the underbrush to escape their righteous wrath.

Harris returned from Texas on June 8, and a meeting was soon arranged at his office on June 10. His personal investigation of the records in Refugio indicated that Antonio de la Garza settled the estate of his father, Francisco de la Garza, in the county of Refugio during May of 1881. The documents of the final estate of Francisco de la Garza in 1881 disclosed that the inventory of February 11, 1874, was correct in regard to the dead livestock found on the de la Garza range. The cattle sale to R. P Clarkson and Henry Scott on

September 18, 1876, was also correct. The 112 horses on hand in May of 1881 were sold and the proceeds distributed equally among the eight heirs or heads of families. Apparently, the 112 horses were sold for $1,000 ($10 each), and each of the family heads received $140. The list of debts paid were as follows: cost of county court, $27.85; L. B. Russell, attorney, $10; Antonio de la Garza, commissions, $89.75; R. A. Wellington, $107. It would be interesting to find the cause of the debt paid to Wellington. There were seven pages of information attached to the final estate.[3]

This was the final estate of Francisco de la Garza, and the names of the heirs as of May 1881 were listed:

1. Trinidad Garza de Lozano, Refugio County.
2. Antonio de la Garza, Goliad County.
3. Genoveva Garza de Lozano, deceased leaving one minor child named Paula Lozano whose guardian *de facto* was her aunt Trinidad Garza de Lozano.
4. Alejándra Garza de Patino, deceased leaving three minor children whose guardian *de facto* was Antonio de la Garza. These three children were Anselmo Patino, eight years old; Ygnacio Patino, six years old; and Gertrudis Patino, four years old.
5. Rosalia Garza de Valdez, deceased leaving one minor child named Cornelio Valdez whose guardian *de facto* was his father, Santos Valdez, who resided in Goliad County.
6. Ynes de la Garza, Goliad County.
7. Alberta de la Garza, Goliad County.
8. Rufino de la Garza, Goliad County; the guardian *de facto* was Antonio de la Garza from Goliad County. Rufino de la Garza was nineteen years old.

Antonio de la Garza was the guardian *de facto* to his two deceased sisters' minor children.[4] This was in addition to his own children who, in 1881, numbered two sons and three daughters. On September 23, 1878, Antonio petitioned the Refugio Court to move the cause of his father's estate to the probate court of Goliad County. He cited the reasons as being that the minor children were then residing in Goliad County. The reply from the court had not been found. The entire herd of horses (112) was also in Goliad County.

Antonio surely must have been having his share of problems, for as early as August 20, 1872, the county clerk, Hough Rea, ordered Sheriff J. L. Billingsly to find the young herdsman de la Garza. Antonio had failed to account for the estate of his father's property. On September 29, 1872, the sheriff finally found Antonio somewhere in the woods and served the papers. The same would happen in Goliad County in 1881, the reasons we were to learn later.

Sheriff Billingsly charged Antonio the sum of five dollars for locating him. Mileage on horseback was five cents per mile, which amounted to two dollars. This meant that the sheriff and his faithful steed traveled forty miles, more or less, before finding the elusive party. For some reason, Antonio chose not to appear in the town of Refugio.[5]

Most interesting, however, Harris could find no records indicating that Antonio disposed of his one-quarter league of land (1,107 acres). This appeared in the inventories for 1874–76, but perhaps more astonishing was the fact that on the final estate of Francisco de la Garza there appeared one-half league of land (2,214 acres). Antonio must have acquired another one-quarter league between November 2, 1876, and May 1881. According to Harris, Antonio never made any conveyances of land to anyone. Harris appeared surprised at finding the additional one-quarter league of land; the fact that 2,214 acres of land were not properly accounted for in Refugio aroused his suspicions. This certainly warranted further investigation of the family records and perhaps a return trip.

There was sufficient cause for rejoicing since Harris had found the additional acreage, but still there were 6,000 unaccounted acres. For certain, someone in Refugio County was in possession of the entire grant. When this information was relayed to Core and the entire family, the majority did not seem overly surprised. We were confronted with a serious land problem. The Becerra land was located somewhere in Refugio County, but where it was located and who was in possession of it was not known. This person, or persons, for all practical purposes, had no valid title.

I vowed never to cease in my present quest. Knowing that someone was enjoying the good things produced by my great-grandfather's land was a bitter pill to swallow, but this only spurred me on to greater activity and leadership within the Becerra family.

Harris knew that things were not as they should be in Refugio. He wanted to pursue the search to a conclusion. He said that our best approach at this time was to obtain maps of Refugio County.

Soon he obtained maps from the General Land Office at Austin. But these were modern and unsuitable for our purposes. Harris promptly dispatched a second request to the General Land Office in Austin. This time, however, he requested maps of Refugio and Goliad counties beginning with the year 1836. The earliest map we received was for 1851.

While in Refugio, Harris had read a local history of the county and found interesting information about the de la Garza family. Harris was particularly impressed with one of our ancestors whose name was Carlos de la Garza. Don Carlos had fought against the Texan army in the rebellion of 1836. He subsequently saved from execution five or more of Colonel James Fannin's men at La Bahía during the murders that occurred there in 1836. Later he served as an Indian fighter under the Texas Republic.[6]

In July 1972, Harris and I met only once. Again we went over the 1851 map, very carefully trying to locate the Becerra grant. The tract had been resurveyed for his heir, so we looked for a de la Garza name on the map. Surveyor David Snively's report on March 12 and 13, 1849, showed the usual markings and boundaries. Snively drew a sketch to indicate exactly where the grant was located. The sketch was certainly vivid proof that the grant existed and exactly where it was in relation to the creeks.

The sketch was drawn on the first page of the surveyor's report. According to Snively, the Becerra tract boundary began about twelve miles east of the old Mission Refugio in the bed of Alamito Creek and across Copano Creek in Refugio County. The original point of the survey began at four cottonwood trees in the bed of Alamito Creek. The west boundary of the Becerra grant was adjacent to a survey made in the name of Don Juan Martin de Veramendi. After feverishly rotating the 1851 map countless times, we finally arrived in the general vicinity where the Becerra tract should be. But we were puzzled, for all the names there were strange to us. Oh Lord, not again, I thought; Satan surely must be greatly delighted in interfering with our research. We were expecting to find Becerra or de la Garza names but none appeared on the map. Needless to say, this led to further frustration. Harris and I wondered why Snively failed to include Becerra's name on the map after the survey of March 12 and 13, 1849.

Previous misconceptions that I may have had about the Becerra grant being a myth were now forgotten. Our ancestors' land grant was very real. Since the survey papers appeared in good order, it seemed reasonable that Becerra or his daughters should be shown on the map. Francisco de la Garza himself was alive and well in Refugio County in 1851. He was no doubt properly occupying a large portion of the land. Something had to be amiss for our family's names to be missing from the maps.

I foresaw a long road ahead of us beset with countless problems, but these, I hoped, could be overcome with courage, determination, intelligence, and, yes, even sacrifice. I prayed that God guide the Becerra family in successfully completing the search. The Becerra grant seemed strangely clouded in mystery in Refugio County.

At this early stage of the search, there was much confusion among the Becerra family in Texas. Apparently some members were not receiving information I had sent after Harris's return from Texas. Harris had not searched the records at the General Land Office at Austin, only those in Refugio County.

By the latter part of July 1972, things were in complete turmoil with the family in Texas. Some complained bitterly of not knowing what was going on; others asked when Harris was leaving for Texas, though Harris had been to Texas and back nearly six weeks. Some did not even know we had engaged a California attorney to do the research of the family records in Refugio. We had problems not only with finding the missing land, but also with a disorganized family. In view of this problem, I decided to take a trip to Texas on August 18.

On his first trip, our California attorney was not impressed with Refugio County. He felt there was something foreboding about the town. He and I began to suspect that something dreadful must have happened to the descendants of Manuel Becerra within the county during the 1870s and perhaps even earlier. As he walked down the streets of Refugio that hot and humid day of June 7, 1972, he wondered what vicissitudes the de la Garza family underwent while living on the isolated ranch, and why the herdsman Antonio de la Garza left over 8,000 acres of land in Refugio County to live the rest of his life in Goliad County in poverty. Harris learned that his clients had good reason for wanting the family records investigated. He told me that he wished that the Becerra family had not waited so long before beginning the search. Time was running out, for there were the finer points of law to be considered in the event of a lawsuit, particularly the statute of limitations. Harris noted that several local people with whom he had spoken at the court-house and library appeared suspicious and not overly friendly. He attributed this to the fact he was an outsider.

On Thursday, August 17, Harris and I held another confer-ence. We again viewed the Refugio map of 1851 without obtaining favorable results. John de la Garza and William Reed were assist-ants to the surveyor, David Snively, for their names appear on the survey papers.[7] On the third examination of the map we found something that would puzzle and mislead us for a while: Essy Reed was one of the names appearing on tracts on the map. We carefully plotted the sketch of Snively's 1849 report on the map of 1851. Reed's tract of land seemed to be in the area where the Becerra grant should be. The sketch of the Becerra tract drawn by Snively appeared to coincide as to length and width with that of Essy Reed. All other maps including one for 1872 revealed the same informa-tion. Almost simultaneously we realized that this could be a big problem.

I thought it strange to have Essy Reed's name in the same area as Becerra. This newly found information prompted Harris to ad-vise a further search of the records in Refugio County. I presented this report to the family during the scheduled meeting with them on August 21.

I had found myself confronted with anxieties which were con-stant reminders of the land situation. The distance between Cali-fornia and Texas was far and costly for me. I felt chained and help-less, totally unable to accomplish what I had a great desire to do. But I never hesitated nor cringed in assuming the responsibility of this investigation, little realizing through my own ignorance how great and awesome it would become.

[3]

Home to
South Texas

Guadalupe (Core), his wife, Olga, and my brother, Guillermo Rubio, Jr., met me at the Houston airport in mid-August 1972. As we walked outside, the hot, humid air reminded me that the next four or five days would be anything but pleasant. After discussing with Core the information found by Harris in Refugio and his advice to the family, Core felt certain that the forthcoming family gathering would prove beneficial to everyone. But I was not so confident. After my long trip, what if no one appeared for the gathering?

Early on the morning of August 19, we were on our way to see Uncle Jesús Rubio, Core's father, at his ranch near Cuero. The weather was bearable early in the morning; but by the time we arrived at the ranch it was intensely hot, very uncomfortable for one not accustomed to the humidity of South Texas. Because of many years away from my native soil, I felt like an outsider. But the genuine friendliness of my hatted and booted relatives reassured me that I, too, was still a Texan. Things generally seemed different from when I was a youth growing up in South Texas, for I had many unpleasant memories.

I was delighted to see Uncle Jesús and Aunt María again. She

29

was the kindest person I have ever had the pleasure of knowing. She immediately began to prepare a huge evening meal.

All the Rubios grew up on cattle ranches in South Texas. The Rubio brothers were some of the last of the Mexican *vaqueros* who herded cattle to earn their livelihood, the possible exception being the youngest of the clan, Tomás Rubio. The wildest of the Rubio brothers was the ill-tempered and hard-drinking Guillermo, my father. As a youth he gave my poor grandmother Francisca de la Garza much cause for concern.

The Jesús Rubio ranch was more or less six miles north of Cuero. It was situated close to the Guadalupe River, with dense mesquite trees typical of the South Texas brush country. Somewhat isolated, it was serene and lonely, peaceful and beautiful. I sat contently under a mesquite tree and gazed at the lone bull and horse in the corral. The young bull had been gored by an older bull that emerged victorious from the fray. Uncle Jesús was doctoring the young, still agitated loser.

For the first time in many years, my mind was absorbed in the tranquility afforded by the lonely ranch. This wonderful moment of solace was abruptly terminated when I remembered the purpose of my journey from California.

The Guadalupe River was famous in Texas history. It was named by the Spanish *conquistador* Captain Alonso de Leon, who came to Texas in search of the French explorer La Salle in the late 1600s. Had the two explorers met face to face in the wilds, the course of Texas history could have been different. But fate in the form of the Karankawa Indians intervened, and La Salle and his colonists ultimately perished in the Texas wilderness. Fate also deemed that the Karankawas be eradicated from the Texas coast by the Anglo-Americans from the north. When the Spanish *conquistadores* made their bold *entradas* into Texas, they were always accompanied by the Franciscan fathers. The missionary priests came for the purpose of bringing Christianity to the Indians. The soldiers came to claim the lands and other booty for the king of Spain — with the sword and the cross, but more often the sword.

While reposing under the old mesquite tree, I thought of this wonderful land being discovered, explored, and settled by the Spanish of so long ago. Now, nearly 200 years later, a descendant of the explorer Manuel Becerra traveled 1,500 miles to find out what happened to his tract of land. Who was to say that Becerra himself with his own eyes did not see the old tree his much-troubled descendant was leaning against?

Very carefully and in Spanish, I explained to Uncle Jesús everything we had accomplished thus far in regard to the land investigation. He agreed that the way in which we were proceeding with the search was the most logical. He was hesitant about Texas attorneys becoming involved in the initial investigation. Uncle Jesús wanted to know everything about our California attorney. I assured him that Harris was trustworthy and very loyal to the family. I mentioned that Harris had found an additional 1,107 acres of land in Refugio County under Antonio de la Garza. At the mention of the name, Uncle Jesús smiled broadly and appeared very pleased with the new discovery. He told me *Tatita* (Grandfather) Antonio never sold nor conveyed his land to anyone.

"Someone is occupying those lands without permission, and we must find out who they are," declared Jesús Rubio.[1]

He agreed to give his full support until the search was thoroughly completed to the satisfaction of everyone. His were the first words of encouragement I had heard since the Becerra grant investigation had begun. Uncle Jesús possessed a strong influence with the de la Garza heirs and he would ably demonstrate this during the meeting of August 21. I no longer felt alone; his wise counsel and advice to me was a tremendous morale booster.

Monclova Rubio, the eldest daughter of Uncle Jesús, and her husband, Richard Gonzales, arrived at the ranch. I had not seen her since 1942; her lovely features were unmistakably Rubio. Señora María Rubio prepared a splendid evening meal typical of those prepared by the South Texas *ranchero* families.

The many years of rich Spanish-Mexican tradition were very prevalent in the Jesús Rubio home. Richard Gonzales finished his chores of looking after the cattle then joined us on the front porch. He owned a cattle ranch in Mexico but had lost 150 head of beeves to cattle rustlers within one year. It was still dangerous below the Rio Grande. Bandits made no distinction between Mexican and American ranchers.

Gonzales and his family experienced a land grant situation similar to ours. Their problem also entailed financial difficulties and lack of communication between families. Gonzales gave his support to financial assistance and encouragement. Perhaps more important than anything else was the fact that he really believed in what we were attempting to do and the way we were approaching the problem.

We left the ranch house for Goliad to visit Core's older brother, Juan Rubio. While passing through this small South Texas town, I thought of its history. It seemed peaceful and quiet, but its past was bathed in blood and violence, perhaps second only to the Alamo in San Antonio.

Core drove very slowly by the Goliad courthouse and pointed out the famous "Hanging Tree." He said that in frontier days they used to hang five poor devils at a time. I asked from which limb of the tree did they send the wretched unfortunates to the hereafter. Core did not know which limb was used the most, but any one was sturdy and certainly capable of holding the weight of five men. It was night, and the tree looked eerie and gruesome.

I wondered if the ugly but famous "Hanging Tree" was reserved exclusively for Anglo-Texans. For the *Tejanos*, the nearest mesquite tree or wagon tongue was deemed sufficient to extract justice. Core said that regardless of race or creed the tree was used impartially; everyone was treated equally. This may have been the only place in Goliad where prejudice was overlooked.

I spent a most enjoyable weekend in Goliad visiting many of the relatives. It was very surprising to meet one by the name of Antonio de la Garza. He was a grandson of the original Antonio de la Garza, the Refugio cattleman. Core and I visited the old cabin Antonio de la Garza brought from Refugio in the middle 1870s. The cabin was across the highway from Presidio de La Bahía, built in 1749. The Spanish explorer Don José de Escandon founded the colony and built the *presidio*. He was one of the greatest explorer-colonizers who came north from Mexico to colonize Texas. Escandon settled South Texas from La Bahía toward the present Mexican border with Mexican settlers.

The original Presidio La Bahía was founded near the Guadalupe River in 1721 by the Spanish governor of Coahuila, the Marquis de San Miguel de Aguayo, who came into Texas for the express purpose of clearing the province of its French inhabitants. Aguayo ably accomplished his mission by asserting Spain's claim to the giant province for nearly 100 years.

I reflected that on November 8, 1930, I was baptized in the beautiful Chapel of Our Lady of Loreto at La Bahía. My sponsors were Trinidad de la Garza and her husband, Candelario Moreno. Trinidad was the eldest daughter of José María de la Garza and Regina Laso. Trinidad de la Garza was born at La Bahía on November 10, 1893, and died on January 22, 1953, while I, her godson, was engaged in combat in faraway Korea. She was a first cousin to my father. The picture on her grave marker showed her to have been a lovely young woman.

When I returned from the Korean War in 1953, I visited Great-aunt Eliza de la Garza who was then living in the old cabin. She was born in Goliad County in 1877. Her eldest sister, Grandmother Francisca, was born in this same cabin in 1869 which was then on the Rancho Alamito homestead in Refugio County. All the children of Antonio de la Garza and Ponposa Bontan were born in this ancient relic of a cabin. Regretfully, I did not ask Aunt Eliza about our ancestry of which she knew a great deal.

The cabin deeply and emotionally fascinated me, and on my visit there in late August 1972, I stood for a long time looking at the walls and carefully inspecting its interior. Considering its age, it was still in remarkable condition, and through genealogical research and family tradition I had, by then, already learned some of its story.

For example, on March 3, 1869, pretty and frail Ponposa Bontan, eighteen-year-old wife of Antonio de la Garza, gave birth to her first-born child whom she and her husband would name Francisca. Green-eyed Ponposa was attended by neighboring cattle ranchers' wives who came several days before and remained a day or two after the child was born. The nearest ranch to the de la Garza homestead was ten or more miles away. On the dawn of this day, Antonio de la Garza rose from his bunk earlier than usual, dressed, and put on a heavy sheepskin coat. The ranchers' wives had prepared breakfast and put a pot of steaming coffee on the pot-bellied stove. Antonio went into Ponposa's room and tenderly held her hand and assured her he would be nearby. As she firmly grasped his hand and weakly smiled up at him, he thought how green her eyes looked — perhaps greener than usual — but maybe he was only imagining things. Attached to Antonio's boots, which were always somewhat run down at the heels, were a pair of enormous spurs; over his trousers were the *chaparajos* (chaps), and attached to his right boot was a dagger. However, he carried no pistol that day. Near the cabin was his horse, the butt of a Winchester rifle protruding from the saddle scabbard. The rawhide twenty-one-year-old de la Garza rancher was prepared for any emergency.

Restless and concerned for his lovely wife, he paced back and forth when suddenly he heard the wailings of an infant. One hundred and three years ago Grandmother Francisca's first cry was heard by the very wall I was looking at this very moment. I desperately wished that I could reach back into the past and touch her.

Presidio La Bahía was equally fascinating to me for it was here that the explorer-colonizer, Don Manuel Becerra, his wife, Juana María Cadena, and their children passed through its massive doors to attend Catholic services over a century and a half ago. Becerra's youngest daughter, Gertrudis, married Francisco de la Garza, and provided my own direct link to Manuel Becerra. All of the Becerra and de la Garza children were baptized in the Chapel of Our Lady of Loreto at La Bahía.

Juan, Core, and I decided to take a trip to visit the General Land Office at Austin on Monday, August 21. I was particularly interested in seeing the original maps of Refugio County for 1851–72. On the way to Austin we again stopped at Uncle Jesús Rubio's ranch in Cuero. The cantankerous old man was in fairly good spirits despite a run-in with a man who dumped some bales of hay much closer to the house than the barn. He was about to get on his horse and go tend to his cattle. I noticed the lone bull and horse were still in the corral. Continuing to Austin, I saw many cattle ranches and many herds of cattle. The grass was a beautiful lush green, and there were many scattered small *arroyos* filled with water. It was a good summer; all the cattle were fat.

We passed through a small town and never in my life had I seen or heard of a town with so many oil wells. Many of these wells were located near the railroad. One well was in the back yard of a run-down shack whose inhabitants appeared to be of Mexican extraction, but apparently not the well's owners. But then these things happened in Texas. I was impressed with the magnificence of the country between the famous old town of Goliad and Austin, the capital of Texas, named in honor of the Texas-American colonist, Stephen F. Austin.

We arrived at the General Land Office where I asked to see maps of Refugio County beginning with the year 1851. An amiable young woman, Lanell Aston, assisted me with the maps and was most helpful. She appeared genuinely sincere in her desire to help me, which she did magnificently. The name Essy Reed appeared on every map of Refugio County, 1851–1921 inclusive. This was most annoying and disappointing because it seemed that she occupied the area where the Becerra tract ought to be.

After viewing the maps, we next visited the Spanish Collection of the Land Office's Archives and Records Division. I was pleasantly surprised to find that Virginia Taylor, the interpreter for the Spanish Collection, spoke Spanish fluently and unquestionably in its proper form. Her ability to translate the difficult handwritten Spanish documents was to be admired. That an Anglo-American, especially a Texan, should take such a great interest in a language other than her own is cause for respect and the enlightenment of one's heart. I do not imply that other Anglo-American Texans cannot speak Spanish for they indeed do, and these help to strengthen the bonds of friendship between the two peoples.

I examined a volume containing the de la Garza land grants which were numerous and far surpassed any other name in land grant ownership. Many of these grants were issued by the Mexican land commissioner, José Jesús Vidaurri, in 1834 in Refugio County. José María de la Garza received eleven leagues of land but not from Vidaurri. In 1838, Francisco de la Garza conveyed one league of land to Antonio Navarro in Bexar County. It is doubtful if this man was the same Francisco de la Garza of Refugio County because our ancestor was on the Rio Grande border about this time. The records also indicated that in 1840 one Cristóbal Rubio conveyed to a man named Johnson 1,477 acres of land for the meager sum of forty dollars. The transaction was made in Bexar County. This also happened before Rubio got clear title to the land. Johnson subsequently conveyed the land to someone else; the title appeared to have been questionable, mostly the doings of Rubio who seemed to have been a devious character. My cousin, Juan Rubio, said that perhaps Cristóbal Rubio was in a hurry to sell the land, and he was probably on the run to save his neck from stretching rope. Years later, in my research I found that Cristóbal Rubio met a violent death at the hands of Texas Rangers in 1842.[2] He was wanted for many crimes in San Antonio and Seguin and was supposedly a spy for the Mexican army. He was described as a desperate villain, an early Texas *desperado*. One of his crimes may have been the faulty land conveyance described above. Rubio's vengeance was no doubt directed at the Anglo-Americans who ruled Texas and were the oppressors of Texas Mexicans. Cristóbal may well have been the first social bandit in Texas history and not the last. Others would follow in the not too distant future.[3]

In terms of acreage, five leagues of land were the equivalent of one *hacienda*. José María de la Garza managed to obtain eleven leagues, comprising over two *haciendas,* or about 48,700 acres. This Mexican *ranchero* seemed to possess a great desire for acquisition of huge tracts of land; but it was doubtful that he or his descendants remained in possession of the land. In the final analysis, the North American Anglo acquired possession of almost all Texas lands — *including the air above.*

I noticed with interest that the most land acquired by Anglo-Americans in Texas was one league, or 4,428 acres. There being very few of these grants, most possessions were for one-quarter league (1,107 acres) or one-half league (2,214 acres) and sometimes one labor (177 acres). These were generally for farmers. While silently viewing this generous system of land distribution to the North Americans, it seemed to me that the Mexican government was overly generous to foreigners. In a few years this generosity would be repaid with the long rifle and the Bowie knife.

Within a very few years after their arrival in the Mexican province, the Americans undisputedly gained possession of Mexican territory. While professing to be Catholics and loyal Mexicans, under the surface there was much treachery. With manifest destiny as their guide, they overcame anyone who dared stand in their way.

Before departing the General Land Office, we paused briefly to view the paintings of Texas heroes hanging on the walls. There were also paintings depicting the earliest Texas settlers, including one of a Spanish *conquistador* wearing an armored vest and helmet, boots and spurs. This was probably Governor Alonso de Leon of Coahuila province. The statue of General Sam Houston was most prominently displayed; Stephen F. Austin's statue was in the capitol. When these two men entered Texas, the years of Mexican rule were numbered. Austin and Houston were of a somewhat different caliber, but their philosophies bore the same results. Central to the motivations of their new society which took root in Texas after 1821 and rebelled in 1836 was the acquisition of land, land, land, and more land.

On the return trip to Goliad I had the opportunity to view this magnificent South Texas country again, with sadness and perhaps a little hurt pride. As we rolled along, I stared out the automobile window. This great country once belonged to citizens of the kingdom of Spain who fought and bled to acquire it, and then finally but regretfully to Mexico. The Spaniards proved themselves to have been shrewd politicians in the course of their dealings with people from other countries. They far surpassed the Mexican leaders in this respect. The most destructive enemy of the Mexican was himself, and the ingredients of this evil were greed, jealousy, personal envy, and lastly disunity, for he appeared to thrive on this.

In the 1820s and 1830s, Mexico was beset by internal strife. Nearly all her former presidents became victims of the turmoil. Her army was constantly in the field stamping out one revolution after another, a sign of bad leadership in Mexico City. The best veteran officers and soldiers were being killed in these uprisings. These useless killings of Mexicans by Mexicans greatly weakened the army. When they were needed in Texas in 1836, they were not there to answer the call. While these revolutions were going on, the disregarded Texas province was literally being overrun by Anglo-Americans. The bold and strong-willed North Americans were solidly and firmly entrenched in Texas by 1830; the province was readied for a takeover.

Through her incompetent leaders, Mexico invited disaster when she allowed the first Anglo-American to settle in Texas. Had her leaders known of the North American's craving for land, her immigration policy may have been different. According to the Mexican settlers of La Bahía, the government in Mexico City appeared to favor the Anglo-American settlers over the native Mexicans. It seemed that the Mexican leaders wanted to impress the Americans with their generosity in land grant distribution. When the *alcalde* of

La Bahía complained bitterly to the government in Mexico City that the Americans were already dispossessing the Mexicans from their land, the leaders in Mexico City remained silent. When they did act in the disputes, they acted in favor of the Americans. These actions were bitterly resented by native Mexicans and La Bahía *alcalde* Rafael A. Manchola.[4]

It is certain that Manuel Becerra and his fellow *regidores* of the illustrious *ayuntamiento* supported their *alcalde*. In spite of this resistance, the American *empresarios* always emerged victorious from the disputes with the Mexicans. The Mexicans recoiled from these encounters, never forgetting how these things came about. After Mexico lost the war with the United States, why did not my ancestors sell what land they had and depart from Texas? Conditions surely must have been unstable in that defeated country. These ancestors must have known that to remain in Texas, they and their descendants would be subjected to abuse and prejudice by the Anglo-Texans. But the descendants of Manuel Becerra were of a rare breed, and they chose to remain where they were born regardless of the consequences.

[4]

Growing Up
Tejano

I was born in Goliad County on a ranch simply called Rancho el Oso or Bear Ranch. It was located about eight miles below La Bahía on the east bank of the San Antonio River. The ranch house was about six miles more or less from the Refugio road, which could easily be seen from the ranch due to the sparse plains area. My father, Guillermo Rubio, worked for the James O'Connor family, whose ranch was in the vicinity. It may well be that the ranch which can be seen from the Refugio road was the O'Connor ranch.

My first vivid memories were when we lived for a time on a farm west of a town called Palacios, near a large body of water we called *la laguna* or *el mar*. This was the Gulf Coast area of South Texas, truly a good place for young boys to fish and hunt. My father moved us to this isolated place from Goliad County where he had worked for the James O'Connor family as a *vaquero*. Father agreed to work the land as a sharecropper for a certain percent of the harvest. He intended to plant cotton and corn because he had five sturdy sons and two daughters to assist him in the hard work. The owner, whom I don't remember, loaned father four mules, five horses, a wagon, and the necessary equipment for planting the seed. Also included were two milk cows with small calves. One of the cows had a crooked horn and appeared to be possessed of a nasty disposition. I took an instant dislike to *la vaca con el cuerno torcido y el becerrito de ella* (the crooked horn cow and her calf), and I subjected both animals to many acts of deviltry which set the stage for near tragic consequences for my mother.

The house was big and livable but had an abundance of cracks in the walls. The outer walls were nailed to two by fours without any inside panelling. The two-by-four studs became the travel route for *ratones* (rats) in their search for food. On cold, windy nights the wind easily penetrated the thin clapboard walls. The howling winds created mournful sounds through the cracks in the walls and combined with the squeals from the fighting rats to terrify my six-year-old mind.

Hunting in the wilderness for the Rubio boys — Rosendo, Guillermo, Guadalupe, and me — was a thrilling adventure. We had four big dogs and tiny Pelón, the hairless one. This poor creature suffered miserably in wintertime. Pelón and I generally brought up the rear on the hunts for skunks and opossums. We were careful not to damage the skins so that the hides could be sold to the country store seven miles away. Redfish and trout abounded in the bay, and these we also sold to the store.

We generally hunted all night with our dogs. On one occasion, they ran back to us whining with tails between their legs. Someone shouted *"Pantera!"* The next thing I realized, we were in full flight with the dogs leading the way.

The following day my brothers searched the area for tracks of a panther while little Pelón and I remained close to home. They found nothing, but the episode put a stop to the all-night hunts for quite some time.

The first year's crop of cotton and corn was bountiful. Our entire family worked the fields especially during cotton picking time, the hottest season of South Texas. I hated to pick cotton. It was wretchedly hot and the stoop labor hurt my back. In my hip pocket I carried my slingshot and in my side pockets an abundance of clay balls the size of marbles as ammunition. To make my work more pleasant, I was constantly on the lookout for birds. By doing so, I lagged far behind the others in my picking, and Father would shout *"Dese prisa muchacho"* (Hurry up, boy!). I would always respond, *"Sí Papá."* But his admonitions only fell on deaf ears. Six-year-old boys do not like to work. All day long, my family heard: *Dese prisa muchacho. Sí, Papá. Dese prisa muchacho. Sí Papá.* It must have gotten old. When the heat became unbearable, I found some relief in the shade of the tall, green cotton plants. Often the only way I could continue picking was by burrowing my bare feet under the soft dry earth because the top of the ground was too hot to stand. My blue denims and heavy jacket made me even more uncomfortable. Only my little straw hat, which resembled a bird's nest, afforded any break from the sun's rays as I stooped to strip the open cotton bolls from their stalks.

Every once in a while a bird or rodent appeared which quickly became a target for my clay missiles when Father was not looking. I spent much of my time looking at the sky hoping to see dark clouds of an impending heavy rain. Only rain would bring a break in our toil and relief from the dreary rigors of cotton picking.

One day while looking for clouds I saw a hawk hovering in the sky. I knew this winged predator was after rats or field mice, and I began to shout and throw cotton bolls in the direction where I thought the creatures were. The hawk drew back its wings, dived for a scurrying field mouse, and managed to snare the creature with its talons. It carried its prey to a barbed-wire fence where it began to feast on the still struggling mouse. Thus, I learned a good lesson in survival. My shoutings at the hawk brought Father with a cotton stalk in his hand. He gave me a thrashing for not doing my share of the work. Father just didn't understand how much his youngest son hated to pick cotton. Sullenly, I continued to finish my row, despising every cotton boll I saw. Soon, however, my young mind began to drift, thinking of ways to torment the crooked horn cow and her calf back at the house.

After all the mischief I did to that cow, it became so temperamental that it gored my mother nearly to death. Father rightly suspected that one of us boys had been responsible for the cow's behavior, and so to make sure he punished the culprit, he whipped all three mischievous younger boys — Guillermo, Guadalupe, and me. My father and mother had such a responsibility with nine children at home. By then my oldest sister, Josephine, had married a fine boy named Antonio Flores and had moved away. Ramón, the last of their children, would later be born on the Peterson Ranch near Midway.

Antonio and Josephine would visit the farm quite often. Their eldest daughter, Elida, was just beginning to walk. Her grandfather and grandmother constantly held on to their first grandchild, while we other kids were amused with the little girl and never failed to play tricks on her. Generally, we tripped little Elida at every opportunity. Sometimes guiding her toward the corrals, we hoped she would step on cow and horse manure which abounded about the place. Josephine would become furious and chase us away, reprimanding us severely. But we defiantly shouted back verbal abuses. We considered her an intruder on the farm, for she was married and had no business trying to order us around.

For three young boys, the nearby lagoon was an irresistible area for exploration and adventure. One cold winter day we got into a small rowboat and struck out for the other side which lay about one and a half miles away. Guillermo, Guadalupe, and I, two of the big hounds, and tiny Pelón all clamored into the little boat for what we thought was a bold journey into the unknown. Considering our ages and the distance we had to navigate, this was a foolhardy and dangerous thing to do, but childish curiosity pushed us on. The trip progressed remarkably well until Guadalupe unintentionally struck me on the side of the head with his oar. Instantly, I struck him back with my oar. In the ensuing melee the boat capsized, spilling everyone into the frigid water, dogs and all.

It was indeed fortunate for us that everyone could swim quite well. We managed to right the boat, and continuing the trip, reached the other side miserably wet and cold. We beached the boat and, dogs running ahead, headed inland. The area was mostly plains with only a few trees. Satisfied that this place was not good for hunting, we returned home the way we had come. Even as adventurous as we three youngsters were, we never went back.

My earliest memories of the farm, I suppose, were ones of ups and downs. It was a hard life, but it had its pleasant moments. One thing it did was make me tough. And believe me, I needed to be tough when I began school because it was there that my worst memories really began. At school I first encountered, on my own, the condition of being a Mexican in an Anglo-American society. It was a physical and mental struggle that I will never forget, and one probably common to most Mexican children at that time.

The Anglo-Americans in that area of South Texas generally

preferred to be called white, and they held a dislike for Mexicans. This prejudice was very prevalent in the 1930s in the South Texas segregated rural school that I had the misfortune to attend. Regardless of the negative experience I endured as a child in segregated schools, I still believed that many of the whites were often compassionate and humane in their dealings with people of other ethnic groups. Unfortunately, the bigots far outnumbered the good ones so that the Mexican child could trust neither because it was difficult to differentiate between the good or bad white on first meeting.

The first Mexican school I attended was approximately 150 yards from the Anglo school. Our school was a one-room shack in the most deplorable condition and, in fact, it was a mockery of what a school should be. The two schools were separated by wooden fences, which indicated that the barefoot Mexicans (many of the poor little wretches did not own shoes) should keep on their side of the partition.

One day a daring blond boy crawled under the fence and came over to where I was and said something. I merely shook my head for I could not as yet understand English. He paused for a moment, then put up his fists and said, *"Quiere combate . . .* want to fight?" This sign language I understood perfectly. Instantly I flew at him with both fists swinging. My fury gained the element of surprise for me and a bloody nose for him. In the encounter I received a bruised lip. The boy was as bold as he was arrogant, but he was ingloriously put to flight. He had the audacity to invade Mexican territory, and he was routed without glory. As the fellow was trying mightily to squeeze through the fence, I continued beating him on the back. Soon a report came from the school principal directed at Miss Vela, the Mexican teacher. The principal protested vigorously that a group of Mexicans had beaten a white child.

Miss Vela, an attractive woman, was from Port Lavaca. Her eyes were like big, green marbles, and she looked more like an Anglo than a Mexican. I never cared much for Miss Vela. In my opinion, she was prejudiced against the Mexican children, for she would not allow us to speak Spanish. I always believed that this was the reason why so many of the children dropped out of school.

My schoolyard fight was the first of many encounters with the Anglos from which I didn't always emerge the victor. Often I went home with a bloody nose and black eyes, suffering the pangs of defeat. I fought the shoeless Mexicans, too, but more often with the whites, for I regarded these as my sworn enemies. In due time, I found that these Anglos thought they were better than the Mexicans (as evidenced by the segregated school, among other things), and due to this sad experience in the segregated Mexican school from the tender age of seven, I grew up despising Anglo-Texans and never trusting them. If these intense hatreds and prejudices were prevalent during modern times, how terrible must it have been for the Mexicans during the frontier days in Texas!

My fights at school became more frequent. I always struck first while the other boy was making his war talk. I would act really scared and my opponent generally always dropped his guard momentarily. When this happened, I would attack him viciously. These deceptive ruses were not always to my advantage, for the reverse happened in some encounters. When my opponent appeared to gain the upper hand I would break off the engagement and retreat in defeat and humiliation. Some of the Anglo-Texan youths were, in my opinion, positively brave fellows, almost to the point of foolhardiness. They were good fighters, such as the blond boy who had trespassed into Mexican territory. You might say these fights were childish versions of the cultural clash between the descendants of the Nordic frontiersmen and the Spanish *conquistadores*.

Once I saw a group of big Anglo boys encouraging two younger ones who were beating up a lone Mexican lad. They shouted "get the ugly Mexican," "get the Mex," "get the greaser," "don't let the greaser get away," and "kill the dirty Meskin." I could clearly hear the screams from the Mexican boy. How cowardly and brutal these Anglos were. I wanted desperately to come to the aid of the fallen Mexican, but I reasoned that to do so would be sheer madness. The beaten boy had walked into an ambush, and I determined never to get caught in the same circumstance. During roll call the next morning, I glanced back and saw an empty chair and knew who its occupant had been.

By the time I reached the age of ten I was an orphan. I was still in the segregated Mexican school, although by this time I could speak English fairly well.

This was clearly a world of survival for me. I got into fights only when the advantage was on my side, generally retreating when the odds seemed unfavorable, and I remained a loner.

My earliest childhood recollections at school hold no pleasant memories. Most youngsters in their first years of school experience a sense of unity and belonging. My own initial introduction into Anglo society was a brutal shock with which I was almost totally unprepared to cope. Perhaps the worst memory of all was the segregated school, far inferior to the white schoolhouse. Our school was in terrible need of repairs and paint, with cracks in the walls, and a lone potbellied stove that was supposed to heat the entire room in wintertime.

The Anglo's dirty name calling continued incessantly: "look at that Mex without shoes," "the greaser is poor," "yeah, all greasers are dirt poor," "Mexes don't eat bread, only totillas and beans." Here they, through the ignorance which they no doubt derived from their parents, missed the letter "r" in the word *tortillas*.

I don't ever remember seeing two Mexican youths eating their lunch together. This seemingly strange behavior was not for lack of friendship, but because of the Anglo behavior toward the Mexican-American children. These children eventually grew up hesitant to be called Mexican, for the Anglo-Texan perpetrators thought the name Mexican to be a dirty word. We Mexican-American children knew little or nothing about our proud Spanish-Mexican cultural heritage, not even of the cultural history of such things as our cuisine. At least we didn't in Goliad County. We didn't even want anyone to see what we ate for lunch each day. Everyone knew it was a rolled *tortilla* with a piece of meat or two; this was the forerunner of what is universally known today as the "burrito."

I would always take my lunch far away from the others, where I would turn my back, pull out the rolled *tortilla*, and quickly look around to see if anyone was looking. Immediately, I gobbled the cold *tortilla* with huge bites to finish in a hurry. We were like monkeys in a zoo cage feasting on peanuts. On rare occasions I saw a few of my classmates bring sandwiches for lunch — made with real bread. I would call them Mexican-Anglos because I was jealous that they fared better than I.

The boys' dilapidated outhouse was a sorry looking affair, dangerously leaning to one side. The girls' facility was no better and was rarely visited by the teacher. It was a source of amusement for us when we saw the teacher heading for the outhouse. I wished that the thing would topple over with her inside; however, this never happened. What a disappointment for me.

The Anglo outhouses were nicely painted white, which I deeply resented for I felt that everything they had was better than the Mexicans. Once I saw a girl with long pigtails go in and just for sheer deviltry and perhaps revenge I peppered it with my slingshot. The missiles for my weapons were clay balls which, when they came into contact with my object, broke into hundreds of small particles. Three girls came running out furious and told their teacher that a Mexican was bombarding their restroom. The girl with the pigtails was bringing up the rear, and to her I delivered a parting shot. The missile landed close to her heels and burst, covering her with dust. She screamed to high heaven and ran even faster.

After the horrible automobile accident which killed my parents and most of my brothers and sisters, the rest of us finally settled with my brother, Daniel, in the little town of Bloomington, and I went to another segregated school. It seemed as if everyone in Bloomington, both Mexican and Anglo, knew about the tragic fate of my family.

The Anglo school was on the other side of town — perhaps that was just as well — but there was a Negro school about two or three hundred yards away. This was my first contact with black people. I wondered if the boys were good fighters. I was most curious about their hair, particularly that of the little girls, because they always seemed to wear little pigtails that stuck straight up. These seemed to me like tiny horns with little bows attached. I felt much compassion for them then for I knew that they, too, were segregated. Even the wretched local movie theater was segregated.

The Mexican school was very nice but we were still segregated, each race in its own area. The school had two huge classrooms. I noticed that there were very few cracks in the walls as compared with my first school.

In the Bloomington Mexican school I would soon come face to face with my first Anglo-American teachers. None of these teachers could speak Spanish, yet they taught in the Mexican school. Luckily, I did not have another Miss Vela.

Even though it is now some thirty-six years later, I still vividly remember my first Anglo-American teacher, Miss Edna Patterson. If I should narrate a glowing account of her, it is because she is so richly deserving. If my attitude changed for the better toward all things in general, it was through the efforts of this wonderful, compassionate teacher whom I greatly respected and came to adore in my own childish way. From the very beginning, Miss Patterson displayed genuine concern and affection for me. Many years later, while on leave from the Marine Corps, I spoke with her parents, and they assured me that their daughter had always been truly concerned about the welfare of her orphan pupil. To learn that my feelings were requited was most gratifying.

Edna Patterson was the first and only Anglo-American teacher who expressed kindness and understanding toward me. Though I was still greatly resentful and bitter toward Anglo-Texans, over the years these ill feelings started to change because of the attitude of that Anglo school teacher toward her Mexican-American pupils. She helped restore my individual dignity as a human being to a certain extent.

She was a very lovely young woman. Her hair was light brown and her eyes were blue. She possessed an amiable, easygoing disposition. When the occasion demanded, however, she was a strict but fair disciplinarian.

At that time, the Texas public school system required that a child of Mexican extraction complete five years of school before transferring to the sixth grade in the all-Anglo school. There were not many of these transfers, for the Mexican child was severely handicapped and doomed to failure from his first day in the Mexican school. Texas educators felt that by the time the Mexican child finished five years of school he was capable of competing with the Anglo child. This grave misconception resulted in tragic and dire consequences for the already defeated Mexican children. The segregated school quickly made him a second-class citizen far inferior to the Anglo. Consequently, by the time he reached the sixth grade, he was fearful and sullen. My Mexican-American friends feared attending the all-white school because they felt that the Anglos were better. The majority of these unfortunate children were unable to cope with Anglo-American society and dropped out of school. They soon drifted to the cotton fields of South Texas, and became *piscadores* for the rest of their lives — truly born losers who lived in chronic poverty. The unfortunate wretches knew no other occupation than the miserable cotton fields. I knew many children who, by the time they reached the age of ten years, were already veteran cotton pickers. I saw these things with my own eyes many, many times.

Miss Patterson did what she could to break that cycle. She succeeded with me, and with some others too. I, and they, will attest to that. Years later, when she contracted a lingering illness which brought her death, we deeply felt the loss.

Miss Patterson had her hands full with us. Since there were no Anglo or Negro boys to fight with, we fought each other. I must confess that generally I was in the center of the action. During one playground melee, I was left lying on the field when Miss Patterson came to my rescue. She kneeled down, helped me get up, and put her arm around my shoulder until we reached the school. She appeared somewhat distressed, for I could feel her arms shaking and hear her voice faltering. I noticed beads of perspiration on her forehead and upper lip.

Once I became involved in a fist fight with a larger boy and was being soundly defeated when a pretty girl named Mamie Mercado intervened. This intervention only increased my fury. Pulling my yellow pencil from my hip pocket I lunged at her. She put up her hand to fend off the blow and I sank the sharp point in her palm. Mamie's screams were frightening. Her girlfriends, seeing her bloody hand and dress, began to wail. At this point, her brother, Stevan Mercado, grabbed me. I was about to plunge the pencil stub into him when the older boys wrested the weapon away. The teachers, including Miss Patterson, were horrified when they saw Mamie's hand bleeding profusely. They seemed confused, but they managed to stop the bleeding. Mamie's parents took her to the doctor in Victoria.

On the school playground there were many cries and accusations that "the long-haired rebel Rubio boy did it." Mamie Mercado's girlfriends said that "the Rubio boy is an evil little monster and ought to be sent back to the farm." They shouted that I was nothing but trouble and should be expelled from school for good. They all felt that I was heading in the direction of an outlaw. The head teacher angrily shouted, "Young man, go to my office immediately." She gave me a thorough and severe reprimand and reported me to the school officials, which resulted in expulsion from school for a week. This I enjoyed, for I needed the respite.

Don Pioquento Mercado, Mamie's father, bitterly complained to the school authorities, the teachers, and my eldest brother, Daniel, about my cruel attack on his daughter. Before long, the story of the fight at the Mexican school was all over town. Clearly, I was labeled as a rebellious orphan boy who had shamefully stabbed a lovely young girl. To make matters worse, someone let out the word that I had also almost stabbed her brother. This brought on more complaints and reprimands from the teachers.

It seemed to me that thereafter every time there was trouble in school I was accused of being the perpetrator by the girls as well as by some cowardly Mexican boys.

"El muchacho Rubio es mal persona, cuando este más grande lo van a mandar al carcel. Él es como un potro ladino de los montes, así son los muchachos cuando no tienen padre y madre, este muchacho Rubio es un demónio." Such was the humble opinion of the elder Mexicans of Bloomington. Indeed, their opinion of my future was a dim one. "The Rubio boy is a bad person. When he grows up they will send him to the penitentiary. He is like the wild colt of the wilderness; this is how boys grow up without father and mother. The Rubio boy is a demon."

This opinion of the elders was shared by the young Mexican boys and girls. I was too busy with my own affairs to care or pay attention to their remarks. Even after these turbulent episodes, Edna Patterson's attitude toward me never changed. I will never forget her belief in me.

Eduardo Reyes and I were constantly at each others' throats. We usually settled our differences after school in a fight. He was tough. In one of these fights one day, I hit Eduardo solidly between the eyes. By the time he arrived home both his eyes were black. His father asked him about the bruises, and Eduardo told him that while trying to catch a ball he had run into a telephone pole! Stella Reyes, his sister, told her father that Eduardo had been fighting with the Rubio boy. Señor Reyes became enraged and grabbing a huge leather belt, dealt a severe thrashing to poor Eduardo. He was made a loser twice in one day.

It seemed to me that the teachers at the Bloomington Mexican school delighted in hearing their Mexican students sing "The Eyes of Texas Are Upon You," and "The Yellow Rose of Texas." I stubbornly refused to join in for I did not consider myself to be a part of

it all. I was in a segregated school and separated from the other citizens who did not consider me an equal. How could I possibly join
in on the Texas songs? I resisted anything which would place the
Mexican beneath the Anglo-Americans. I felt that singing the
Texan songs was an affront to my individual dignity. It was simply
impossible for the teachers to make Anglos out of Mexicans, and I
was penalized severely for my rebellious attitude. Usually, the
teacher would draw a circle on the blackboard. Standing on my
toes with my hands behind my back, I had to keep my nose in that
ring. These penalties resulted in deeper hatred and resentful ill feelings toward Anglo-Texans. I never heard the teachers tell us we
were Americans. How could I join in singing the American songs
when I was not considered one? Some of my Mexican friends made
a feeble effort to sing just to escape the punishment.

After Miss Patterson died, despite her best efforts, I dropped
out of school unable to cope with the educational system as it was
then. From there I became a migrant laborer — first in San Benito
and Robstown picking cotton. Thereafter, I drifted to Wisconsin to
work in the cherry fields; thence to Illinois to work in the corn
fields. In Indiana, I worked in the tomato fields doing backbreak-
ing labor. Many times I stood by the side of the road with all my
worldly possessions in a brown paper bag, hitchhiking back to Goliad. I was constantly on the move, never really having a perma-
nent home. Tiring of this hobo existence, I joined the United States
Marine Corps in 1947, where I finally found a home and learned
what it was to be an American. One of the things they taught me
was never to give up, whether in combat or otherwise. The disci-
pline and methodical training the Marine Corps imparted to me
was now being put to the supreme test.

The memories of my tumultuous, unhappy childhood filled
my head as I gazed from the car window across the rolling South
Texas country. My thoughts were finally interrupted when we arrived at Uncle Jesús Rubio's ranch in Cuero. The past had to wait.
There were more pressing matters of the present at hand. We remained at my uncle's house for a while, and he assured me that he
would be at the meeting in Goliad later that evening. Before long,
we were back on the road to Goliad and a family confab.

[5]

A Century of Becerras

On August 21,1972, my cousins Juan and Core and I visited with Don Nicolas Cabrera in Goliad. He has been a resident of that town all his life. Señor Cabrera was born in 1895, so when we spoke with him in 1972 he was seventy-seven years of age. Despite his age, he appeared very alert and keen of mind. He was tall and somewhat slight of frame but stood very proud, and his skin was crisply sunburned. This venerable old man was one of those few remaining Mexican *vaqueros* in Texas.

Don Nicolas sadly related to us that his father, Macario Cabrera, once owned a small plot of land about ten miles southeast of Goliad. When asked where, he said *"El terrano está para el rumbo de Refugio* ("The land is in the general direction of Refugio"), indicating the direction with a sweep of his arm. Cabrera said that about 1902 or 1903 there were many people found hanging from the limbs of mesquite trees. All the victims were Mexicans who owned small plots of land. Sometimes the victim's family also disappeared completely.

The elderly *vaquero* settled in his chair comfortably and his mind wandered back to the early years. He said that the hangings without benefit of trial in a court of law were a terrible injustice to the Mexicans. These evil doings happened in Goliad County and perhaps in Refugio County, for he had heard of many strange things having occurred there.

For example, when Don Nicolas was only an eight-year-old child, about three o'clock one morning hooded men with pistols and rifles entered the home of their neighbor, dragging the protesting Mexican outside. The hooded killers unceremoniously strung him up in front of his family, but the fiends moved the body to a spot near the Cabrera farm apparently to give a warning to other local Mexicans. Young Nicolas had risen with the crack of dawn that day and, rubbing the sleep from his eyes, was soon on his way to the outhouse. The young Cabrera boy, still somewhat sleepy, was unprepared for the sight that greeted him. On nearing the outhouse the boy glanced toward the nearby mesquite trees. What he saw seemed unreal. Quickly he rubbed his eyes, and an object dangling from the tree came into clear focus. He recognized the object as being the unfortunate neighbor. Letting out a terrified shriek, he fled toward his home screaming at the top of his lungs.

His parents heard him and came out of their cabin. Don Nicolas related that he would never again go near the outhouse. Soon his entire family fled the area. The Cabrera family read the terrifying sight of the hanging man as an unmistakable warning: *Vacate the land or suffer the fate of your neighbor.* They loaded their belongings in their wagon and left, followed by the milk cow and a lone bleating goat. Don Nicolas said the marauding hooded night killers were, as expected, Anglos.

He recalled that by 1905 none of his Mexican friends who had owned small plots of land between Refugio and Goliad still occupied their property. Juan, Core, and I wondered who had those lands now and how in the world they could claim valid title. Don Nicolas said they could not have valid deeds.

He also claimed to be a relative of the Rubio family, a cousin of Grandfather Juan Rubio. The old man was entirely correct because my later research revealed that his grandfather, Macario Cabrera, and Juan Rubio's mother, Teresita Cabrera, were brother and sister. Don Nicolas was a truthful man who told us what he remembered after almost seven decades.

The early maps of Refugio and Goliad counties revealed a substantial number of Mexican landowners in these areas. This is particularly true of the de la Garzas of Refugio County. However, by 1872 these landowners' names began to disappear, and by 1883 only a few remained in Refugio County. These were the fortunate few but not for long. By 1900, the Refugio County map was covered with Anglo-American names with only three or four owners with Spanish surnames. The once powerful Mexican landowning *dons* were no more.

The family gathering on the evening of August 21, 1972, was attended by between sixty and seventy of the Becerra heirs. The Manuel Becerra heirs at this gathering were the sons and daughters and grandchildren of Francisca de la Garza and her brother, José María de la Garza, the eldest son of Antonio de la Garza and Ponposa Bontan. It was the first and largest gathering in the history of the family. I was particularly struck by the beauty of the de la Garza women, some of whom were quite old but still retaining their beauty. I warmly and affectionately embraced all these kinfolk. They would strongly support me on the long road that lay ahead.

I knew that a detailed and patient explanation was in order and on that basis I proceeded. Mention was made of the trip to the General Land Office at Austin to inspect the Refugio County maps for 1851–1921. When I stated that Manuel Becerra failed to appear on the maps, I noticed expressions of disappointment and anger on their faces. The relatives seemed genuinely interested and enthusiastic with the progress we had made to date. They inspected the displayed maps and, not finding the name of Manuel Becerra, voiced their opinions as to the reasons why the Becerra name failed to appear.

Their opinions varied somewhat, but all believed that our grandfather, Antonio de la Garza, had lost the land through fraud and murder in Refugio County. Some even alleged that Manuel Becerra himself had been killed over a land boundary dispute even before his grandson, Antonio de la Garza, had been born. This was not factual, but very nearly so as later research proved that Antonio de la Garza was born on March 21, 1848, and the last document on record signed by Manuel Becerra and his wife, Juana María Cadena, was dated October 14, 1848, in Refugio County.

According to Jesús and Daniel Rubio and Antonio de la Garza (a namesake of the Refugio cattleman), a similar search for the lost land was begun in 1952 by Olivia Ybarbo and Candido Artero from Victoria, but nothing was accomplished as there was no family support in that endeavor. So our meeting of August 1972 was a fresh beginning of a long struggle.

It was most gratifying when everyone gave enthusiastic approval to the continued investigation. This gathering was an emotional and traumatic one, and many family members met for the first time in their lives. Yesterday they were strangers, but on that day they were united as a family. I felt honored for having been responsible for this first Becerra family reunion, and I was overwhelmed with emotion and joy. I had never expected such a reception.

During this gathering, I tried to be fair and loyal to the family cause and answered their questions fairly and impartially. Perhaps this prompted them to support me as they did. I warmly thanked my aunts and uncles for their belief and trust in our present quest. All wished us Godspeed in our search for the lost Becerra land, and they insisted the investigation be pursued quickly and vigorously.

The family was magnificent that evening of August 21, 1972. My journey from California to Texas to rally family support was totally successful and well worth the time and effort expended. My spirits and morale were soaring. Before concluding the meeting, I informed them about the required expenses to send Alvin L. Harris to Texas for at least three days. Upon my return to California, I would arrange a meeting with Harris to decide when to make a return trip to Texas.

The day after the family meeting I left for Refugio to search out the family records. Anxiety coupled with fear of not finding my ancestors in the old records was disturbing. About six miles out of Goliad on the Refugio road, I glanced to my left, vainly hoping to catch a glimpse of the old ranch house where my sister had told me I was born. It was fruitless. All that could be seen were some large white buildings; the small barren plain was still there, lonely and desolate.

The town of Refugio had a somewhat dejected appearance associated with poverty, or so it seemed to me. It was my impression that this town owed its very existence to a few of the wealthiest landowners in the area. The fact that my ancestors were early colonists of Refugio did not alter my poor impression of this Texas town.

Father J. William Hennel, pastor of Our Lady of Refugio Church, met me at the door of his church. After informing Father Hennel of the purpose of my visit, he assured me that the records would be made available to conduct my search. He was very kind and understanding. Eagerly I searched the church files for Becerra's name but experienced failure once again. Becerra did not appear in the church records, and neither did his wife, Juana María Cadena.

Despite my disappointment, I continued the search and was rewarded by finding the names of Francisco de la Garza and his children. Perhaps my most joyous moment came when I found Antonio de la Garza (Francisco's only son by his first marriage) and Ponposa Bontan and their two children. Don Manuel's daughter María Josefa Becerra was also in the baptismal records; she had been a sponsor for one of Francisco de la Garza's and second wife Gertrudis Garcia's children. I noticed all these de la Garza children had been born between 1856 and 1861. This appears to have been the last recorded information left by Manuel Becerra's daughter María Josefa Becerra.

The actual copies of the birth and baptismal certificates for de la Garza and allied families were not on file. When I mentioned this to Father Hennel, he said that original birth certificates of those persons born before the year 1850 were sent to Mexico by order of the bishop. Father Hennel was certain that the records were sent to Our Lady of Guadalupe Church in Zacatecas. I expressed my sincere appreciation to him for his assistance. It was indeed fortunate that I found the Becerra-de la Garza names in his church. Our Lady of Guadalupe Church in Zacatecas might reveal additional information.

I went to the local library in Refugio and found excellent material on the county's earliest history. A great many of the de la Garzas were mentioned, as well as Manuel Becerra.[1]

While deeply involved with my research at the Refugio library, I was somewhat distracted by the presence of several booted Anglo-Texans. Here I had the opportunity to observe and listen to their earnest conversations. It seemed to me these Anglos pronounced the name Refugio "Rafurio," apparently content or accustomed to change the sound to conform to their own brand of Texas vernacular. Their unique and colorful manner of talking, particularly the

Texan drawl, was quite fascinating. I became engrossed in listening and nearly forgot the research task at hand. I noticed that when pronouncing "Rafurio," their upper lip seemed to protrude. By the expression on their faces they seemed to endure a certain pain when pronouncing the odd Spanish name.

At the county courthouse I was shown an ancient-looking volume concerning marriages dating to the year 1829. Here I found Manuel Becerra's name. This volume was in Spanish, and again I was unable to translate.

Perhaps the most historical of the volumes was one known as *Libro Becerra*, which pertains to town lots in Refugio dating back to the Mexican era. It appears that Manuel Becerra authenticated the recordings in the volume, for his signature is prominently displayed on the front page. This was the *Libro Becerra* mentioned in Hubert Howe Bancroft's *History of the North Mexican States and Texas*. However, Hobart Huson in his *History of Refugio County* titles the volume *Libro Becerra de la villa de Refugio*, properly named after its originator or keeper, Manuel Becerra.[2]

Patiently continuing my search, I located the marriage certificate of my great-great-grandfather, Francisco de la Garza, to Gertrudis Garcia. The marriage took place at his ranch known as Rancho Alamito on August 18, 1851. This was the *don's* second marriage. Father James Girandon solemnized the rites of matrimony between Francisco and Gertrudis. He then filed the certificate for record on September 16, 1851. W. M. McFarland was the county clerk and Patrick Shelly the deputy clerk, all from Refugio.[3]

I felt there was something strange and almost sinister about the town of Refugio. Perhaps it had to do with what Don Nicolas Cabrera had told me the previous day. However, I strongly suspected it went back much farther than the years 1902–03. I had begun to feel that it involved my great-grandfather, Antonio de la Garza, and his family.

Many of the people with whom I came into contact in Refugio appeared annoyed and even suspicious. Except for Father Hennel, I sensed that local residents were reluctant to assist me. Prejudice against Mexican-Americans still existed, perhaps as much as in any other town in Texas. But I considered myself very fortunate indeed for I had established contact with my ancestors of so long ago.

Concluding my preliminary examination of the records in Refugio, I departed believing that one day I would return. There was more information to be found, and I meant to find what I sought regardless of the obstacles in my path. I was in a jubilant state of mind when I arrived at Goliad. I informed Uncle Tomás Rubio and Aunt Juanita Gonzales of what I had found about our ancestors' history in Refugio County. Uncle Tomás and I talked until the wee hours of the morning, the conversation relating to the family history with which he was quite familiar.

Years before, on the day of the funeral services for my family at La Bahía, I had left the cemetery and gone to the home of Uncle Tomás and Aunt Juanita. Throughout the years I had never neglected to visit them. On that day in 1942, there had been many people at my aunt and uncle's house, mostly relatives. To escape the people, I retreated to their bedroom. When I looked up with swollen eyes I saw a picture of a lovely young woman with a smile on her face. Over thirty years later, as a grown man, I once again was gazing intently at the picture of the green-eyed woman. She was my grandmother, Francisca de la Garza, who was about thirty-four years old when the picture was taken. She greatly resembled her father, Antonio.

Uncle Tomás told me that Grandmother Francisca was a courageous woman born and reared on the rugged Texas frontier. She and my grandfather, Juan Rubio, were the parents of ten children. Their youngest son, Uncle Tomás, was born on March 18, 1903, in Goliad County. Juan died on February 24, 1903, before his son was born. Grandmother became a widow with ten children to raise — an awesome task for a woman. Her father, Antonio, assisted his eldest daughter when he was able. But he had two daughters and two sons still at home, and these were hard times. He visited his daughter and her family almost daily, for he was concerned about their well-being.

Uncle Tomás told me that when Antonio de la Garza, fifty-five years old in 1903, entered his daughter's home and saw her suffering with her children, he brooded and became bitter. He often recalled the good life on Rancho Alamito in Refugio County when he had large herds of cattle and an abundance of fowl, pigs, and goats. His family had never been in want of food or shelter; but bad American gunmen in Refugio County had changed all that.

Life on the Alamito Ranch in the early 1870s had been pleasant and serene for him and his young bride, Ponposa Bontan. During the cool evenings he and Ponposa would sit on the porch and view their herd of grazing cattle. This tract of land had belonged to his grandfather, Manuel Becerra, but by 1870 Antonio reigned supreme on the Becerra lands.

Antonio was the only grandson of Manuel Becerra, and his older sisters — Trinidad, Genoveva, and Rosalia — saw to it that he assumed the leadership after the death of their father. Uncle Tomás told me again that Antonio's downfall and ultimate ruin came as a result of his violent encounters with vicious Anglo-American *pistoleros*.

Antonio became a widower on March 3, 1891. He would visit his wife's grave at the de la Garza cemetery, and he never forgot to take flowers even if they were wildflowers which grew in abundance behind his cabin. Antonio would kneel by Ponposa's grave and pray for her, wishing desperately that God could bring her back to him.

Antonio told his grandchildren that, while on the Alamito Ranch, he always carried plenty of cash in his pockets, particularly gold coins. In 1903, while at the home of his daughter, Francisca, he knew all these things were of the past. By 1903, he considered himself fortunate if he carried a lowly nickel in his pocket.

Antonio took his recently widowed and destitute daughter, now with child (Tomás Rubio would be born within two weeks), a large bag of coffee, a good supply of sugar and flour, a bag of beans, and two rabbits. Antonio's eldest granddaughter, fourteen-year-old Sálome Rubio, adored her grandfather and would immediately make coffee for him. Francisca's children would sit around their grandfather and the eldest would pepper him with countless questions. He always commented on their smoky green eyes.

Juan Rubio served as deputy sheriff of Goliad County from 1890 to 1903. Before his death he had been reappointed by Sheriff George S. Petty to another term of either two or four years. He was about thirty years old when first appointed deputy in 1890. The job provided the large family with the necessities for their daily existence. Rubio supplemented his income by cutting and hauling wood to residents of the town.

About 1896, Juan Rubio and his son, Guillermo, were bringing a load of wood to town when they were stopped by Texas Rangers about three miles from town. The Rangers suspected that Juan was a Mexican bandit in disguise. Grandfather explained to the Rangers that the rancher had given him permission to cut wood from his land. The persistent Rangers demanded identification, whereupon Grandfather brought forth the deputy's badge. After viewing the badge, the Rangers wheeled about their mounts and rode into town to ask the sheriff about Juan Rubio.

Sheriff Petty informed them that his deputy was one of the best peace officers in that area. Furthermore, he had known the deputy for many years.

After Juan's death, Francisca de la Garza returned her husband's pistol, rifle, and cartridge belts to the sheriff. The destitute woman soon petitioned the officials of Goliad County for assistance which was a task she did not care to do, but under the pressing circumstances she had but little choice. Francisca knew that her husband had been an efficient peace officer of Goliad County for nearly fourteen years. Many were the times when his life was in danger while pursuing and capturing dangerous Mexican bandits and other undesirables. Juan Rubio had done his duty for his community, and that is why Francisca decided to apply for assistance.

It was solely through the efforts of the kind sheriff that she was awarded a small amount of income with which to sustain herself and ten children. By this time Tomás was a few months old, and Francisca was a happy woman indeed because her children would have enough to eat. The sheriff saw the terrible predicament facing his former deputy's widow. However, the assistance was only for winter months when there was no field work available for the children.

Francisca had greatly feared the approach of winter for she knew there would be suffering and possibly hunger for her family. This first winter of 1903 would be the first without her husband since their marriage on January 29, 1887. She was well acquainted with the brutal Texas northers that easily penetrated the thin walls of her cabin. She instructed her eldest sons, Guillermo and Stevan, and daughter Sálome to begin patching up the cracks in the cabin walls and roof. She wanted her home well prepared to meet winter's first onslaught. Also, she made sure there was plenty of firewood stacked behind the potbellied stove in the corner.

Francisca and her children did indeed suffer miserably that

winter of 1903–04. In spite of the destitute conditions and the terrors of hunger and cold, this remarkable woman and her children survived nature's ravages. She was a very religious woman and at night she would kneel down and pray for guidance in this time of peril.

When conditions were at their worst, the family barely survived. Grandmother was extremely careful when measuring flour to bake the bread in a half-inch deep pan. She dared not spill any of the precious flour and, if she did, she would pick it up. She would divide the baked bread into ten equal pieces and distribute one to each child. The same procedure was followed with the beans and coffee. Countless nights she went to bed feeling the pangs of hunger so the children could have their ration of food.

During cold and moonlit nights, she would stand behind the potbellied stove and stare out toward the road where her husband rode for so many years on his way home. At times it seemed she saw her husband riding toward the cabin. She would say a prayer and go to bed lonely and hungry.

Francisca's eldest sons were in the brush constantly hunting for birds and rabbits. Tomás Rubio said that by the year 1905 the rabbit population had been reduced drastically. As a consequence, the Rubio hunters had to go farther into the brush. The Rubios were not solely responsible for the rabbit decline in Goliad County. Others, mostly Mexicans, were in competition for food.

Antonio de la Garza had given his widowed daughter two and three-quarter acres of land from his tiny eighteen-acre plot. The two and three-quarter acres still remain in the Rubio family to this day. He also gave her a good mule and a plow. With this she would plant corn, beans, and chili. The harvest, particularly the corn and beans, she would save for winter. During the winter of 1903 and thereafter, Antonio would slaughter several pigs and give his daughter half or more. She would make *chicharones,* meaty pork skins, and store them in a large barrel filled with salt. When winter came, she would take a mortgage on the mule and use the cash to purchase flour and coffee. These, together with the *chicharones,* the beans, and the corn she had stored for corn tortillas, barely sustained the family. During the summer months when field work was plentiful, the children picked cotton and Francisca would scrupulously repay her mortgage and again acquire clear title to her mule

before winter. This unique method of survival was repeated year after year.

Francisca was greatly concerned about the welfare of her faithful mule. She had the boys build a shed to shelter the beast from the cold. This beast of burden was a valued asset to the family, for it meant the dividing line between survival and hunger.

Grandmother was of average height and her appearance could suggest that she was frail and delicate. In reality, she was possessed of great courage and endurance. Her ten children became solid, God-fearing and law-abiding citizens. She was very religious, and she clung to the Catholic faith of her ancestors. Her father was a devout Catholic, and her children and grandchildren attend Sunday services at Our Lady of Loreto at La Bahía to this day.

By mid-year 1905, my father (Guillermo) was nearly sixteen years old and restless. He was proficient with a Colt 45 pistol he used for target practice. Ismael de la Garza, Grandmother's younger brother, coached his nephew with the pistol. Grandmother severely reprimanded her brother for teaching her son the use of what she considered the devil's weapon. Ismael assured his older sister that her son must learn how to defend himself with a pistol and knife if necessary. All of this was pure nonsense as far as Grandmother Francisca was concerned, and she told her brother to stop the foolishness as it would lead to trouble. Grandmother knew that her brother, Ismael, possessed a "mean streak" which was common among the de la Garza men, and she was aware that Ismael sometimes vanished from Goliad County for many days and sometimes weeks. She wondered if he crossed the border into Mexico on wild escapades, perhaps even in company with Mexican bandits.

Ismael, born at La Bahía on September 30, 1879, was twenty-six years old, and Francisca felt he ought to marry a local girl and settle down. Meanwhile, her son, Guillermo, was becoming restless and sullen and seemed to change for the worse. Francisca blamed her son's ill behavior on Ismael, who seemed to be a bad influence. She told her father about the matter, but her concern fell on deaf ears, for Antonio also believed in making his Rubio grandsons good fighters with pistols or knives. Guillermo could have easily acquired a pistol and a fast horse and become a *desperado*. Instead, the spirited and sometimes rebellious youth chose to remain and help his mother rear the younger children.

During the latter part of 1905, my father began to work as a *vaquero* for one of the big cattle ranchers in the area. He still carried the Colt 45 pistol for protection against rattlesnakes and bandits. The majority of the cattle rustlers were marauding bandits from across the Rio Grande. These *desgraciados* greatly delighted in raiding Texas cattle ranches, making no distinction between Anglo and Mexican ranchers. Uncle Tomás said Father often told him that the brigands and killers from across the border even stole chickens, anything which would yield a dishonest *peso*.

Stevan Rubio soon joined Father to work as a *vaquero*. Eventually all of the Rubios pursued this time-honored occupation and worked for the largest cattle ranchers of the area, the Thomas O'Connor family. Uncle Stevan resided to the day of his death in 1979 on the O'Connor family's ranch in Victoria County. Uncles Stevan and Guadalupe Rubio served honorably in World War I, fighting in France and suffering from being gassed by the Germans.

Guillermo Rubio also entered the military, but the great war ended while he was en route to Victoria. Francisca de la Garza feared daily for the lives of her two soldier sons who were fighting the war so many thousands of miles away from her cabin at La Bahía. She knew that the United States Army did not feed the soldiers *tortillas* and beans because her sons had written and told her they missed those at mealtimes. She could not read or write, but upon being told these things she would break down and cry.

Many years later her grandsons, the Rubios, Floreses, and Carabajals, would return to similar battlefields and fight the same enemy her sons had fought in 1917–18. There would also be other conflicts in which the name Rubio would be deeply involved; many would pay the supreme sacrifice for their country.

By 1909, Guillermo Rubio was twenty-one years old, ill-tempered, and in the prime of life. He wanted to follow in the footsteps of his uncle, Ismael de la Garza. By 1910, the Mexican revolution was being fought across the Rio Grande, and for the young *vaquero* it must have been a great temptation. His loyalty and responsibility to Francisca prevailed; however, he still caroused around the local *cantinas* with his uncle.

Francisca de la Garza died of cancer on August 22, 1935.[4] According to her son, Tomás, she suffered greatly from want of finances to buy the necessary medicine to ease the pain. During the last few days of her life, her father would approach the head of her bed and make the sign of the cross. She would open her eyes and smile, and the eighty-seven-year-old man would kneel and begin praying for his daughter to get well. After praying, he had to be assisted to his feet by his grandsons. His leathery, wrinkled face bespoke the torment and grief he felt for his eldest daughter. It was usually Tomás Rubio who assisted his grandfather to the porch where they had a rocking chair for him.

On August 23, 1972, I left Texas after a most informative talk with Uncle Tomás. It was remarkable what could be learned about history and a family's past by listening to elder members. My uncles and aunts had already begun to serve me well in this regard.

Manuel Garcia and Lily Rubio assured me that funds would be made available for the attorney's return trip to Texas.

During the last week of August 1972, after I had returned to California, a large family gathering was held at the home of John Artero in Victoria. At this gathering was Olivia Ybarbo de la Garza of California, who had the original Manuel Becerra land grant documents. Also present were members of the Rubio, Garcia, Martinez, and Ybarbo families. Family interest in our land search was running high by this time.

The family had asked Olivia to send them the original deed papers, but she chose to bring the valuable and ancient papers personally. They reminded Olivia that some twenty years previously she had been involved in a similar investigation and had accomplished little except to abruptly leave Texas with the original deeds the family had loaned her, creating much suspicion among family members.

Some family members were strongly opposed to having an out-of-state attorney conduct the investigation of the family records. Others insisted they did not want a Texas attorney involved at this time. In the final vote, the heirs from Goliad County won in favor of Harris.

Tomás and Jesús Rubio strongly appealed to Don Plácido Martinez to side with the Goliad families. Plácido and his Rubio cousins grew up together in Goliad. These two family branches had always been closely united.

The trip I had made on August 21, 1972, to attend the gathering at Goliad indeed had generated family support. I returned to Texas on October 6 and was warmly met by first cousins Eva Rubio and Lucinda Carbajal, who took me to meet and interview Aunt Sálome, a matriarch of our family.

Sálome R. Lambardia, next to my father in age, was born in Goliad County on April 22, 1889. Upon seeing her for the first time I was struck by her smoky green eyes. She immediately said that I looked like her eldest brother, Guillermo Rubio.

Although she was eighty-three years old, Aunt Sálome possessed a very keen mind and was remarkably alert.[5] It was clear to me when I first set eyes on her that she, like Uncle Tomás, was my closest living link to the past. In 1902, when she was nearly thirteen years old, she was told many things by her mother and father and also by her grandfather Antonio de la Garza, who often visited their cabin at La Bahía. Her grandfather vividly recalled the Texas frontier from the late 1850s to 1900, and the old man had a good listener in his granddaughter. There were details in Aunt Sálome's account which later proved to be slightly in error, but the errors were not so great that I was misled. Indeed, it was quite the opposite. At this point I was a beginner in research and her oral accounts of what had been passed down to her by her elders were very helpful. It was then up to me to clarify some of the details which had become obscured over the years.

Aunt Sálome told me that Manuel Becerra and Juana María Cadena were blessed with two children, a son and a daughter. She said the son died when he was very young, leaving María Josefa Becerra as the only surviving child. The lone Becerra girl, María Josefa, became wealthy, so much so that she eventually was known as *la rica* — the rich one. María Josefa came into possession of the entire Becerra grant.

Later I discovered that Manuel and Juana María actually had three children, two daughters and a son. By 1850, however, María Josefa was the sole surviving heir; the other children had died. Her husband, José María de la Garza, became involved in the 1836 Texan war for independence and served with the Anglo-American revolutionary army.

"Hijito, todos tuyos abuelitos, Becerra, de la Garza, Rubio, y los padres

y los bisabuelitos de ellos fueron Tejano macizos toda la vida. Ellos no se fueron para el otro lado del Río Grande para escaparse de la guerra de México y Tejas." ["My son, your grandfathers Becerra, de la Garza, Rubio, and their grandfathers were strong-willed Texans all their lives. They did not flee across the Rio Grande during the war between Mexico and Texas."]

"They served their country as soldiers and Texas peace officers and faithful tax-paying cattle ranchers and farmers," she said, and as an afterthought: "Mother was in mourning for seven years after the passing of my father; this was from February 24, 1903, to February 24, 1910."

In February 1902, she continued, the entire sky turned pitch dark and a tornado struck Goliad and the surrounding country with swift and horrible fury. She thought that God was telling bad citizens (American outlaws, Mexican bandits, killers and their cohorts, including saloon girls), "Repent you evil sinners or suffer the consequences." The tornado offered little warning. Aunt Sálome recalled seeing many saddle horses running and neighing and kicking their hoofs into the air. She saw a horse impaled by a tree, a horrible sight. The horses were followed by long-eared mules, some still with halters on. She reckoned these creatures had broken loose from a farmer's plow or wagon. The young girl noticed that some of the mules had their blinders on; and on some of the beasts the blinders had become loose, thereby obscuring the creatures' view or restricting the view to one eye, which only terrified them that much more. The blinded one-eyed mules ran headlong into trees and fences, injuring themselves. Last came the *burros* and their incessant braying. The hardy little creatures were terrified. Some of the burros carried loads of firewood, and Aunt Sálome knew that the owners were Mexicans for they could not afford the luxury of a horse.

In Goliad the commotion and confusion was horrid. All over town the people were scurrying for cover wherever they could find it. Horses broke from the hitching rails and fled in terror, vigorously chased by yapping dogs. Mules fled with the wagons, some of which were loaded with the farmers' provisions. Bleary-eyed, drunk Mexican *vaqueros* and their Anglo-American *compadres* ran out of the local *cantinas*. In their drunken haste to untie the reigns from the hitching rails, some lost their mounts. Others managed to get aboard their cow ponies and, reeling drunkenly, applied the *riata* and spur to the frightened animals and fled to their ranches where they no doubt arrived literally cured from the effects of the liquid spirits.

Aunt Sálome claimed that Francisco de la Garza was the first husband of Mariá Josefa Becerra. She also asserted that Francisco married a second time. Her claim as to the second marriage is correct, for I found the marriage certificate dated August 18, 1851, to Gertrudis Garcia, a copy of which is in my possession. Aunt Sálome was mistaken in regard to Francisco de la Garza's first marriage. Francisco was never married to Mariá Josefa Becerra. But more on that later. What is important here is that Aunt Sálome told me that Francisco de la Garza had married into the Becerra family in his first marriage, and it was through that first marriage that Francisco would come into possession of Becerra lands. But, again, more on that later as my research actually unfolded the exact details. Of equal importance, the family matriarch put me in more direct touch with my great-grandfather, Antonio. She told me that on April 8, 1937, Antonio de la Garza breathed his last in his ancient cabin near Presidio La Bahía. It was only proper that the elderly gentleman should die in the very room where he took his first breath in 1848. The wildflowers, such as those he used to take to the grave of his beloved wife, Ponposa Bontan, in 1891, were in bloom.

Huge throngs of relatives and friends came to pay their last respects to the old herdsman as he was the last of the flamboyant de la Garza *rancheros* of Refugio County. However, at the time of his death he was a very poor and broken man. His sons, Ismael and Guadalupe, and daughters, Eliza, Adela, and Petra, were by his bedside; numerous grandchildren and great-grandchildren were always near.

Sálome had many stories to share about her father, Juan Rubio. She told me that she had seen the weapons carried by her deputy father. He made many arrests of bad men, both Anglo and Mexican. Juan was once escorting a desperate Mexican bandit to the Goliad County Jail on horseback. Before reaching town, the villain made a lunge for Juan's pistol and actually got his hands on it. Juan desperately fought for the weapon and managed to get it back.

He never made the same careless mistake again. There is no doubt that as senior deputy he was duty bound to witness the hangings of many outlaws and killers, perhaps even fitting the dreadful black hood and rope around the victims' necks.

Before becoming deputy sheriff, Juan was a *vaquero* and made the cattle drives to Kansas City. The last trail drive he made was in 1885 while employed by the Fant brothers of Goliad County. Juan was very young and religious when he began to work for the Fant brothers. On January 15, 1887, Judge William N. Fant united Juan Rubio and Francisca de la Garza in marriage. Judge Fant probably was a relative of the Fant brothers. The youthful *vaquero* was no doubt under the protective wing of the Fant brothers while on the long and lonely cattle drives to faraway Kansas.

The brothers would ask Juan to say evening prayer for the cowboys and *vaqueros* while camped for the night. The Fant brothers were also very religious men. One can easily form a mental picture of a very youthful Mexican boy with a prayer book, given to him by his mother, Teresita Cabrera, in his hands zealously praying to the Almighty that no trouble should befall men and livestock.

On the trail drives, around the campfire after supper, the Mexicans always rolled their *cigarrillos* and tuned the strings of their guitars. As if by magic, the songs they so beautifully sang penetrated the night. The songs usually related to a hidden and lonely past, or a wild Texas *vaquero* on the run from the law. Some of the songs related to a *vaquero,* spurned by a lovely señorita. The brokenhearted *vaquero* would hit the trail, only to be killed in a blazing gunfight along the Texas-Mexican border. Other songs related to a *caballo quebrado* (broken-down horse) or a vicious Spanish longhorn bull who would fight anything on earth. Still others related to Texas cowboys and *vaqueros* being hunted down by the dreaded Texas Rangers. The songs began smooth and low toned, and gradually rose to a high pitch which seemed barbaric to young Juan Rubio.

Then there was talk of *bultos en la noche* (strange and odd objects in the night) and *brujas en la noche* (witches in the night). There was talk of clanking chains and the doleful sounds of a person in great pain as if the poor wretch was being sacrificed by *el diablo* (the devil). Juan usually moved his saddle and blankets closer to a place where the Fant brothers were lying when these stories began. Next

to Rubio was the oldest cowboy in the group; he had herded cattle for over forty years. He was a long-haired old man, attired in buckskin clothing, and he assured his young companion not to pay any mind to the *vaqueros'* and cowboys' gruesome tales.

Early every morning while the stars still shone, the men woke to the rattling of pots and pans, for this was the way the grumpy Mexican cook generally woke up the men. Everyone griped and moaned but soon there was the wonderful smell of brewing coffee. After a hearty breakfast, the Fant brothers told the men to double check their weapons. They were nearing Kansas, and there was danger of cattle rustlers as well as Indians, for this was the land of the fierce Comanche and their numerous allies. Soon the great herd was in motion and dust could be seen for miles.

Juan Rubio was almost always near the grizzled old Anglo-Texan in buckskin clothing. The man was so sunburned that his face and neck were crispy brown, giving him the appearance of a Mexican except for his blue eyes. The boy noticed that the old man constantly cleaned his huge pistol and rifle. On the left side of the belt he carried a sinister-looking knife. He was a loner, and none dared molest him. Juan became attached to the strange *americano* who taught the boy many tricks of the trail. The boy was quick to learn, which pleased the old man. The man, an Indian fighter and *pistolero*, told Juan that the Comanches always struck the outlying Texas settlements during the full moon, called the Comanche moon. Their raids were swift and devastating. He told his avid listener that the Comanches were the bravest and deadliest warriors in North America, surpassing even the dreaded Apaches who themselves were known as the scourge of the plains and mountains.

On reaching their destination a few miles outside Kansas City, the men bedded down the cattle, and the Fant brothers went to town and bargained over the price of beef with the cattle buyers. The brothers returned to camp with bags full of gold coins. They were accompanied by three or four cowboys who acted as guards. Then came the best and happiest moment of all — payday. That evening Juan Rubio and his old *compadre* rode into town, hitched their horses, and entered the nearest saloon. The boy *vaquero* was astounded at the sight in the saloon. Everywhere there were drunken cowboys and *vaqueros* and many, many saloon girls, some of whom were quite pretty.

The old man and the boy found a corner table. Juan always noticed that the man chose to sit with his back toward the wall. Soon a pretty American saloon girl came to take their order. The flirty girl whispered something to Juan, whose face instantly changed to the color of a beet. The Texan noticed the expression on Juan's face and nearly fell off the chair from laughing so much. Juan did not partake of the liquid spirits; he merely drank a cold soda while his companion became soused. The same girl kept glancing at young Rubio and beckoning him to join her, but he declined, much to the amusement of the old Texan.

Grandfather Juan Rubio survived the rigors of the long cattle trails: the hot sun, the terrible cold rains, the hail and snow storms, not to mention the swollen rivers they had to cross. By 1885, during the last trail drive to Kansas, he had informed the Fant family that he intended to go into law enforcement. The older of the Fant brothers warned him that a peace officer's duty on the rugged Texas frontier was an extremely dangerous undertaking. He tried to dissuade his *vaquero* from applying for such a job with the sheriff of Goliad County. Aunt Sálome spoke very highly of the Fant brothers. During the interview she made frequent references to the fine Fant family and how her father grew up on the trail with the big men from Goliad County.

Juan Rubio's father, Juan Rubio, Sr., was born in Cameron County on June 24, 1833.[6] According to his granddaughter, he was in the *policia secreta* of Texas. During times of trouble he would investigate disturbances within his district. It is not known what law enforcement agency he belonged to; however, both father and son were Texas peace officers for many years on the frontier. The elder Rubio served in the Confederate army during the Civil War.

Both public records and family tradition indicated that Juan Rubio, Sr. was quite a frontiersman. He was a stoic individual whom most people approached with reservation and caution. His quiet aloofness could have come from the Indian blood which flowed in his veins. His complexion was very dark, which caused him trouble with the more light-skinned Mexicans.

Juan Rubio, Sr. married Teresita Cabrera, who was born about 1840 in Cameron County.[7] Her brother, Macario Cabrera, was born on March 23, 1842, also in Cameron County. Their parents were Mariano Cabrera and Mageline Maucha. Macario was a farmer in Goliad County and died there on July 7, 1913. He and his younger brothers were vigorously opposed to the marriage of their sister Teresita to Juan. Teresita was very light complected, and her brothers tried to prevent the marriage because Juan was dark-skinned. Their efforts came to nought; however, these sentiments over Juan Rubio's complexion caused such ill feelings that a rift developed between the Cabrera and Rubio branches of the family that lasted until 1913.

Teresita Cabrera was the aunt of Don Nicolas Cabrera, who discovered the hanging man behind their cabin in Goliad County about 1903. Señor Cabrera asserted that he was the cousin of Grandfather Juan Rubio. My subsequent search revealed that he was correct. His father, Macario, Jr., was the first cousin of the deputy sheriff Juan Rubio, Jr.

Aunt Sálome made some other important family connections for me regarding the Bontan line. Benito Bontan was born in Texas in 1808 and his wife, Jesúsa Esparza, in 1830. They had three children: José Bontan, born in 1848; Gregorio Bontan, born in 1850; and daughter, Ponposa Bontan, born in 1852. All the children were born in Goliad County. Benito and Jesúsa were probably born in Bexar County, San Antonio. Their daughter, Ponposa, married Antonio de la Garza from Refugio County.

Benito Bontan was a guard at the Alamo fortress in San Antonio, but Aunt Sálome could not recall the year. Bontan may have been a Texas courier as were most of the patriotic Mexicans from Texas who ultimately perished there in 1836. All of these Mexican-Texan couriers were swift horsemen and knew the country well. Benito Bontan may have been under the command of Colonel Juan Seguin who had a company of mounted volunteers. Bontan's presence at the Alamo assures us that he was definitely on the side of the Texas rebels and detested the tyranny of the Mexican government in 1836. These ancient Mexican-Texans loved their freedom and a great many of them paid the supreme sacrifice for their beliefs. The Bontan family settled at La Bahía probably before the year 1847.[8] In later life, Benito became a butcher to earn a livelihood for his family.

Benito Bontan and his son José were murdered at Goliad by some killers from Blanco. The dispute arose over a horse race Anglo-Americans lost to the Bontans. The cowardly murderers waited for the dark of the night and shot father and son through the windows of their home. In performing their evil deed, the murderers used rifles, shotguns, and pistols. The Bontans were literally riddled with bullets and pellets from the deadly shotgun blasts. This tragic event in the lives of our ancestors happened in 1870 or 1871. The night killers fled from Goliad County and were never heard from again. Aunt Sálome did not know if the law ever caught up with them.

The widow, Jesúsa Esparza, chose to have her husband, Benito, and son, José, interred near the entrance door to the Chapel of Our Lady of Loreto at La Bahía. The funeral was attended by a great many people as the Bontan family was well known in Goliad. There were many horses, wagons, and buckboards all about Presidio La Bahía. The Mexican *vaqueros* were dreased in their finest attire. The Anglo-Americans dressed in suits or long black frock coats. The priest in his long black robes began chanting the Mass, then the bell atop the chapel began its tolling.

Kathryn Stoner O'Connor, in her history of Presidio La Bahía, indicated the location of the graves of Benito Bontan and son, José Bontan.[9] The information was pointed out to Mrs. O'Connor by Eliza de la Garza, daughter of Ponposa Bontan and Antonio de la Garza. Ponposa pinpointed the grave locations and names to her daughter prior to her death on March 3, 1891.

Before concluding this memorable interview with the grand matriarch of the Rubio family, Aunt Sálome, I inquired why some members of the Rubio family had been gifted with green eyes. I thought this was due to one of our ancestors of long ago. She smiled and quickly agreed. Aunt Sálome said that we had inherited the green eyes from the very beautiful Ponposa Bontan, who was of French and Spanish ancestry.

Ponposa Bontan was a direct descendant of early French settlers in Texas. Her father, Benito Bontan, was born in 1808 at La Bahía.[10] There were others of the Bontans residing in the old pueblo as well. The first Frenchman to appear at La Bahía was one Francisco Bontan, a carpenter. Bontan first made his appearance at this Spanish outpost in 1757, claiming to have been a native of France.[11] By 1792, Bontan was quite elderly and blind. He and his wife had three sons and several grandsons; although a Spanish subject and longtime settler of the La Bahía region, Francisco Bontan was still considered a foreigner by the Spanish.[12] The census of 1825 listed Benito Bontan, Julian Bontan, and Nepomenceno Bontan in the household of María Josefa de Luna, widow, aged sixty. Eusebio Bontan was shown in the household of Don José Trejo. The census taker was Manuel Becerra, and the *alcalde* was Juan José Hernandez.[13]

Sálome's grandfather, the young Refugio County *ranchero* Antonio de la Garza, who was then twenty years old, fell in love with the sixteen-year-old Ponposa from La Bahía. A beautiful courtship developed between the two young people. Antonio soon asked Benito Bontan for permission to marry his daughter and such was given about 1868.[14]

After their marriage at Our Lady of Loreto at La Bahía, Antonio took his young wife to his Rancho Alamito in Refugio County. After the death of his wife, Antonio never remarried.

Inside the Alamo fortress, which I visited after my interview with Aunt Sálome in San Antonio, are the names of the 187 Texas heroes who chose to perish there rather than surrender to General Santa Anna. Their names are engraved in bronze plaques with the lone star of Texas prominently displayed. Nine Mexican-Texans perished with their Anglo-Texan comrades. Alejandro de la Garza was a Texan courier, as were most of the Mexican-Texans who defended the old *presidio*. Gregorio Esparza was cruelly and most brutally bayoneted to death in front of the church by Mexican troops of the Matamoras Battalion. Esparza was probably the first Texas martyr to die in defense of the ancient Spanish fortress. His body was the only one not consumed by fire, and he was probably the only Texan to receive Christian burial.

The Mexican troops attacking the Alamo surely must have possessed a certain amount of raw courage. Some historians sadly neglect to mention this, perhaps due to their partiality to the Anglo-American. What about the other side? The Mexican soldiers had to face the determined and lethal fire from the defenders of the Alamo. Most alarming, however, the early biased accounts of the battle of the Alamo have been very damaging to native Mexican-Texans and have resulted in prejudicing our position in this society, a society which we have defended since we became a part of it in the early nineteenth century. Mexican-Americans were not responsible for the actions of the dictator, Antonio López de Santa Anna, but this has not stopped those looking for scapegoats. Bigots never seem to be able to separate Mexican-Texan citizens and the atrocities committed by Santa Anna in 1836.

Benito Bontan and his wife, Jesúsa Esparza, named their son Gregorio Esparza Bontan, the same name as the Alamo hero, Gregorio Esparza. There was tragic irony in this because it was an example of how the prejudice engendered over the years by people's misunderstanding of historical events such as the Alamo negatively affected the lives of Texas Mexicans. Young Gregorio Esparza Bontan, Aunt Sálome told me, met his death at the hands of non-Hispanic persecutors in Refugio County in 1874 when our family was being dispossessed of its land.

Indeed, Aunt Sálome described in great detail what she had been told by her grandfather, Antonio, about how he had been forceably driven off our ancestral Rancho Alamito, apparently by the same group that killed young Bontan. I sat fascinated by what she told me about her youthful association with old Antonio.

Antonio de la Garza was forced from his lands by villainous land-grabbers beginning in 1875. He and his family on their isolated property became targets of these predators in Refugio County. They were among many Mexican-Texans who became victims and lost their lands.

I will elaborate upon these details later as I begin to piece together the full story. For now, suffice it to say that my interview with Aunt Sálome, one of the few remaining family members who knew my great-grandfather Antonio, had provided me with much insight into my family's past and would serve, along with my conversations with uncles Tomás and Jesús, as a point of departure in my historical research of the lost Becerra land grant. Family tradition and documentary research were becoming inextricably intertwined in my relentless search into our past.

[6]

New Light on
an Old Grant

On the morning of October 10, 1972, Harris, the California attorney, and I once again visited the Spanish Collection at the General Land Office in Austin. We proceeded to search available records pertaining to landowners of Refugio back to the time when it was still a Mexican pueblo. Manuel Becerra was not on the list of landowners from the county and neither were the de la Garzas. The list of landowners of Refugio by Matagorda land commisioners included a woman named Essy Reed as having received one league and one labor of land — 4,605 acres — while she was residing in Matagorda County in 1838. However, her patent was cancelled in 1893 by Refugio County officials. Until the ultimate cancellation, her name was on the Refugio County map of 1851 and possibly other earlier maps. Dennis M. O'Connor from Refugio County finally claimed the Reed tract in 1892 by virtue of a headright certificate. It appeared that the tract was again resurveyed and finalized by O'Connor the same year. The Reed patent seemed to have been faulty from its inception.[1]

The Essy Reed tract was granted by the Republic of Texas on July 3, 1845. On January 29, 1875, James Dieterich, son of Essy Reed and Francis Dieterich, initially conveyed to Thomas O'Connor, father of Dennis, the Reed tract. James, the surviving son, was then residing in Travis County.[2] The year 1875, I learned, was crucial for O'Connor land acquisitions.

On the original documents we possessed, the district surveyor of Refugio County, David Snively, had drawn a small rectangular plat indicating the measurements of the Becerra tract as being one and one-fourth inches by two and one-half inches, which comprised two leagues or 8,856 acres. The Reed tract of 4,605 acres was therefore much smaller, which obviously cast doubt that her land covered the exact area as Becerra's.[3] But our suspicion still lingered about their relationship to one another.

I indicated to the Spanish archivist, Virginia Taylor, that I wanted to obtain a copy of the Manuel Becerra diary which he apparently kept very diligently while on his exploring journey with Stephen F. Austin in September of 1821. Becerra's ancient handwritten diary in Spanish had been translated into English.[4] Attached to Becerra's diary was a report made to Governor Antonio Martinez by the *alcalde* of La Bahía, Tomás Buentello, on September 15, 1821. The officials of Goliad appeared suspicious of Austin, and the Becerra report no doubt had much to do with the evaluation of the *norte americano* by the town fathers of the little La Bahía settlement.

Whether the *ayuntamiento* of La Bahía liked it or not, Austin had been duly authorized and commissioned by the governor of the Texas province to explore certain portions of the Texas coast for his settlers who would soon arrive. Buentello and his fellow *regidores* received Austin cordially, but with suspicion and distrust. Austin's arrival at La Bahía marked the first time since the *presidio* was established in 1749 that any foreigner came in peace, particularly North Americans. Great must have been the surprise to the local citizenry, since in previous times the fortress had been bombarded, captured and recaptured by the Mexicans, the Spanish, and the boldest intruders of all — the American filibusters.

Harris and I left Austin and arrived in Refugio in mid-afternoon on October 10, 1972. Again I got a strange feeling when visiting this town. It was a feeling of mixed emotions — nostalgia, suspicion, hatred, even revenge. Brutal crimes were committed against my ancestors in Refugio in the 1870s. I was reticent to have bad feelings against the town; yet, even at this early stage, the bad feelings were there in my heart.

Entering the courthouse we went directly to the district clerk's office. Those persons laboring within appeared much surprised at seeing us, and one merely grunted, "I thought you two were in this together." The clerk seemed irritated and annoyed. I wondered if certain people in Refugio County resented our presence and preferred us to leave, but this was not to be for we would come back to the old town again and again until we found all the information we sought. This reception may well have had something to do with the letter of inquiry Harris had previously sent to the Refugio Mission Title Abstract Company. Also, I had sent the clerk a letter requesting certain information. Someone knew that something was in the wind regarding the Becerra family.

The examination of the family records began immediately, and we were rewarded by finding transactions made by Manuel Becerra, Francisco de la Garza, María Josefa Becerra, her husband, José María de la Garza, and Antonio de la Garza. Before departing for the day, Harris informed one of the clerks that we would be back at 8:00 A.M. the following day. Again a grunt and shake of the head, clear signs of unwelcome for us, were all we received.

Returning to Goliad, Harris indicated he wished to see Presidio La Bahía and Our Lady of Loreto Chapel. We saw the statue of General Ignacio Zaragosa, hero of the battle of Puebla on May 5, 1862, when he and his Mexican troops defeated the French legions sent against him. General Zaragosa was a native-born Texan from La Bahía. He was born in 1829 in a stone house outside the walls of the *presidio*. General Zaragosa was not a professional soldier, but he and his officers were seasoned guerrilla fighters. They heroically met the onslaught of the French legions and cut those forces to pieces. It was the first time that one of Europe's finest armies was defeated by a poorly equipped Mexican army. The defeat of the elite French army stunned all of Europe. Such a stunning defeat was dealt by the hand of a Texas Mexican who is annually honored throughout Mexico and Texas. Texan officials and Texas Mexicans also celebrate the great victory on Cinco de Mayo (May 5) every year. The state erected a historical marker at La Bahía, Zaragosa's birthplace — a mute reminder that Texas had produced great soldiers, both Anglos and Mexicans.

We visited the grave of Grandmother Francisca de la Garza, and Harris asked to see the grave of Juan Rubio, but I did not know the location. Their son, Juan Rubio, Jr., was killed by a deputy sheriff of Goliad County on May 23, 1936; his brother Stevan suffered a gunshot wound but survived. Both Stevan and Juan were unarmed.

I pointed out the monument dedicated to Colonel James Fannin and his men, who were murdered by direct order of General Santa Anna on Palm Sunday, 1836. We also visited the cabin Antonio de la Garza brought from Refugio County in 1875.

Early the following Wednesday morning, Harris and I returned to Refugio to continue to search the records. We obtained papers of all land transactions made by the Becerra-de la Garza families and their heirs. Harris obtained a copy of the tax rolls for 1861 showing that Carlos, José María, and Francisco de la Garza paid taxes on 4,428 acres of land. All of these de la Garza *rancheros* were owners of many herds of cattle and horses. Carlos de la Garza owned over 100 head of horses in addition to an immense herd of cattle. José María de la Garza possessed two oxen, the only one to own such animals. By 1870, he had four or five, which were eventually acquired by Antonio de la Garza. Antonio also came into possession of all the land and livestock belonging to his father, Francisco, as well as that belonging to José María de la Garza and wife, María Josefa Becerra.[5]

It was in these records that I began to clarify some of the things Aunt Sálome had told me, especially about the relationship between María Josefa Becerra and Francisco de la Garza. Sálome had said they were married, but I soon began to see that they were not. The records indicated that by 1850 María Josefa, oldest daughter of Manuel Becerra, was a grown woman married to José María de la Garza for many years. Both apparently were well known in Goliad and Refugio counties. In the Refugio County records there was a land transaction whereby María Josefa and her husband gave Francisco de la Garza 1,107 acres of their land. The transaction was made in Goliad County on June 19, 1853, and recorded in Refugio County, April 9, 1855. It was clear to me that Francisco and María Josefa could never have been married. They were in-laws, as I was to discover.

We visited the district surveyor's office where I saw a map of Refugio County for 1900. Harris examined the map which mentioned Alamito Creek; none of the others we saw at the General

Land Office mentioned such a name. (The General Land Office did not have the 1900 map.) Prior to our trip to Refugio County, Harris had written to the district surveyor's office requesting maps. The reply was that they did not have the requested maps and advised Harris to seek the information at the General Land Office in Austin.

We concluded the search of the records — reluctantly, I may add — but I knew that sooner or later I would return to Refugio. I was not entirely satisfied as yet; there was more information buried deep in the old records somewhere, and I was intent on finding such regardless of how unwelcome I was made to feel. The final land transaction we found was made by Antonia de la Garza[6] on July 1, 1884, when she leased for one-third interest 1,000 acres to a Mrs. M. K. Plummer. After the July 1, 1884, transaction, no further records of the de la Garzas appeared in Refugio County records.[7]

The lease was made from the original deed granted to Antonia Cruz de la Garza on March 17, 1853, from María Josefa Becerra and husband, José María de la Garza.[8] Antonia de la Garza also leased to E. P. Upton of Aransas County her lands (no amount mentioned). The lands lie on both sides of Copano Creek running back to Alamito Creek. This lease was filed for the record in Refugio County on June 30, 1884; and the same was made in Goliad County.[9] The two de la Garza leases of 1884 were made by the same person.

In 1884, there were two women named de la Garza in Goliad. The first of these was Antonia Cruz, wife of Carlos de la Garza. By 1884, of course, she was his widow. The second one was Ponposa Bontan, wife of Antonio de la Garza. The lease to the Uptons as mentioned above was definitely not made by Ponposa.

Tax records for 1861 show Carlos de la Garza as owning 2,214 acres deeded to him by Manuel Becerra. No conveyance was found for this, only the tax record. Since Carlos married Antonia Cruz, it was her lease that was filed for record on June 30, 1884, as Mrs. Antonia de la Garza. By this time the Uptons were deeply involved in the de la Garza lands. The leases were properly made and recorded according to law, for we found them eighty-eight years after the fact. What happened after 1884 is not known and perhaps never will be.

Harris asked the Refugio County clerk about the leases of 1884 and inquired why there were no further records after that year. The clerk agreed that this was indeed a mystery; but Harris did not press the matter further because the clerk seemed upset and somewhat irritated.

Harris politely but firmly reminded the frustrated and nervous clerk that while visiting her office on June 8, 1972, he saw a particular document bearing the signature of Manuel Becerra and that this time we failed to find it in the records. The clerk immediately denied seeing such a document in her records. Harris was certain that they were evading his questions and that some documents were either hidden or missing from the records.

Bitterly disappointed, I wondered why the flamboyant explorer-colonist, Manuel Becerra, chose this wretched place to settle his family. It is something I will probably never be able to understand. Since he was thoroughly familiar with all the lands along the Gulf Coast of Texas, he apparently saw something in the Refugio area which prompted him to settle in the area I had begun to detest almost to a point of vengeance. Becerra's huge cattle ranch lay on both sides of Alamito Creek, which flows into the larger Copano Creek. These creeks are apparently never dry and thus perhaps Becerra saw this as the ideal place to establish his ranch; but he apparently did not reckon with the aggressive intruders from the north.

The documents we found during our search still had to be carefully analyzed upon our return to California. Knowing that some items were still missing only added to my frustration and disappointment. Perhaps after my seemingly fruitless trips from California to Texas the strain was beginning to take effect. Things appeared dismal for the Becerra heirs.

But still, according to the documents we found in Refugio County, Great-grandfather Antonio de la Garza never sold nor conveyed his lands to anyone. Of this we were certain. This brought on renewed hope. All was not lost as yet, for I would return to Refugio County again and again if necessary.

Harris and I had been more fortunate than we thought because the documents proved very valuable for our cause. While on the way to California I studied some of the material we had found. Of particular significance was a document dated January 25, 1834, at Monclova, Coahuila, Mexico, bearing the signatures of F. Vidaurri and J. Miguel Falcón. It appears that Vidaurri and Falcón were ranking officials of the Mexican government for the provinces of Coahuila and Texas. Their signatures appear after the approval of the original Becerra petition at Villa de Goliad by Juan José Hernandez, the *alcalde*, J. Antonio Vasquez, secretary for the town government, and Manuel Becerra on May 14, 1832.[10]

The January 25, 1834, document was translated from Spanish to English rather poorly but nonetheless was properly recorded into the deed records of Refugio. Who were the two men from Coahuila, Mexico, and what positions did they hold in the Mexican government? These questions had to be answered, and research was in order. I conducted this undertaking.

Mexican land grants — particularly those signed by the governors — are complex and difficult even for an experienced research historian. As an amateur, at best, I would soon fall into this quagmire. But family honor was at stake and I had no recourse but to claw my way out of the nightmare which seemed like a dark bottomless pit.

It should be noted here that if the old-time Refugio County clerks had been involved in shady and devious land transactions, our research would have ended in complete failure, but such, as far as I could tell, was not the case. The integrity of these clerks after July 1, 1884, however, cannot be ascertained regarding the de la Garza family lands.

From available records and other old documents found, it appears that Manuel Becerra was the only one who was well versed in reading and writing Spanish. His writings are unmistakable evidence that he was well educated. During the Spanish era there were no schools at La Bahía nor Refugio and probably in all the Texas province where Spanish or Mexican children could be educated. Becerra must have received his education in Mexico. Becerra's wife and daughters could not even sign their names. Here again is ample evidence of the lack of schools in the Goliad and Refugio areas. Such conditions were even worse during the Mexican era.

The Spanish Franciscan priests in charge of the missions, Espíritu Santo at La Bahía and Nuestra Señora de Refugio, were highly educated men. But it appears that their sole purpose was to bring the teachings of God to the Indians who congregated about the missions. The fathers even taught natives a trade and kept them fed. Neither the fathers nor the officials in Mexico City saw fit to establish schools for Spanish children at Goliad or Refugio. Their primary duty, with the blessing of officials in Mexico City, was to convert the Indians, principally the Karankawa and Coco tribes. These Indians were not very responsive to such efforts, and often fled back into the wilderness and reverted to their former ways.

Spanish and Mexican settlers and their families were the forgotten orphans of the Texas wilderness. Bitter must have been their feelings when they saw the mission Indians with better food than they possessed.

Spanish governors of Texas, as well as those in New Mexico and their *presidio* commanders, were constantly at odds with the priests. The veteran frontier commanders and their soldiers favored dealing with the natives with the sword and fire, but they dared not for the priests generally took the side of the Indians. And they had the ear of the viceroy in Mexico City. The priests constantly complained of the wicked, licentious bachelor troops of the local garrison. They accused the soldiers of molesting Indian women and being notorious gamblers among other things. The much hounded soldiers, on the other hand, grumbled that the priests were too exacting in their ways. They grumbled at being constantly summoned to mass or made to perform religious duties such as helping to baptize an Indian child or convert a "heathen" from the wilds to Christianity. The pious *padres* greatly preferred that the government send married soldiers and their families to be stationed at the lonely Texas frontier outposts. Single and adventurous young soldiers were too troublesome; some behaved worse than the Indians and were poor examples to the Texas natives. But what soldier and his wife would be willing to bring children to an outpost in the outer fringes of Spanish civilization where there were no schools?

The royal treasurer for *Nueva España* in Mexico City kept providing thousands and thousands of pesos at the requests of the *padres* in the province of Texas. The zealous fathers pleaded constantly for funds with which to build missions and schools for the natives. These requests were rarely disapproved, for if it meant spending a thousand pesos to convert an Indian to Christianity, it was worth the rewards. Pesos were also squandered in purchasing gifts for the natives. The intention was to buy their friendship.

Meanwhile, my beloved great-great-grandmothers, little girls on the Texas frontier of the 1700s, became illiterate for want of education. The Spanish government spent millions of dollars on the Indians and not one peso to better the welfare of the Spanish-Mexican settlers, most especially the children. It was a miracle that they survived. The fearsome Karankawa Indians and their equally warlike allies, the Cocos, were never subdued by the Holy Cross or force of arms. These Texas Indians were extremely hostile, unlike those of New Mexico and farther west who were for the most part sedentary in nature.

Had the Spanish government been able to spend a small portion from the royal treasury to bring Spanish-Mexican colonists to colonize the Goliad and Refugio areas, the end result no doubt would have paid off handsomely. The Spanish-Mexican settlers would fight to keep intruders away from their lands, and the daughters would provide wives for the lonely Spanish soldiers stationed at the *presidios*. It seems that this was the prudent thing to do under the circumstances, for how else could a Christian civilization begin flourishing in the wilderness?

My research in Refugio records had revealed that the Becerras were early recognized colonists in those parts. Manuel Becerra and his wife, Juana María Cadena, were sponsors for baptismals at Nuestra Señora del Refugio mission between the years 1813 and 1820; their daughter, María Josefa, in 1819, and her husband, José María de la Garza, in 1812–16 were also baptismal sponsors.[11]

Upon my return to California in an agitated frame of mind, I began a methodical analysis of the documents and the identity and position in the Mexican government of the signers F. Vidaurri and J. Miguel Falcón at Coahuila, Mexico, on January 25, 1834. In the process of constant analysis of the document, I suddenly recalled the name José Jesús Vidaurri while visiting the General Land Office on August 21, 1972; but the latter was not the Vidaurri I was seeking.[12]

This Vidaurri appears to have been related to F. Vidaurri of Coahuila, Mexico. The Mexican government ordered the former to Texas sometime in 1834 or possibly before to become land commissioner for the Power and Hewetson Irish colony of Refugio County, Texas. Before Vidaurri's arrival in Refugio, the Mexican settlers were already well settled and occupying the lands in the county when James Power came to Texas

On February 8, 1830, the inventories for the missions at Refugio and Espíritu Santo at La Bahía and the order of secularization of the Nuestra Señora de Refugio were signed by Father Antonio Diaz de Leon. The ceremony was witnessed by the *alcalde* of La Bahía, José Miguel Aldrete, secretary Manuel Becerra, and *procurador* Juan Escalera.

The *empresario* James Power in April 1830 petitioned the supreme government for the choicest portions of the lands including the lands where the Refugio mission had been established in 1795.

Refugio was the last Spanish mission erected in Texas, and it was coming to its official conclusion. The reverend fathers de Leon and Muro must have reluctantly affixed their signatures to the secularization document for this mission. Even before secularization, a sacred event to the local Mexicans, the foreigners Power and Hewetson had coveted those lands. It seemed the Mexican government was inviting disaster. After secularization, the lands became open for settlement as public lands.

When James Power petitioned for the mission lands and when the Mexican settlers found out, they raised a great furor and resented Power for his claim to what they considered premium lands. This discontent was soon equalled by those Mexican settlers from La Bahía. Power's arrival in Texas created problems for the small Mexican settlement of Refugio, and bitter disputes arose as the *Tejanos* accused the Mexican government of showing favoritism to Power and the other foreigners coming to Texas.[13]

It was, of course, soon after this transpired that Manuel Becerra in 1832 applied for his grant in Refugio from the *ayuntamiento* of La Bahía and later from Governor Francisco Vidaurri. At that time, Power and Hewtson had no legal documentation or valid claim from the governor to any land claimed by Becerra.

Some of the tracts belonging to local Refugio and La Bahía Mexicans definitely fell within the boundaries that Power and Hewetson claimed for their colony. Thus, by 1830, heated boundary disputes arose between the La Bahía Mexicans and the Irish *empresarios*, with men like *alcalde* Rafael A. Manchola and secretary Manuel Becerra being the most vocal to Mexican authorities over the intrusion of these newcomers.[14]

Mexican settlers of Refugio and especially the elders of La Bahía vigorously asserted that the lands stretching from the La

Bahía settlement to the Refugio settlement ran red with the very blood of their ancestors in their constant encounters with the Indians. They had also endured the infernal weather, disease, and hunger, in addition to the intruders who came to claim the land. The Mexican settlers actually had no valid titles from the Mexican government, but no doubt they were claiming the lands by right of occupancy, based on old Roman law.

It was about this time in 1832 that one of the oldest colonists of the entire area, Don Manuel Becerra, petitioned the supreme government for his land grant. Becerra had been occupying his land in the Refugio settlement many years before Power's arrival there; and since there was no town government in Refugio, he went directly to the officials of La Bahía and applied there for his grant. Becerra bypassed *empresario* James Power, probably because he mistrusted the latter's attitude toward Mexican settlers. Hence, he wasted little time in applying for the federal land grant from the supreme government headquartered in Monclova, Coahuila.

The bitterness and discontent of the Mexican colonists toward the Irish and Anglo-American settlers encroaching upon their lands was soon felt in Monclova. Officials there immediately ordered José Jesús Vidaurri to establish an *ayuntamiento*, which he promptly did and named it Villa de Refugio. Vidaurri was to distribute the lands and issue good titles to the Mexican and American colonists according to the colonization laws of the provinces of Coahuila and Texas. Power, the ranking official of the colony, saw to it that his settlers received good titles and that they professed the Catholic religion.[15]

With great effort, Vidaurri somehow restored order in the Refugio settlement; however, the seeds of discontent had been firmly planted between the Mexicans, Irish, and American settlers. The offspring of three proud cultural heritages had met in this remote Texas wilderness area and soon clashed. Doubtless, Manuel Becerra and the de la Garza *rancheros* were deeply involved in the fierce disputes.

Manuel Becerra was one of the leading figures of the Refugio settlement. The de la Garzas were fighters and were quick to use force of arms to protect their lands. Becerra, on the other hand, was a politician, later involved in the Refugio town government. Becerra was methodical and unyielding in his dealings with others; he was an able critic of the powerful Irish *empresarios*. Still, by 1834, Becerra was busy at the Refugio *ayuntamiento* assisting Power and Commissioner Vidaurri, and he himself signed nearly 60,000 acres of land for the Refugio colonists.

All the town officials of Goliad were his close personal friends, as well as the Mexican colonizer and founder of Victoria, Don Martin de Leon, who himself was at odds with the Americans and especially the Irish.

Before 1825, the de la Garza families were well entrenched on their remote *ranchos* in Refugio. During these turbulent years there were many Indian depredations being committed on the settlements, including La Bahía and Refugio. The special targets for the warriors were the outlying ranches. The Indians never ventured forth into the de la Garza range lands. The de la Garzas constantly patrolled their vast wilderness domain against all intruders. Tradition has remembered them as "the de la Garza horsemen." They were in fact mounted gunmen, perhaps the earliest of such in Texas history. Among this unique breed of men was Francisco de la Garza, the youngest of the clan but possessed with the daring of his forefathers. During the land disputes already mentioned, no one ousted a de la Garza rancher from his home or land, though several of these firebrands eventually received proper title to the lands from Power and from Vidaurri in 1834.

The titles received by the Refugio colonists were honored by the Mexican government and later the Republic of Texas, but the huge Power and Hewetson grant comprising 242,000 acres appears to have been fraught with errors since its inception for one reason or another. A portion of these problems confronting Power may have been due to his claiming lands already settled by the Mexicans before his appearance in Refugio. Indications are that this huge tract of land was declared void by the Republic of Texas courts as early as 1841.[16]

The maps of Refugio County for 1850 through 1872, and the earlier Willard Richardson map of 1841, failed to show the names of James Power and his partner James Hewetson as owners of the largest land grant in the county. The district surveyor of Refugio County, David Snively, stated in his report of September 21, 1850, that all county surveys up to August 1, 1850, were correct. The strange disappearance of the *empresarios'* names from the county

maps suggests that the grant was faulty; the Texas courts apparently found errors and thence voided it from the records. The
Power grant was dated October 20, 1834; and the Hewetson grant
bore the date of November 19, 1834. Subsequently, a portion of the
James Power land grant was claimed by Thomas O'Connor, a
nephew of Power.[17] Father William Herman Oberste, a noted historian of Refugio, stated that both *empresarios* received over 242,440
acres and that James Hewetson had no heirs.[18]

José Jesús Vidaurri did not approve the Manuel Becerra petition of 1832. The approval had been granted by the *ayuntamiento* of
Goliad, as already mentioned; however, the name Vidaurri appeared in the petition. A painstaking and exhaustive search led me
to discover at this time just exactly who were F. Vidaurri and J.
Miguel Falcón. The former was governor Francisco Vidaurri for
the provinces of Coahuila and Texas; the latter was the secretary
general.[19]

These findings made the Becerra papers even more valuable
than otherwise thought possible. My relentless pursuit into the past
had been richly rewarded. I had been studying the copy of the original grant with the governor's signature; also, we had the copy
which W. M. McFarland, the clerk of Refugio County, had translated from Spanish into English and recorded as a deed on September 6, 1848.[20] With the approval of Governor Vidaurri and J. Miguel Falcón, the Manuel Becerra petition became a federal land
grant, the best in Texas and elsewhere. Falcón later became governor. The governors of Coahuila and Texas were the ranking civil officials either to approve or disapprove land grant petitions, and this
included those petitions submitted by the *empresarios* themselves.
Don Manuel Becerra unquestionably carried out scrupulously all
the laws of colonization. McFarland accepted it as a deed from the
government of Mexico and recorded it as such into the record.

The Becerra grant was a first-class grant which in truth was
most desired by Texas settlers. It took precedence over those issued
by the *empresarios*. Manuel Becerra was a member of the town government at Villa de Goliad for many years; it was perhaps for this
reason that he applied to the highest authority for his grant on May
14, 1832. Becerra eventually settled permanently in Refugio
County. Evidently, he had been busily clearing and improving his
land in Refugio a number of years before 1832.

After a lonely and tedious search into my ancestors' dim and obscured past, an ever so tiny ray of light hidden for over 150 years was beginning to appear. It was as if my ancestors had left a beacon for one of their offspring to follow, and the light was destined to shine brighter as I relentlessly pursued the search.

Harris was very optimistic when I informed him of the two men named Vidaurri. He was convinced that we had all the necessary information, but it was imperative that Governor Vidaurri's signature be verified. This was soon accomplished with the assistance of Virginia Taylor of the Spanish Collection at the General Land Office in Austin.

Taylor sent us a copy of Spanish Law 128, article 12, which governed land grant distribution in Texas in 1832–34. (Becerra, however, applied under article 15.) She also sent copies of Mexican land grants signed by Governor Vidaurri, and the signatures matched perfectly with that on the Becerra petition!

Indeed, the documents we gathered in Texas and my continuing research were bearing fruit.

[7]

The Original *Tejanos*: A Fresh Look

While in California, before my next trip to Texas, I consolidated the interviews, secondary materials, and primary documents I had gathered to draw a more complete picture of the Becerra and de la Garza families. These ancestors had not been squatters; rather, their legitimate presence dated from the very beginning of this area's history and formed some of the more interesting and important pages of Texas history, even into the twentieth century.

When Stephen Fuller Austin first came to Texas, my ancestors were there to greet and assist him. Manuel Becerra was born in the La Bahía settlement in 1765 and his parents had probably been original La Bahía residents. According to earliest Spanish records, he and Juana María Cadena, also a child of a La Bahía settler, married by at least 1805. As a young man, even before he married, Becerra explored the Texas Gulf Coast and came to know the territory and all its inhabitants, especially the fearsome Indian tribes.

Austin appeared at the small Spanish settlement of La Bahía on August 26, 1821. With him were ten huge bearded *norte americanos*. Austin presented his Spanish commission from the Texas governor, Colonel Antonio Martinez, to the *alcalde*, Tomás Buentello, who must have scrutinized the document several times over, vainly

trying to find fault. Buentello and his *regidores* received Austin and his party with courtesy but with no small amount of suspicion as regarded their true intentions in Texas. Austin then crossed the San Antonio River and appeared before the commander of Presidio La Bahía. He requested soldiers to serve as guides for his forthcoming explorations. The commander politely informed the American that he was sorry but could not spare a single soldier.

Austin wrote to Governor Martinez informing him of his need of soldiers for guides. Martinez wrote back saying that if the *presidio* commander could not spare the soldiers then he must seek assistance from the *alcalde,* who would recommend a competent civilian guide. Thus, Austin spent a week from August 26 to September 1 awaiting the governor's reply; during this wait he spent time viewing the town and undoubtedly arousing the curiosity of the Spanish population. Upon learning that the soldiers were not to be furnished, Austin appealed to Buentello for assistance in locating a competent guide from the local population. This did not take long.

Buentello advised Austin to engage the *regidor* Manuel Becerra, as he was familiar with the area on the Colorado River and beyond. Austin then hired Becerra to act as guide. Every household knew of the North Americans in their midst. Austin, a very observant man, reported that the people were very poor and appeared in dire circumstances. These had been and still were Spain's abandoned children in the Texas wilds. Their suffering due to hunger and disease and Indian depredations must have been terrible, yet when Austin arrived in 1821, these people had been enduring hardships for many years. Their indomitable courage should be crowned with a laureate. The Spanish and later Mexican governments are worthy of shame and disgrace for their neglect of these people.

Austin's credentials were in proper order, and the orders of Governor Antonio Martinez had to be carried out, albeit reluctantly. Nonetheless, they were carried out.[1]

North Americans were not strangers to the inhabitants of La Bahía settlement. Adventurous spirits that they were, the Americans had actually made inroads into the Texas province and once or twice captured the settlement and the Presidio La Bahía even before the year 1819. Small wonder that the population was jittery upon Austin's arrival there. Buentello and his *ayuntamiento* ordered Becerra to observe carefully and report the movements of the foreigners while in the wilderness. The last paragraph of Becerra's diary states: "I report this observance according to the orders issued on the matter."[2]

Becerra carried out the orders of the town government to the letter. Austin was delayed nearly three days due to Becerra's preparations, and the expedition did not get under way until September 3, 1821.[3]

Eugene C. Barker, in his book *The Life of Stephen F. Austin,* declares that Austin dismissed Becerra because the latter was wandering around lost and knew nothing of the area under exploration. Barker further implies that Becerra's dismissal was in the field. Barker's statement is generally taken as fact by other Texas historians without bothering to investigate Becerra's diary for another side to the journey. Both the Austin journal and the Becerra diary state that Austin returned to the La Bahía settlement where he dismissed the guides. Austin would not leave the guides in the wilderness where they would become prey for the coastal indians which constantly roamed the area. Austin wrote:

Sunday, September 10, 1821, the men went hunting. I went with the Spaniard (Becerra) and one man to examine the site of old La Baddie [meaning the original site of Our Lady of Loreto La Bahía, which was established in 1721 by the governor of Coahuila province, the Marques San Miguel de Aguayo, who came to clear the Texas province of the French intruders]. The Spaniard, the Indians, and I didn't know the country; the food supply being low, I decided to discharge all the guides. Two Indians went toward the Guadalupe River, and the other Indian and Spaniard came with me. The Spaniard and the Indian fell back and left me without saying a word of their intentions. At that place we saw that it would not be possible to continue because the different creeks flowing into the lakes prevented our passage.[4]

Becerra noted, however, that

the said Austin agreed to suspend his commission and start home, saying that on his arrival he would send some experienced men in a schooner to examine all those lands and that bay and then make a report to our government. Since this seemed a wise decision, he returned to this presidio omitting the trip to the Colorado River, which was ordered by the government. On the way back, that commissioner proposed that the establishment of the new town should be on the middle road which goes from this presidio to Nacogdoches because he noticed that the coast was very low.[5]

On September 5, 1821, Becerra, Austin, and ten Americans with the Indian guides set out and reached Lake Ortiz. Becerra had knowledge that this lake was named for a deceased Spaniard named Ortiz, and his statement concerning Lake Ortiz clearly indicates that he was quite familiar with the area. This refutes the distorted statements alluded to by Barker. Becerra stated that departure was made from the *presidio* La Bahía del Espíritu Santo on September 3, 1821. The purpose of the trek into the wilderness was to explore the Colorado River area to find a suitable site for establishing the Austin colony. Becerra mentioned no Indians in the exploring party but Austin stated there were three, which were probably Xaraname mission Indians. The journey was ordered by Governor Martinez, and only the Colorado River was to be explored.

On Monday, September 4, 1821, Don Manuel Becerra became suspicious of the American's intentions, for the route was not lead-

jaxon·83

ing to the Colorado River. Austin wanted to be taken to examine the site of the old Mission Nuestra Señora de Refugio and its *presidio,* upon which Becerra politely informed Austin he was ordered by the government to proceed straight to the margins of the Colorado River. When Austin told Becerra it was also necessary for him to examine those places, Becerra reluctantly granted Austin the request though he had no such authority.[6]

Austin certainly must have had good reasons for insisting on examining the coastal areas. Had it not been for the presence of the ever watchful Manuel Becerra, he no doubt would have explored the coast from Corpus Christi to Galveston Bay.

On September 4, 1821, Austin disregarded and thus violated the orders of Governor Antonio Martinez; at the same time he created friction between himself and Manuel Becerra. The clash between the North American and the Spaniard was inevitable. The persistent Austin would have his way for the time being, but the wily Becerra would soon oust Austin and the Americans from the forbidden Spanish territory.

On Saturday, September 9, 1821, they proceeded east recon-noitering the environs of the old *presidio*. This was the *presidio* of Nuestra Señora de Refugio Becerra had visited various times from 1813 to 1820, which further suggests that historians distorted the truth with their assertions that Becerra was lost. Becerra noted:

> Having noticed that they were mapping all those places it seemed that it was not proper to give them information about those lands; and on the pretext that the said examination would be impeded by several intervening creeks, we went up a creek until a crossing was found. We spent the night at the mouth of the creek. It was not possible to continue and the said Austin agreed to suspend his commission and start home.

On this day of September 9, 1821, Manuel Becerra, a deeply frustrated man, had no recourse but to misguide and remove Austin and his men from the wrong territory. Becerra was rather late when he made his decision to remove the Americans; by this time, Austin had mapped a good portion of the territory, which further attests to Becerra's patience.[7]

On September 15, 1821, Becerra reported to the *alcalde* of La Bahía, Tomás Buentello, that Austin's only purpose had been to map the Guadalupe River, the old Mission of Refugio, the vicinity of the old *presidio,* and the port of Matagorda Bay. Becerra reported that in spite of having resisted he could do no less than to go along with them; it appears that Becerra considered the Americans as heretic, and that they did not profess the Catholic religion.[8]

Manuel Becerra's diary and his verbal report to Buentello prompted that official to become greatly alarmed. Buentello informed Governor Antonio Martinez that it seemed to him the North Americans would be more harmful than beneficial to the country. It appeared that Buentello's predictions proved to be correct. Unknowingly, the *alcalde* was telling Governor Martinez about the North American's vision of "Manifest Destiny."[9]

Austin stated in his journal that Becerra demanded ten dollars payable in advance and a promise to pay him one dollar per day. It was not known if Austin paid him his dollar every day while in the wilderness or upon their return to La Bahía. Being an honorable man, Austin undoubtedly kept his word.

It appears that historian Barker failed to examine Manuel Becerra's diary closely concerning his activities during his journey with Austin. Barker asserts that Becerra was ignorant of the areas under exploration; but Becerra, as we have seen, was in and about the old mission of Refugio and its *presidio* as early as 1813 and perhaps even much earlier.

Without question Becerra knew the Gulf Coast of Texas, including the Colorado and Brazos Rivers (the latter named by the Spanish explorers as *Brazos de Dios* or Arms of God River). But Barker and countless other historians always appear most sensitive and equally careful lest they injure the reputation of Austin. Their careless oversight resulted in a one-sided account of that important moment of Texas history when Manuel Becerra guided Stephen F. Austin into the wilderness.

The reports of Becerra and Buentello to Governor Antonio Martinez at San Antonio on September 15, 1821, expressed fear of the Americans. Their warning of the true intentions of the American foreigners went unheeded. Becerra's strange behavior and consequent guiding of Austin erratically during the journey have been unjustly criticized by historians. However, his loyalty was to the governor of Texas and the Spanish government. In the same instance, these writers completely exonerated Austin of any wrongdoing during his wandering about in the wrong territory in 1821.

The Austin-Becerra journey was unique as this was the last exploration for the purpose of founding a settlement under the Spanish regime. It was authorized by Antonio Martinez, who was the last Spanish governor of Texas. Becerra's small diary to Governor Martinez written on a tiny remote peninsula along the Texas coast is most interesting. It is without a doubt the last recorded document involving explorations of Texas under the Spanish government. Spanish explorations into New Spain began in 1521 by the *conquistador* Hernando Cortez, the conqueror of Mexico; and it ended 300 years later in Texas with Manuel Becerra, a minor official of the small Spanish settlement of La Bahía.

In the *Libro de Becerra* in Refugio County are recorded numerous works by Becerra, his work for the *ayuntamiento* of Refugio and José Jesús Vidaurri, as well as involvement for many years with the *ayuntamiento* of Goliad and subsequently with Austin. Becerra was deeply involved in the colonization of the Refugio-Goliad settlements. This man, who was responsible for much of the earliest history of Goliad and Refugio counties, has remained an obscure figure in Texas history.

Austin and Becerra were destined to meet again at the plaza at Villa de Guadalupe Victoria, presently Victoria, on May 13, 1827, to discuss articles of a peace treaty proposed by the Karankawa and Coco Indian tribes.[10] At the time of the treaty signing at Villa de Goliad which took place on May 27, 1827, Becerra was *síndico procurador* or law officer. As such, he signed the treaty for the town of Goliad.

The cunning Karankawas, called *Carancajuases* by the Mexicans, and the Cocos had committed many depredations against the settlements. So bold were the tribes that they had the audacity to plunder settlements in the Austin colony. Austin and his colonists soon caught up with them and in the ensuing battle severely thrashed and routed them. The furiosity and bravery of the Americans must have astounded the Indians who broke off the engagement and fled for La Bahía and safety. The flight of the Indians to La Bahía seeking the protection of the officials and priests clearly indicated that at one time or another they had been attached to the Espíritu Santo and Refugio missions. The aborigines arrived at La Bahía and begged the officials and mission *padres* to intercede on their behalf. The officials and *padres* informed Austin that the Indians wished to sue for peace. Austin agreed to the proposed peace treaty at the urging of the La Bahía officials, all of whom he knew personally.

On May 13, 1827, the following men met at Guadalupe Victoria to discuss the articles of the treaty: General Anastacio Bustamente, commander of the Eastern Internal Provinces; Don Martin de Leon, founder of the Victoria colony, and his son, Fernando de Leon; *el síndico procurador* Don Manuel Becerra, representing the La Bahía and Refugio settlements; Father Miguel Muro, representing the Goliad mission of Espíritu Santo; James Kerr of the Kerr colony; Green Dewitt of the Dewitt colony; Jacob Betts, representing the Austin colony (Austin apparently did not attend but sent Betts in his place); and Colonel Jose M. Guerra, secretary to General Bustamente.

Had it not been for the intercession of the Goliad officials, Austin and his colonists would have most assuredly put the Indians to the sword. The *alcalde* of La Bahía and his councilmen, as well as the Mexican settlers, urged their representative Becerra to agree with the treaty. Otherwise, the Indians would continue the depredations and steal every cow the settlers possessed on their *ranchos*. Already the Mexicans had lost much stock to the thieves. The settlers bewailed their misfortunes and implored Becerra to do everything possible to alleviate their suffering by agreeing to the articles of the treaty. The Mexicans looked at the mission *padres* with suspicious eyes because these Indians were supposed to be under their care and supervision. Otherwise, why had they come running to the *padres* for protection after Austin had chased them out of the woods?

Becerra assured the jittery settlers that he would do what was expected of him. He reminded them that he himself had lost cattle to unknown thieves. On May 13, 1827, Manuel Becerra and fathers Muro and Valdez traveled from La Bahía settlement to the Victoria settlement on the Guadalupe River to discuss the articles of the treaty. They were escorted by a small but heavily armed Mexican cavalry patrol providing for their safety. On May 27, 1827, the treaty was officially signed at La Bahía, the mission *padres* signing for the Indians of the Refugio and Espíritu Santo Mission at Goliad.[11]

Romana de la Garza, a cousin of mine and a resolute researcher of the Becerra-de la Garza family history, relates that Manuel Becerra, along with Martin de Leon and the latter's brother, were ordered by Governor Vidaurri to bring Mexican colonists to Texas.[12] These men were instrumental in colonizing the town now known as Refugio. Martin de Leon and his brother departed from Refugio and brought colonists to Victoria, which is now one of the wealthiest and most prosperous cities in South Texas.

After Manuel Becerra had distributed the lands to his colonists as per Vidaurri's instructions, the Irishmen Power and Hewetson talked to Becerra and wanted to find out how they could bring Irish settlers to this land. Becerra then took Power to Monclova to talk to Governor Vidaurri. Vidaurri gave Power authority to act in the same capacity as Becerra. Power was to distribute land to Irish settlers he said he could bring to the Mexican settlement of Refugio. With his settlers, Power wanted to settle on land that had been cleared by the Mexican colonists brought in by Becerra. Becerra told Power that he would have to settle on unimproved land just as the Mexicans had done. Contemporary histories of the region do not show De Leon as being a colonizer of the Refugio area; however, Spanish documents show Becerra and De Leon at La Bahía in 1809, and in Refugio in 1813.

Manuel Becerra was well known in Coahuila, Mexico, for his work in Texas. Hence, Becerra was well qualified to take Power to Coahuila and introduce him to Governor Vidaurri. The Irish *empresario* James Power had not issued a single title to the Irish colonists in the Refugio settlement previous to August 4, 1834; [13] and, under the pressing circumstances, he needed Becerra's assistance.

Between August 4, 1834, and December 30, 1834, José Jesús Vidaurri issued 201 land titles. Of these titles, thirty-six went to the Mexican colonists with the remaining 165 going to the Irish and a sprinkling of other foreigners. For their colonizing venture in the Refugio settlement, James Power and his partner James Hewetson were granted fifty-six and three-quarter leagues of land, or about 251,289 acres.[14]

Trouble plagued these two Irishmen from their first appearance in the Refugio settlement. Their apparent greed for the prime lands — all 251,289 acres — undoubtedly contributed to their problems with Mexican officials, and especially the old-time Mexican settlers who had lived near the Refugio mission since 1795. It seems incredible that within the span of five years or less, these two men, Power and Hewetson, acquired over a quarter of a million acres of the very best land in Refugio County. But it should also be pointed out that these two men, especially Power, endured no small amount of hardships in their colonization efforts. The role of *empresario* was also open to any Mexican with the capability for leadership, but none dared to take the challenge. There were very few native Mexicans who qualified for the role of *empresario;* among these men were Tomás Buentello, Juan José Hernandez, José Miguel Aldrete, J. Antonio Vasquez, Manuel Becerra, and perhaps Juan Escalera. All of these men were politicians from La Bahía and devoted their lives to working for the government.

The land grants of many settlers in the Refugio region bear the signature of Manuel Becerra, especially in 1834. These lands total 59,778 acres. This was a full one-quarter of the entire amount of land issued to the colonists in the Power and Hewetson Irish colony in Refugio. Clearly, Becerra, the public man of Goliad and Refugio, did his part in this settlement effort. Becerra's name helped place the stamp of formal legality on these documents forever more.[15]

Becerra seemed to have been the only one who came from La Bahía to colonize the Refugio settlement, and he himself acquired land in the region. Governor Francisco Vidaurri was invested with executive power by Decree 246 on January 8, 1834.[16] Approximately two weeks after taking office, on January 25, 1834, he signed the Manuel Becerra petition of May 14, 1832.

It is regrettable that many valuable records of the Mexican and Irish colonists from Refugio County were ultimately destroyed during the Texans' fight for freedom in 1836, but it is remarkable that some of these records survived and are now preserved in the Refugio Courthouse. A majority of the records pertained to Mexican land grants and deeds. Unfortunately, much of the history concerning Manuel Becerra and the de la Garza families as well as the county was destroyed by fire. The last fire in Refugio was in 1903; and in Goliad County in 1870. Such convenient fires have made it difficult for families such as ours to trace ownership of our ancestral land.

Besides the important episodes involving Stephen F. Austin, the Karankawa Indians, and Refugio colonization, Manuel Becerra was well known in those parts for his day-to-day activity in the lives of the people in the community. For example, primary records kept by meticulous mission *padres* reveal that between 1813 and 1820 Becerra and his wife, Juana María Cadena, were sponsors to numerous baptismals at the Refugio mission. The list of children they sponsored is too long to enter here, but suffice it to say that such was a sacred duty which leading citizens were required to perform, both for Mexicans and Indian children.[17]

Becerra lived at least until October of 1848. He died sometime between October 1848 and March 12, 1849, when Snively surveyed the Becerra tract for his heirs. Becerra was at least eighty-three years old at the time of his death. Indeed, he refused to leave Texas after 1836 as it was his native soil, and he would remain true as it sought its own destiny. He apparently took no part in the fighting.

The Becerra and de la Garza families were long associated with one another in South Texas. I had learned that this association was bonded by the marriage of Becerra's daughters to younger kinsmen of the powerful Don Carlos de la Garza.

By 1824, Don Carlos de la Garza was in possession of a flourishing *rancho* eight miles north of the settlement of La Bahía on the
south side of the San Antonio River. By that year, the de la Garza
clan, led by Don Carlos, was emerging as a potent force in the region. No one dared harm them or their property. The de la Garzas
were a proud and noble family on that frontier, their fathers and
grandfathers having been Spanish soldiers stationed in the various
Texas *presidios,* mainly at La Bahía.

The de la Garza land grants issued north of the Rio Grande by
the royal Spanish government and later the Mexican government
are unquestionably the most famous in the annals of Texas history.
From the Rio Grande border to the San Antonio River and the
margins of the Guadalupe River, the old and colorful de la Garza
dons controlled their famous grants with an iron hand. Not even the
Karankawa and Coco Indians, marauders of the Texas Gulf Coast,
dared venture forth into these lands.

The de la Garza families from the La Bahía and Refugio settlements — including relatives from the Texas side of the Rio Grande
border — were not always united. This became most visible when
the moment of truth arrived and the bloody struggle for Texas independence began. In 1835, Carlos de la Garza dispatched swift riders to the outlying *ranchos* with a summons for his brothers and
many cousins to gather at his large ranch on the San Antonio
River. Within hours his home was packed with his family. He discussed with them the best possible course of action to take, for he
had information that the Americans planned to wrest Texas away
from Mexico. Action against Mexico was imminent, and he expected his family to side with their native country. Out of this emotional gathering emerged two men who chose to fight against Mexico: Carlos's close relatives, José María de la Garza (husband of
Manuel Becerra's daughter, María Josefa) and Paulino de la
Garza. Spanish documents of La Bahía indicate that José María
and Paulino were very likely uncles of Don Carlos. Later documents suggest that the men may have been cousins of Carlos de la
Garza.

After having served under the command of Captain Philip
Dimitt and Colonel John W. Bower at Goliad in 1835, José María
de la Garza became a volunteer under the command of Lieutenant
Plácido Benavides and proceeded to San Antonio, then under siege

by the Texas rebels. Lieutenant Benavides, upon reaching Bexar, placed his small volunteer group under the company of Captain Juan N. Seguin. Seguin and his company of horsemen rendered great service to Texas, participating in the storming of Bexar in December 1835. According to the testimony given by Colonel Seguin at district court of Bexar on April 19, 1861, José María de la Garza served as a soldier in his company from December 1835 to June or July 1836. For this service to the cause of Texas, de la Garza petitioned the commissioner's court of Refugio County and the district court of Bexar for a headright certificate comprising one league and one labor of land. The records found do not indicate if he ever received his bounty of land.[18] The witnesses, Canuto Diaz and eighty-seven-year-old Bonilio Delgado, stated that José María de la Garza was of pure Spanish blood. The son of Spanish-born Texan parents, he was born at La Bahía about 1798. De la Garza stated in his petition that during the war there was no town government at La Bahía, and for a long time afterwards, the citizens, he said, had scattered all over the country.

Paulino de la Garza, the younger brother of José María, participated in the attack on San Antonio in December 1835. José and Paulino, who were in the same unit, served in the Texas army for four months or until April 1836. They both became spies and scouts for the Americans. On August 11, 1855, Paulino was issued a warrant entitling him to 320 acres of land for his four months of service in the army. He located 120 acres in Medina County and 120 acres in Bexar County. Also on August 11, 1855, Paulino was issued a certificate entitling him to 640 acres of land for having participated in the storming of Bexar in December 1835. He located his 640 acres in Bandera County. However, on November 20, 1855, Paulino sold his right to the warrant for 320 acres to Ben E. Edwards; and on November 21, 1855, he sold his right to the 640 acres in Bandera County to James E. Sewal.[19]

The entire family must have been upset at the defection of two of their own. Supposing that during the struggle the two men became the targets of their deadly gun sights, what were they to do? Were they told to use their own discretion under the circumstances? Surely Carlos de la Garza knew what he would do and prayed that such an encounter should not happen for the sake of the family.

The Becerra ranch on Alamito Creek was about fifteen miles

from the Carlos Ranch, which was on the San Antonio River. Manuel Becerra had known the de la Garzas for many years; they were connected through marriage. His eldest daughter, María Josefa, was already married to José María de la Garza, who had joined the Americans. Francisco, the eighteen-year-old and youngest de la Garza brother, by 1835, already had his eye on Becerra's youngest daughter, seventeen-year-old Gertrudis Becerra. Becerra must have wondered if Francisco would remain by the side of his eldest brother, Carlos, in this time of trouble. Old Manuel was the kind of contemplative individual who would be very disturbed over the family division that had apparently affected his illustrious neighbors and in-laws.

Becerra's daughter, María Josefa, had every reason to worry about her husband's decision to join the rebels. She would remain on her father's ranch and await his return. The cautious Becerra may well have related to Francisco de la Garza, when he came to visit Gertrudis, that as early as 1821 he and the officials of La Bahía had informed Governor Martinez of the troubles Mexico would one day have with the North Americans. Governor Martinez had not heeded that early warning and neither had the officials in faraway Coahuila. Now Becerra's worst fears had come to pass. Government neglect of those Mexicans in *Tejas* had left them to fend for themselves. If the de la Garzas and Becerras and their fellow settlers survived in the wilderness, it was solely through their own hard labor and industry. Such policies, combined with dictatorial and unstable rule from Mexico City, could only result in divided loyalties. Perhaps Paulino and José María were responding to the long years of uncertainty by siding with the newcomers who seemed to know how to provide security to the local region.

Carlos de la Garza and the other members of his family remained loyal to Mexico. In the violent events of late 1835 and 1836, the de la Garzas never resorted to murder or other acts of violence which Santa Anna ordered against the prisoners they captured. When Don Carlos learned that Americans were to be executed at Goliad, he and his men rode to La Bahía where they managed to save six or seven Texan soldiers from execution. These included some Irish settlers from Refugio County. Among those Irish colonists saved from execution by Don Carlos were his close personal friends, Nicholas Fagan and son, John Fagan. I would later dis-

cover a historic friendship between these two Texan families. Regardless of many of the distortions in Texas tradition which have
come down to us against men like Carlos de la Garza for siding
with Mexico, it must be remembered that he and his brothers and
cousins are blamed essentially for remaining loyal and faithful to
their nation.

It has been asserted by some historians that the de la Garzas
captured a fleeing American, probably in early March of 1836, and
then destroyed the Refugio archives. Actually, the de la Garzas
would have gained nothing by the wanton destruction of the archives. The archives contained the records of their own land grants,
in Refugio County. Carlos de la Garza owned a large grant in Victoria County, which he lost to the Republic of Texas because he es-
poused the Mexican cause during the battles of 1836. The government of the Republic of Texas shamefully confiscated the Carlos de
la Garza grant if for no other reason than his patriotism for his native land. Who can be called a traitor for loyalty to and love of his
country?

The de la Garza family, it must again be emphasized, was split
during these turbulent times into opposing groups. They were a
family caught in the crossfire between the Anglo-Americans in
Texas and a despot in Mexico. Don Carlos was made to suffer for
his loyalty during the days of the Texas Republic when he chose to
remain in his native territory.

The huge and somewhat rusty Spanish sword worn by Don
Carlos de la Garza hangs in the museum at Presidio La Bahía. The
ancient relic was donated by the de la Garza family. Carlos is buried next to the wall of Our Lady of Loreto Chapel where he was
baptized in 1801. It seemed only right that he come back to the
place of his beginning.

Father William H. Oberste refers to these men as the de la
Garza *rancheros* in his two important volumes on the Refugio area.
As a direct descendant of these flamboyant men, I prefer to call the
old Mexican *dons* the "de la Garza horsemen." After the death of
my great-great-grandfather Francisco de la Garza, the youngest of
these brothers, in 1870, these magnificent Texas brothers ceased to
exist.

The de la Garzas saw Texas being wrested away from Mexico.
What seemed more incredible was the fact that within a mere four

months the huge province was solidly under the control of the rugged Irishmen and North Americans. The predictions of Manuel Becerra and Tomás Buentello some fifteen years before had come true. The firebrand Francisco de la Garza remained loyal to his eldest brother, Carlos, and undoubtedly rode with this group of horsemen. When the bloody conflict was over, they vanished back into the woods as suddenly as they had appeared. Carlos de la Garza and Francisco nursed their fiercely wounded pride, for their cause was lost forever. The brothers, Paulino and José María de la Garza, emerged as victorious as the Anglo-Americans.

Francisco, the youngest in this colorful group, married Gertrudis Becerra in 1837; and their eldest daughter, Trinidad de la Garza, was born in 1839.[20] This marriage served to further bind the two proud Texas families. They would not leave Texas, for it had been their home for several generations.

The county records that I took home to California from Texas held specific information. Carlos, José María, Paulino, and Francisco de la Garza appear in the Refugio County census of September 30, 1850. All of these, with the exception of Paulino, possessed portions of the Manuel Becerra lands. In 1858, the Carlos de la Garza estate was worth $7,000.50 — a prosperous man by the standards of that era. Francisco's was $1,760.50 and José María, $968.50.[21]

Carlos de la Garza had been granted title to his 5,535-acre grant on the San Antonio River by José Jesús Vidaurri on October 28, 1834. According to his petition he had been improving and occupying the land for more than nine years, or since 1824 or 1825. He also petitioned for one-quarter league, or 1,107 acres (included in the 5,535 acres) for his son Rafael, who in 1858 married Elizabeth Montgomery of Victoria County.[22]

A painstaking search for the Refugio County tax rolls for 1836–46 had revealed these records were missing, the years coinciding with the Republic of Texas. The possibility that these historical and important documents were purposely destroyed should not be overlooked. It is also possible that the fire of 1903 may have destroyed the ancient records. The Texas census for 1840 failed to show the inhabitants of both Refugio and Goliad counties. The 1830 census taken during the Mexican era is practically all Anglo-American and other foreigners, except for San Antonio and the settlement of Nacogdoches in East Texas. These settlements, for a change, had more Mexicans than Anglos. San Antonio has always remained the stronghold of the ancient Mexicans since the founding of the land of the *Tejas*; the same may be said of the La Bahía settlement.

Antonio de la Garza, the man who last possessed the Becerra lands, was born on the Alamito Ranch about twelve miles east of Refugio on March 20, 1848. He was the only surviving son of Francisco de la Garza and Gertrudis Becerra. I was to learn more about this fascinating man the more I researched. According to his grandson Tomás Rubio, Antonio had the appearance of an Anglo-Texan — including a pink scalp. *Puro Español* — he was of pure Spanish ancestry. Tomás Rubio related to me the following episode told to him by his grandfather Antonio.

Antonio had a quick temper, which was well known among family and friends. In 1875, while residing on his Alamito Ranch in Refugio County, Antonio was vainly trying to put the saddle on a stubborn horse. The horse snorted and ran back and forth in the corral, kicking at him many times. The furious Antonio finally roped the creature and snubbed it closely to a stout corral post. Thinking that he could saddle the horse, Antonio was in for a rude awakening, for the beast reared up and pawed at him with his forefeet, still refusing to be saddled. In a rage, Antonio pulled a long knife from his boot. At every chance he began unmercifully stabbing the poor creature who desperately fought for his life. The struggle between man and beast continued for some time amid a cloud of dust. Antonio finally pulled his Colt 45 pistol and was about to dispatch the stubborn animal when his wife, Ponposa Bontan, intervened and saved the creature from certain death. Ponposa, who was always kind and gentle to animals, somehow managed to doctor the horse back to good health.

Tomás Rubio also remembered that Antonio's advice to his grandsons was to drink, smoke, raise hell, and carry pistols and long knives. In this manner, he felt they could become tough and strong. The old hellion advised them that at the first sign of trouble to take the long knife and quickly plunge it into an opponent, be it man or beast, preferably between the ribs. His eldest daughter Francisca, however, had different ideas about raising her seven sons.

The old man noticed that his grandsons always seemed to have sores on their feet and legs. He told them that he knew of a remedy which would eventually make the sores disappear. He would go into the woods and later emerge with a dead skunk. Carefully, he would skin the animal and build a fire to roast it. With both arms outstretched the old man would motion to his grandsons, *"Hijos, vengan a comer zorillo frito para que se les quitan los granos."* ("Sons, come and partake of this fried skunk so that your sores may disappear.") The boys stood around their grandfather and wondered if indeed it would make their sores disappear. My uncle Tomás Rubio, then a small child, broke and ran through the woods to inform his mother what his grandfather was preparing. Francisca, on hearing of this latest episode, merely shook her head and wondered when her father was going to stop this deviltry. Uncle Daniel Rubio told me that so far as he knew none of the boys ate any of the fried skunk, but instead preferred to keep their sores.

Many years later I asked a native Mexican if he had ever heard of such a remedy. He replied that indeed he had. In Texas, as elsewhere in the Southwest, Mexicans knew of various remedies to cure ailments. Antonio de la Garza doubtless had at least heard of the potent remedy from one of his forefathers, who had heard of it from one of his own ancestors. Perhaps the folk remedy was the invention of an ancient Texas Mexican or Indian which was later adopted by the Mexican people as part of their culture.

Antonio always purchased tobacco leaves and ground them for smoking. The old man had the seven Rubio boys under his wings. They avidly listened to everything he said. All the boys became smokers and liked whiskey. Francisca disapproved of everything her father was teaching her sons and was quick to remind the old man that such excesses were ways of the devil. Antonio was equally quick to remind her that he wanted his grandsons to become rawhide strong. Francisca realized that while his ways were crude and ancient products of the old Texas frontier, he nevertheless meant well.

What the old man most importantly imparted to his grandsons was a frontier legacy he had inherited from his father, Francisco, the youngest brother of the daring Carlos de la Garza. Antonio's father had been the son-in-law of Manuel Becerra from whom they had inherited the lands in Refugio County. I knew the exact lineage now. And from Antonio, his grandsons and granddaughters had learned that the family had been wrongfully dispossessed of their lands; lands they had inherited from the man who had guided Stephen F. Austin when he first came to their homeland.

As I talked with elders of the de la Garza family, I found out that the turbulent de la Garza history did not end in the nineteenth century. Indeed, fate deemed that Ismael de la Garza, grandson of Francisco de la Garza, be the principal participant in what was to be the final but violent gun-blazing episode at La Bahía in 1915. Perhaps fate also deemed it appropriate that the final chapter of the de la Garza *pistoleros* be terminated so near the place where these men were born and baptized.

Ismael, the middle son of Antonio and Ponposa, was born after their flight from Refugio. He was reared by his father with gun and knife in hand — typical frontier style. The young man was quick to adapt to his father's hellish ways. He was very dangerous and lethal with the pistol and rifle. In 1906, he married Caroline Lee, who was born at La Bahía on August 15, 1886. Ismael always tried to impart this deadly knowledge to his nephew, Guillermo Rubio, much to the disapproval of his sister, Francisca. Other than the violent episode to be narrated shortly there were others in the life of Ismael de la Garza. He would mysteriously disappear from Goliad County for weeks at a time. Being the *pistolero* that he was, many concluded that those disappearances involved violence of one form or another. There were two other killings in Goliad County attributed to him. Unfortunately, the brave young man was not around when his father was being intimidated into vacating his lands in Refugio County. Had José, the eldest, and Ismael and Guadalupe been there, things might have turned out differently for our family.

A feud had been developing since the early 1900s between the de la Garza, Reyes, and Flores families.[23] The other two families were not from Goliad County and may have been considered intruders by the de la Garzas. Relatives chose not to elaborate on the reasons for the feud; but whatever the reasons, the results were devastating.

The feud had begun among the older men; but in the confrontation, the younger men of the Reyes and Flores families bore the brunt of the de la Garza wrath. By this time Ismael was thirty-six years old and his brother, José María, forty-five. On Christmas Eve, 1915, the intruders set an ambush on the trail leading to La Bahía. Three well-armed men sat on their horses behind some thicket a short distance from the trail, and with vengeance waited for the de la Garzas. Tiring of the long wait and keenly disappointed that their carefully laid plans had not worked, the men rode on to a dance hall and *cantina* where they demanded a corner table. The proprietor, noting the resolute look of the strangers, promptly complied. The de la Garzas, like their forefathers, knew every trail leading in and out of La Bahía for many miles. Perhaps sensing treachery or a bad omen, they had chosen to ride to La Bahía by a tiny trail only they knew and by doing so saved their lives.

The night was quite cold and Ismael and José María wore similar attire including long overcoats. Ismael's black boots were nearly knee length with the trousers tucked inside; strapped to his right boot was a Colt 45 pistol and another on his waist positioned for easy reach. On the left boot he carried a long knife securely strapped. On this frigid night the two grandsons of Francisco de la Garza were heavily armed and ready to do battle. The two proud men who bore their grandfather's noble name were riding to keep their appointment with destiny.

They entered the *cantina* and within seconds the deadly climax to the long-standing feud erupted into gunfire. When the smoke from the pistols cleared, the nightmarish scene revealed two men had been killed and the third man critically wounded and left for dead. José María and Alejandro Reyes were the first to fall mortally wounded; Ismael shot Reyes, and Adrian Flores shot José María. The thoroughly enraged Ismael turned with smoking pistol and shot Adrian Flores. Adrian, who had been shot twice, miraculously survived though he carried the scars and limped badly for the rest of his life.[24]

The young witness to all this killing was Daniel Rubio. He had been born in Goliad on June 19, 1900, the son of Francisca de la Garza and Juan Rubio. The boy had asked his mother for permission to go and listen to the music at the dance hall, and she had reluctantly conceded. The youth of fifteen years was standing across the road listening to the music blaring from the dance hall. The far-

thest thing from his mind was the violent drama he was about to witness.

Daniel recognized his de la Garza uncles as they rode in, dismounted, and hitched their horses to the wooden hitching rail. The brothers spoke to each other for a few moments then walked into the *cantina*. He said that when the shooting started there were many terrified screams from the women, including *cantineras* or saloon girls, and cursing men came flying out of the broken and narrow windows. Blue smoke began to drift through the broken windows; and the yellow light cast by the lamps presented an eerie sight which he never forgot. The youth was greatly astounded to see men making what appeared to be nearly perfect dives through such narrow windows, particularly those men who were portly of frame. He reckoned that the wretches were pushed by the mob in their haste to vacate the *cantina*.

There was such cursing as he had never heard; people were running into each other in their haste to get away. Several men became embroiled in fist fights; other men fled drunkenly into the woods from whence he heard more cursing, as they, in their drunken stupor, ran into trees. The entire *cantina* was in complete turmoil. It never reopened for business. Saddled horses became terrified of the screaming mob and broke from the hitching rails and fled snorting and kicking. Long-eared mules began braying in terror and also broke the hitching rails.

Daniel observed two big women frantically trying to squeeze through the front door, only to become stuck. The frenzied crowd literally pushed the poor women, and they rolled to the bottom of the wooden stairs. As the women rolled to the bottom of the stairs, one of the combatants flew through a broken window and headed in the direction of the San Antonio River with Ismael in pursuit. The de la Garza *pistolero* continued firing and caught up with the stranger on the banks of the San Antonio River and killed him. The critically wounded Flores had been shot twice and was in great pain. Ismael emerged from the gunfight unscathed.

When the fight began, Guadalupe, one of the de la Garza brothers, instantly became involved. Two men who sided with Flores and Reyes stabbed him in the chest, a wound he would suffer from for the rest of his life. Before the two attackers could finish their work, however, Guadalupe's nephew, seventeen-year-old Antonio, jumped to his defense, long knife in hand. This young man was a namesake of the old Refugio hellion, lean and pale, but ferocious with a blade. Young Antonio had startling green eyes and long black hair. In a rage, he flew at the two men who had Guadalupe at bay and sent them fleeing in terror with blood streaming from the wounds he inflicted.

When word reached Antonio at his ranch that his sons had been involved in a gunfight and that his eldest son, José María, had been killed, the ill-tempered old demon, sixty-five years old at this time, began ranting and swearing terrible revenge on the killers of his son. Preparing to continue the fight, he strapped on his pistol, loaded a rifle, saddled his horse, and headed for La Bahía.

Upon seeing the body of his eldest son, Antonio kneeled down, made the sign of the cross, and wept bitterly. The old man wanted to find the wounded Adrian Flores; however, he was persuaded by the peace officers to return home. The sheriff knew Antonio's temperament and detailed two deputies to escort him.

Adrian Flores soon married Teresita Rubio, a granddaughter

of Antonio de la Garza. Flores was never made welcome at any of the de la Garza homes in Goliad County or anywhere in Texas for that matter.

Several months into 1916, young Antonio de la Garza (he of the evil knife) succumbed to consumption. His grandfather remained by his bedside while the boy slowly died. (Early that year a son, Antonio, was born to Regina Laso, widow of José María. I met him during the first family gathering on August 21, 1972.)

Ironically, it seems that fate willed that a de la Garza be involved in that last bloody encounter almost under the cross of Our Lady of Loreto Chapel near the Presidio La Bahía. In 1957, seventy-eight-year-old Ismael de la Garza, the last *pistolero*, died. He was brought into the beautiful Chapel of Our Lady of Loreto for the requiem mass, as he had been brought in on September 30, 1879, for his baptism. Ismael was interred in the de la Garza cemetery next to his father, Antonio.

There has been no violence in and about Presidio La Bahía involving our family since December 24, 1915. De la Garza pistols were silent at last.

[8]

Pay Dirt in Texas Soil

The documents gathered from county records in Texas shed further light on several other important issues. First of all, the records named the de la Garzas residing on the Becerra lands and dates of their residences. Secondly, only one conveyance of Becerra lands was made to anyone outside our family. Thirdly, they gave further credibility to the validity of Becerra and his heirs' legitimate title to the land in question. And fourthly, it seemed as if a man named O'Connor came into possession of land where our grant was once located.

The Refugio County census of September 1850 showed Francisco de la Garza's occupation as herdsman or rancher. He owned 4,428 acres of land on Alamito and Copano creeks. María Josefa Becerra and her husband, José María de la Garza, owned the other 4,428 acres.[1] Thus, to the year 1850, the entire Manuel Becerra grant was being occupied by his daughters and two sons-in-law, José and Francisco. By 1853, records showed Carlos de la Garza on 2,214 acres of this land, Francisco on 1,107 acres, and José on 1,107 acres — a total of 4,428 acres, or half the Becerra tract. Carlos de la Garza had received the 2,214 acres through a conveyance to his wife, Antonia Cruz, from the Becerra family on March 17, 1853,

113

after Manuel's death. María Josefa and José had given to Francisco the 1,107 acres he occupied. This transaction was made in Goliad County on June 19, 1853, and was recorded in Refugio County, April 9, 1855.[2]

This transaction must have been a reallocation of the property among the de la Garza families in response to a conveyance of 4,428 acres which, we discovered, Manuel Becerra and his wife made on October 14, 1848, to a man named Henry Koehler, a resident of Cameron County on the Mexican border. By 1850, Koehler owned one-half of the Becerra tract, and the de la Garzas, who, according to the census of that year, were occupying all the property, undoubtedly realized they had to share the remaining half in some fashion. They reallocated this acreage among themselves by 1853.

Conveyance to Henry Koehler of the 4,428 acres (known as the "lower half") was the only portion of the Becerra grant ever deeded to someone out of the family. There was another conveyance of Becerra lands involving a ten-acre parcel to a later family member. This small conveyance was made by José María de la Garza and María Josefa Becerra in 1861. The importance of their conveyance rests in the fact that the transaction was officially made by the Refugio notary, Richard J. Bryant, on Rancho Alamito, February 6, 1861, again verifying the existence of our family's property known as Rancho Alamito.

Before explaining the situation I encountered with Henry Koehler, I must note that by this time I discovered that my family's claim to the Becerra tract had likewise met the criteria of ownership under the Texas Land Relinquishment Law of 1852. This law pertained to unrecorded and unarchived Mexican land grant titles issued before November 13, 1835. It provided that field notes of all surveys made before the passage of the said act were to be filed in the General Land Office by August 31, 1853, or be null and void, thus becoming vacant land suspect to relocation and survey by persons holding land certificates or other legal claim to land.

The amended 1876 Texas Constitution simply stated that unrecorded or unarchived surveys issued prior to November 13, 1835, were invalid as to junior titles. Section 2, Article 10 of the 1869 Constitution of Texas had provided that all land surveys (always directed at the grantees or their descendants of Spanish and Mexican land grants) not promptly returned to the General Land Office in compliance with the provisions of the 1852 act were null and void.

These laws of 1852 and the provisions of 1869 and 1876 led me to suspect that they were enacted as much for the benefit of people eager to get their hands on land as for the grantees, whether Mexican or Anglo. It seemed to me that such laws would open the door for some frontier land-grabbers to pounce on an unknowing, semiliterate settler who spent more time working his land than hanging around the county courthouse.

In 1886, in *Gonzales v. Ross*, the United States Supreme Court ruled against these statutes saying that before the adoption of the 1876 Constitution, Texas laws did not require that a Mexican land grant title be registered in the county or deposited in the archives of the General Land Office in order to give it validity.

We had discovered that the Manuel Becerra deed to Antonia Cruz, wife of Carlos de la Garza, on March 17, 1853, clearly stated in Spanish that said grant was issued by the government of Mexico at Monclova, and that it was properly archived in the district court clerk's office, Refugio County. Thus, the tracts belonging to María Josefa Becerra and her husband, José María de la Garza, as well as Francisco de la Garza, and Carlos and Antonia, were in compliance with the law of 1852. The grant was properly archived. Any pretense to the contrary was false.

In addition, County Clerk W. M. McFarland had recorded the Becerra grant on June 6, 1848. The filing fee was $1.35, which made it official. The conveyance from Becerra and Cadena to Henry Koehler on October 14, 1848, stated on the deed that it was a grant from the government of Mexico. The grant was further confirmed on March 12 and 13, 1849, by District Surveyor David Snively as duly recorded. Again, this land was properly archived according to law.

It is not clear whose responsibility it was to forward the documents to the General Land Office. Surely the county clerk should have forwarded duplicates of such important information to Austin. My exhaustive search into those records in Austin revealed that there were very few resurvey notes or documents from Refugio County colonists. Becerra would have never forwarded the original documents to Austin. Like most other colonists in Refugio, who after 1850 balked at attempts by the state to have them lay out extra money to resurvey their tracts, the Becerra children would have rested their claim on their valid original documents. Although it was unfortunate that it was not registered in the General Land Office, that did not negate the validity of ownership.

In regard to Henry Koehler, the county records revealed that he appeared to have been in debt to the sum of $2,052.64 by May 4, 1866. Saloma Young, executrix of John Young, obtained a writ and order of sale at Goliad County against Phillip Koehler, sole heir of Henry Koehler. The land acquired by the heirs of John Young was one league, again it being the "lower half" of two leagues granted by the Republic of Mexico to Manuel Becerra; the said lower league had been transferred to Henry Koehler in 1848. Sheriff James M. Doughty of Refugio County on May 10, 1867, seized all the estate, rights, title, and interests. And on the first week of July 1867, he sold the premises at public vendue in Refugio County. The sheriff gave public notice twenty days prior to the sale. The premises were struck off to the highest bidder, John Young, Jr., for the sum of $200. The instrument was duly recorded on August 20, 1867. It is very important to note here that the Young-Koehler transaction does not question the validity of title to the old Becerra grant.[3]

Desperately hoping to locate the John Young family on the Refugio County maps, I was spurred on to great activity. Since that family had acquired half of the Becerra tract it seemed reasonable that they might appear on the maps. With that thought in mind, I began a vigorous search for an 1870 map. Since the transaction had been made in 1866 by Saloma Young and maps are generally made every ten years, it seemed that they should be on the 1870 map. But this map was not to be found. The only map found was for the year 1872. I methodically scrutinized the 1872 map many times, but found nothing. Undaunted, I reviewed the 1875, 1883, 1896, 1900, and 1921 maps. I still could not locate the Young name on any of those maps.

It seemed to me that someone in Refugio County had seen to it that neither Manuel Becerra nor the John Young family appeared on county maps as far back as 1870. I particularly noticed that on the 1875 map there appeared at the junction of Copano and Alamito creeks, where the Becerra tract begins, the initials I & GNRR Co., which stood for the International and Great Northern Railroad Company. These I&GNRR Co. tracts had numbers that appeared to be patents or survey numbers. The 1896 map shows D. M. O'Connor in place of the I&GNRR Co. with the same patent or survey numbers. I was startled that a railroad and then a man named O'Connor would come into possession of our lands without there being recorded conveyances from Becerra, the de la Garzas, or the Youngs. I would not forget those numbers. Aunt Sálome had first mentioned to me the O'Connor name in reference to the loss of our ancestral lands.

Dennis M. O'Connor was the son of Thomas O'Connor, who was the original O'Connor settler in Refugio County in 1834. Although some standard histories of the region note that the original Thomas O'Connor had received a Mexican land grant, it did not show up in the General Land Office when I searched it exhaustively. However, there was a Thomas <u>Connor</u> whose 4,428-acre grant was dated September 28, 1834. Apparently, this was the same person. At that time, O'Connor was a lad of fifteen years of age. It seems strange that the Mexican government would grant so much land to a youngster unattended by family other than his uncle, James Power. We know, however, that Power, in his haste to complete his colonization decree, might have circumvented the letter of the law by granting lands to unauthorized young people.

As shown on the 1875 map, Thomas O'Connor had already begun to acquire property in Refugio County. By the 1896 map his son, Dennis, claimed land which obviously overlapped the Becerra tract which had been shown as I&GNRR Co. land patents or surveys.

With the appearance of the O'Connor name where the Becerra grant was located, I realized once again that family tradition and documentary evidence were intertwined.

The records we had gathered clarified how Antonio came into possession of the lands on Rancho Alamito. María Josefa de la Garza and Francisco de la Garza in 1850 were listed with the same tax-paying number. Certainly, Francisco and María Josefa and her husband, José María de la Garza, connected by marriage and blood, remained close because when Alberta de la Garza, the daughter of Francisco and his second wife Gertrudis Garcia, was born on September 13, 1859, María Josefa served as godmother at the October 14, 1860, baptism.[4] The death of Gertrudis Becerra,

María Josefa's younger sister and Francisco's first wife, had not ended the family ties.

By the time Francisco de la Garza died in March of 1870 in Refugio County, he had already inherited the 1,107 acres belonging to María Josefa and José María. At the time of his death in 1870, Francisco owned 2,214 acres of Rancho Alamito which was then inherited by his son by Gertrudis Becerra, Antonio de la Garza. Antonio had three sisters, Trinidad, Genoveva, and Rosalia, all from the union between Francisco and Gertrudis Becerra.[5]

José María and María Josefa had no children. Antonio de la Garza was thus the only grandson of Manuel Becerra. He was the head of the de la Garza family after 1870 and the sole male heir to the Becerra lands.

Harris and I had studied the material in California that we had gathered during our stay in Texas. Virginia Taylor at the General Land Office sent us sample documents signed by the leading officials of Coahuila-Texas, Governor Francisco Vidaurri and Secretary General J. Miguel Falcón. She also sent a copy of Spanish Law 128 and Article 12 governing land grant distribution during the Mexican era; however, nothing was found on Article 15. (Taylor indicated in a note that the documents we had received were incomplete, though just what she meant was not clear at that time.) Governor Vidaurri's concession on the Manuel Becerra petition granted the latter the lands specified and fully described on the petition. Vidaurri's signature of approval as well as Falcón's on the Becerra petition matched perfectly with the signatures on the documents we received from the General Land Office. There was no longer any doubt as to the legality of the Becerra grant. It was a federal government grant and not in any way connected in similarity or any manner with those issued by the Irish *empresarios* in Refugio County, Texas.

Don Manuel Becerra did not appear in Title Book 17 of Original Titles which lists colonists receiving titles from José Jesús Vidaurri; however, the Refugio County tax rolls of September 4, 1849, showed Becerra on his *special* grant of 8,856 acres.

Manuel Becerra had paid the *ayuntamiento* of Goliad 100 reales when he signed his petition on May 14, 1832. The officials — probably the *alcalde* Juan José Hernandez — accepted the payment which amounted to twelve and one-half Mexican pesos. Becerra recorded the deed (filing fee was $1.35) which was accepted as such on April 6, 1848. W. M. McFarland, the clerk of Refugio County, apparently found the documents in proper order. The clerk, familiar with Mexican land grants, entered the documents into the records as a deed from the Mexican government. Had the documents been faulty, McFarland would not have allowed their entry into the records; or if they were faulty, he would surely have made a note.[6]

In response to a later inquiry made by Harris, Hobart Huson of the Refugio Mission Title Abstract Company on February 25, 1974, replied in writing that he had found a petition made by Becerra in 1832; but Huson asserted that he could not find a grant made by Governor Vidaurri to Becerra in 1834. This was understandable because the probate clerk McFarland on April 6, 1848, while copying a duplicate from the original, neglected to include Governor Vidaurri's initial F. for Francisco. It should be remembered that there were two men named Vidaurri in Coahuila and Texas in 1834 and both of these were officials of the Mexican government. Governor Vidaurri was at Monclova, and Commissioner José Jesús Vidaurri was issuing land titles in Refugio. José Jesús was at the Power and Hewetson Irish colony. Hobart Huson must have assumed that the signature on the Becerra documents was that of Land Commissioner José Jesús Vidaurri.

Governor Vidaurri remained in office a relatively short period of time — from January 8, 1834, to August of 1834 — certainly not sufficient time to fairly acquaint Vidaurri or his successors with the terrible conditions in faraway Texas. One of the last communications written by Governor Vidaurri was especially meant for the ears of the *empresarios* Power and Hewetson, though the letter was communicated directly to Ramón Musquiz, political chief (the highest civil authority in Texas) on August 28, 1834.[7] The letter was finally transmitted by the new political chief, Angel Navarro, to the Refugio *ayuntamiento.* By this late date, the governor and Musquiz had been out of office for many months. Governor Vidaurri made it known to *empresario* Power that the Mexican colonists residing in Refugio should be guaranteed their rights to the property in their possession. Vidaurri's letter to Power came as a result of many complaints voiced by the bitter Mexican colonists.

By December 28, 1834, there were only two men representing the Mexican government in the Refugio *ayuntamiento:* Ramirez, the *encargado* (intendent), and Manuel Becerra, the secretary and notary. The two men were the last vestiges of Mexican authority in Refugio. Both signed the land titles or certified them for Coahuila and Texas in 1834 and 1835.[8]

Having scrupulously examined and re-examined the documents thus far found during the search, many of the Becerra family were convinced that there was enough evidence to claim the lost land. However, determining who occupied the land and where exactly it was situated was still a great challenge. Suspicion pointed toward persons in Refugio County, but suspicion alone was not enough evidence to make accusations. This would come about in due course.

It is important to note here again that Essy Reed supposedly arrived in Texas in 1832; in 1838, she petitioned the Board of Land Commissioners of Matagorda County for a grant of one league and one labor of land, or about 4,605 acres in Refugio County, half the size of the Becerra property. The petition was approved by the commissioners and subsequently by Anson Jones, secretary of state for the Republic of Texas.[9] It appears that Essy Reed was deceased when approval of her petition was made by the Texas authorities. The petition was fraught with errors in the surveys and resurveys, particularly the boundaries; the patent was finally cancelled in 1893.

This cancellation notwithstanding, it was still called the Essy Reed tract, and in 1849, the taxes on the Reed tract in Refugio County were paid by Francis Dieterich, a Refugio County colonist. Dieterich was probably Reed's husband; and on December 29, 1875, their son, James Dieterich of Travis County, conveyed the entire tract to Thomas O'Connor of Refugio County.[10]

Manuel Becerra, or heirs in his name, also paid taxes on his tract of land in the same month as Francis Dieterich. Had there been any violations regarding the boundaries, Becerra or his heirs most assuredly would have contested with Dieterich. Moreover, on a more careful scrutiny of the maps it began to be apparent that the Essy Reed tract was located to the north of the Becerra grant, which was at the confluence of Copano and Alamito creeks. It appeared that the Becerra and Reed tracts were two separate land grants, though perhaps adjacent to one another. These tracts were probably not in conflict with each other in any way. This laid to rest any suspicion previously entertained that the Reed tract was in the exact area as that of Becerra land.

Our suspicions were now directed more toward the I&GNRR Co. scrips obtained by the O'Connors.

Since we had not received all the information we sought, Harris once again contacted Virginia Taylor at the Land Office in Austin. In December 1972, he requested copies of a completed Mexican land grant deed of the 1832–34 era. Many weeks passed and no reply came from the Spanish archivist. Harris, now somewhat frustrated, made another request for a valid deed specifically relating to Spanish Law 128 and most especially Article 15. None was forthcoming. Harris was certain that the best qualified authority in Texas regarding Spanish and Mexican land grants was Taylor; therefore, if the information sought was not forthcoming we were doomed, or so Harris thought. Should we be unable to obtain a completed deed in all its formality at the Land Office archives in Austin, the only other source would be at the archives in Monclova, Coahuila, Mexico. By the year 1834, Monclova was the capital for the state of Coahuila-Texas; therefore, we assumed that duplicate copies of all transactions pertaining to granting of lands in Texas were sent to the central government headquarters at Monclova. A great deal of information from the Texas *ayuntamientos* was also sent to Monclova. Included in the communications from the *ayuntamiento* were bitter complaints from the Mexican settlers against tyrannical Irish *empresarios*, notably those from the Refugio colony. The exception was the Austin colony, Stephen F. Austin being the most proficient of all the Texas *empresarios*. The Irish *empresarios*, the most notorious, ruled their colonies like dictators.[11]

The prospect of conducting a search in the Monclova archives in the forseeable future appeared dim. Such a search would require a specialist. Spanish Law 128 was easily found, but Article 15 under which Manuel Becerra applied for his grant remained elusive, and I was at least temporarily disappointed and frustrated. Even though we now knew a great deal more than we had about the disposition of our ancestral lands, and suspected even more, I knew that I would have to return to Texas. Only there could I relieve the frustration of uncertainty about more of the finer points of our land ownership during the nineteenth century.

[9]

The Search
Bears Fruit

Before I made my third trip to Texas in search of more documentation regarding ownership of Rancho Alamito, Benito Martinez sent me a copy of a most fascinating letter written in Spanish by his grandmother, Paula Lozano de Martinez. I translated the letter into English, and as I read it, I was overwhelmed with emotion as I had been when I had heard the reminiscences of my uncles Daniel and Tomás, and during my memorable interview with Aunt Sálome. Here, in the letter from Benito's now deceased grandmother, was another family account of what had actually happened to our lands.

Doña Paula had been born on the Alamito Ranch in Refugio County in 1871. Her letter spoke of how she remembered, as a girl of seven, that Anglo-American night riders intimidated her family into fleeing from the lands forever in 1877–78. This was incredible; yet, it corresponded with what the other elders of my family had related.

I took a plane to Houston on January 27, 1973. When I arrived, Core Rubio was waiting for me at the airport. We drove to the Houston residence of the venerable Don Plácido Martinez, the leader of the Martinez family. Don Plácido was born in Goliad on

122

November 3, 1897. Even at seventy-seven years of age, he still retained his massive size, being six feet four inches in height. All of his six sons are tall and strong as well.

Don Plácido is a man known for his hard work, truthfulness, and good works in the community, whether at his old birthplace, La Bahía, or the city of Houston. Don Plácido spoke no idle talk — always the truth as he knew it to be. That day at his house he told me what he knew as his mother, Paula Lozano de Martinez, had told him. His story supplemented the information contained in her letter, the copy of which Benito had sent to me. While Martinez spoke, I took notes. Although Don Plácido is a patriotic American and raised his family the same way, I could see his anger and emotion rise as he told me of the injustices to our family in Refugio County in the 1870s. As the old man spoke, I was fascinated, but my emotion rose as well. Visions of what Aunt Sálome had told me, of what my uncles Daniel and Tomás had told me, and what I had already gathered in my research raced through my mind. Before Don Plácido had finished, I began to despise Refugio. I realized that the injustices against my ancestors there had caused them to live lives of base poverty and humiliation. But in spite of the adverse conditions under which they lived, my forefathers kept their noble Spanish-Mexican heritage intact.

Don Plácido told me of the climate of injustice and prejudice against Mexican Texans in the very early 1900s when he was a boy. Clearly, things had not changed much between the 1870s and 1900 in South Texas. Even as patriotic as he was, Don Plácido harbored a mistrust of many Anglo Texans, especially for the injustices that he knew our people suffered at the hands of all-Anglo juries when he was a young man. Our interview lasted three hours, and from it I gathered much detail.

The following day, January 28, I spent visiting relatives in Goliad, seeing uncles Tomás, Jesús and Daniel Rubio, and my aunts. It was indeed a happy family gathering. Once again I had returned like a wayward son to La Bahía, the land of my birth as well as that of my ancestors of so long ago. At dusk on Saturday, January 28, as if driven by sheer impulse, I crossed the San Antonio River and appeared before the Presidio La Bahía. The magnets which had drawn me there — the ancient bells and the cross — were still there, like beacons, quite visible for all of God's creatures who might come forth to seek a moment of solace with Him in troubled times. One of the bells had a crack, perhaps due to battles fought there between Mexicans against the Spanish and later Anglo-Americans. Standing alone staring at the old bell, I wondered if Manuel Becerra's daughter, Gertrudis, had seen this very bell when she was a little girl in 1822.

Saturday night I stayed at the home of Uncle Tomás Rubio. Once again, he spoke in great detail of the stories he had heard as a youngster. At dawn the next morning I was awakened by the vigorous crowing of roosters (the Rubio dwellings are all on the outer town limits and quite close to the woods), and the wonderful fragrance of brewing coffee. Aunt Juanita Gonzales was preparing an early breakfast assisted by Uncle Tomás. The atmosphere reminded me of the old ranch where I grew up. I remembered my tiny Mexican hairless dog Pelón and wondered what had happened to the little creature after we left the ranch in 1942. Everything seemed so serene on this morning, but this peaceful moment was abruptly interrupted when I remembered Article 15 and the true purpose of my trip to Texas. On Sunday morning during breakfast and before my departure for Austin, Uncle Tomás, perhaps sensing that I was troubled, simply stated, *"Hijo,* you and your family are too far away from us and should return home. You do not belong in California; Texas has been the homeland of your grandfathers for over 200 years and you belong here. Take my advice and return." Uncle Tomás would make the same statement to me again, but under different, sadder circumstances.

The descendants of Francisca, José María, Ismael, and Guadalupe de la Garza were the only ones involved in our struggle, eventually aimed at laying claim to the entire Manuel Becerra grant. Descendants of other members of the family chose to remain aloof and showed no interest in their ancestors' land or in rectifying the injustices against them.

On a bitterly cold morning, January 29, 1973, I drove to the General Land Office in Austin and anxiously proceeded to the Spanish Collection. The amiable Lanell Aston asked if she could be of assistance, to which I indicated a desire to speak with the Spanish archivist. The request was promptly and graciously granted. Aston's past help with the various documents and maps had been of immense value to the search.

Virginia Taylor greeted me with sincere kindness. I indicated my desire to locate a completed deed issued under Decree 128, Article 15, which governed land grants in southeastern Texas for the period of 1832–34. Petitioners for these land grants were all native-born Mexican settlers. Others applied directly to their *empresarios* for lands desired, but no more than one sitio per person or head of family. Sometimes the settler applied for an additional 1,107 acres for a son or daughter, making the total acreage 5,535 acres under family control. The petitioners for these grants applied directly to the *ayuntamiento*, which sent the petition to the governor of Coahuila and Texas.

We made an exhaustive search through the many volumes but to no avail. A deed under Decree 128, Article 15 did not seem to exist in the collection.

The following day, I was on my way back to California, already planning my next meeting with our lawyer. Though I had not found the completed deed, the meetings with Don Plácido Martinez and uncles Tomás and Daniel Rubio had made my travel costs, which were mounting, well worth the expenditure.

Meeting with Harris, I decided the final phase of the Becerra grant search must either be conducted by Harris or with the help of Texas attorneys. Harris rightfully felt that to have outsiders conduct any portion of the investigation, especially in Refugio, at that crucial period was risky. He had little faith in Texas lawyers, particularly in regard to Spanish and Mexican land grants, and especially when the claimants to such grants were Mexican-Americans. Harris was now better versed in Texas history. He was acutely aware of the state's traditional prejudice and mistreatment of Mexican-Americans.

The only solution was to send Harris to Texas. Soon I contacted Manuel Garcia, Core Rubio, and Raul Martinez and explained the situation. They agreed to furnish the necessary funds. Harris advised family members not to talk about the search with outsiders. We all agreed.

Shortly after I returned to California, my persistence paid off and I located the legal wording of Article 15. The article under which Manuel Becerra applied for his grant on May 14, 1832, was the one settlers used who desired more than 4,605 acres. Like Article 12 under Decree 128, it governed lands granted exclusively to

native Mexicans, and stated that a certificate from the ayuntamiento had to be presented, noting the number of years the petitioner had been settled and the services he had rendered.

The wording of the certificate was just the mere technicality of
the law that Becerra, a methodical government officer, followed
scrupulously in obtaining 8,856 acres. Article 15 was used by the
government to grant land to public officials, as was the case with
Manuel Becerra. Becerra was the only colonist in Refugio County
that I could find who ever received a land grant under Article 15
and signed by the governor of Coahuila and Texas. It was indeed a
unique instrument over which *no other* land grant could take precedence.[1]

Back in Texas the Becerra family was in a quagmire. Manuel
Garcia reported some members were becoming dissatisfied in the
cause. Rallying the family required no small amount of effort since
the distance from California to Texas was great. Among those spirited souls who helped were Ponposa de la Garza and Romana de la
Garza.

Meanwhile, Harris wrote to the archivist at Austin requesting
the location of tax records for Refugio County residents for the
years 1833 through 1881. The archivist directed Harris to the state
comptroller's office.

My arrival in Austin on June 19 to search for the family tax
records was indeed a crucial moment. The tax records would provide more essential proof of ownership of the land. But suppose the
tax records showed a strange name as the new owner? Uncle Daniel
Rubio had said that when his grandfather, Antonio de la Garza,
was chased out of Refugio County in the middle 1870s, he brought
bags of gold coins and could have easily purchased thousands of
acres of land in Goliad County. Whatever money Antonio brought
from Refugio County to Goliad County disappeared. He was definitely capable of doing whatever struck his fancy, but family members say he was not a gambler. His father's estate was equally
shared among his brothers and sisters, and Antonio's share was relatively small. Nonetheless, the possibility of finding another person's name as the owner of the land troubled me.

Anxiously and swiftly I began the search and quickly located
records where Don Manuel Becerra paid taxes for 1847–49, and
records of taxes paid by Carlos, José María, and Francisco de la

Garza for 1850–58. The 1850 tax rolls showed only the de la Garzas as paying the taxes, and Manuel Becerra as the grantee. Had Manuel Becerra been alive, he alone would have paid the taxes. This 1850 document further confirmed my belief that Becerra died after October 14, 1848, and before March 10, 1849.

The taxes paid by the de la Garza *rancheros* was for 4,428 acres. These findings confirmed that Becerra not only got his grant but also paid county taxes. However, the tax rolls for 1836–46, the years of the Republic of Texas, were conspicuously missing from the files. After 1850, the de la Garza family was in control of the Becerra lands, but I had not yet been able to locate Antonio de la Garza, whom I considered the most important figure at this time since he was the last holder of the Becerra grant. This was a crushing blow, for the most vital piece of information was still missing; proof that Antonio paid the taxes for his land from 1870 to 1881 had to be found.

Several days later, after a painfully slow search without success, I visited the microfilm department. There, with the able assistance of Ruth B. Pickle, I found Antonio de la Garza had paid his taxes from 1870 to 1877! The records showed that Antonio was not a grantor to anyone.[2] Had he been a grantor he would have made a conveyance.

As I drove to Victoria, there was only one thought in my mind. On his deathbed, Antonio had whispered to his daughter, Eliza, to claim the land in Refugio County because he had never disposed of it nor conveyed it in any way whatsoever. The records proved he was correct. There was no longer any doubt as to the validity of the family records involving the land. However, the tax records for 1878 through 1881 had to be found, and these could only be found in Refugio County, a place that I could barely bring myself to visit. The picture of villainy committed against my ancestors in that area long ago had become clear to me through persistent research and family traditions.

At my request, on June 25, 1973, a large gathering of the Becerra family was held at Goliad. For the first time the family was presented with tax records belonging to Manuel Becerra and the de la Garza family for the years 1847–77, proving ownership of the land in Refugio County. Previous information had been based on family tradition and on the old grant with its attendant documents that Core had first shown me. These tax records proved that family members were correct in their vigorous assertions regarding the Becerra land in Refugio County. Elderly family members were joyous to hear this information.

We were fortunate indeed in having located the tax records for 1847–77, but there still remained those after 1877 to be searched out. These were not at Austin, or else had been overlooked during the search there. I was compelled to proceed with the search in Refugio.

Leaving Victoria on Highway 77 South, I looped through Tivoli and soon turned onto Road 774 going west to Refugio. Approximately fifteen miles from Refugio, I noticed wooded areas extending for miles across both sides of the road had been neatly cut. But several miles farther down Road 774, a heavily wooded area with large clearings remained in its original wild state. Soon I crossed two creeks. Stopping and turning around, I proceeded to the first one and knew this had to be Copano Creek and the one some distance ahead must surely be the Alamito. Standing approximately between both creeks and somberly reflecting on the strange workings of destiny, I looked toward the four winds and wondered if God had finally guided his curious and persistent wandering creature to the Becerra lands. If I was not actually standing on the Becerra land, then it must be very near, dissected by Road 774.

Becerra trekked across southern Texas in the early 1800s and guarded these lands for the kingdom of Spain, even though the lands were still claimed by the Karankawa Indians. Becerra's footsteps in this wilderness area have been traced to the Refugio mission as early as 1813. Now, over 150 years later, his deeply troubled descendant stood on the edge of his domain with the avowed purpose of wresting the lost land from intruders. We had good claim to the Becerra lands, and there was now absolutely no doubt in my mind that in the end those responsible would be found.

At Refugio, I proceeded directly to the courthouse and then to the tax records office. Fear of failure was ever present with me. After informing the woman in charge of this department the purpose of my visit, I was assigned two clerks to help me.

The tax records were stored in the basement, a most unimpressive place; it had the appearance of a dungeon. Politely the clerks were requested to bring out records for the 1860s and, in like manner, they replied that there were no such records. Upon a casual inquiry one of the clerks remarked that the Thomas O'Connor family were the largest landowners in Refugio County. I knew this to be so, but it was good to hear a native affirm it.

After digging through the ancient records for a long time, I finally found the tax records for 1878 through 1881, in which Antonio de la Garza had paid the taxes on 2,214 acres of land![3] The search at Austin and Refugio for the old tax records had been a complete success. The records for the period 1847 through 1881 showed that the Becerra family had been in control of the land for thirty-four years, beginning with Manuel Becerra in 1847 and ending with Antonio de la Garza in 1881. Triumphantly, I left Refugio. The search, *gracias a Dios*, for my stolen heritage was nearly over.

[10]

Night Riders
and Murder

By the time I had located all the pertinent records indicating that the de la Garzas had eventually paid their taxes on the Becerra land grant, I had also accumulated enough research to outline the change in actual possession of this land from my ancestors into the hands of others. I had examined and reexamined such things as standard histories of the area, county records, original maps, and Spanish documents, but it seemed this was not enough. Also, the story became more complete through my gathering and assimilating oral tradition handed down to the elders of my family from many of their parents and elders who had lived through the trying times of the late nineteenth century in Refugio and Goliad counties. During my trip to Texas in the early summer of 1973, I was ready to piece together a complete narrative based on those family stories. What emerged was an account of many of the particulars of the dispossession of the families of Antonio de la Garza and his sister Trinidad between 1874 and 1878.

By the year 1877, the largest landowner in Refugio County was Thomas O'Connor, a nephew of the *empresario* James Power. By this time O'Connor had amassed over 24,000 acres of land and about 33,514 acres of the Power and Hewetson grant, for a total of

57,514 acres in Refugio County.[1] The Refugio County tax rolls for 1871–81 reflected this most impressive accomplishment for a penniless Irish immigrant who set foot on Mexican soil in 1834. He must have indeed possessed an insatiable appetite for land. The census tracts show him to have been in his late fifties by the mid-1870s — at the height of a man's energy and activity.

The Power tract was granted by Governor Vidaurri with the stipulation that it should not be located on lands already occupied by Mexican and American settlers; it was to be established on vacant state lands, and the governor was most specific to James Power that he adhere strictly to the decree.[2]

The Becerra survey copied from Snively's original survey report of 1849 clearly shows where the Becerra grant was located. Becerra had occupied that property for many years before he was granted title, which in turn was several years before Power received his title. Becerra probably had been there since 1820. The beginning point of the Snively survey was at the bed of Alamito Creek and included the junction of Copano and Alamito creeks.

The boundaries crossed both creeks on an east and west course. The grant extended slightly west of Alamito Creek and into Aransas County. The Power grant began exactly on the west side (headwaters of Copano Creek) and crossed west of Alamito Creek. Thus, a portion of the Becerra tract was already located where the Power grant was established in 1834, according to the Refugio County maps of 1883 and 1896 (Alamito Creek was shown on the 1896 map). The Becerra survey copied from the original survey report of 1849 clearly showed where the land was located. Becerra had applied for his grant before James Power; his grant was approved by Governor Vidaurri before that of Power.

Thus, the *empresario* mistakenly and unfortunately established his grant on a portion of the Becerra tract, this being in direct violation of the sovereignty which forbade him from claiming lands already occupied by other prior settlers. The Power grant had never been shown on any of the Refugio County maps beginning in 1834. On the 1872 map, Power's name appears only on the upper portion of the huge grant. But on the 1875 map, like a bad omen, the Power name covered the entire grant. This monstrous grant was fraught with errors from its inception. Its appearance on the 1872 and 1875 maps may have been due to the efforts of Power's descendants or

Thomas O'Connor, who may have attempted to correct the errors. The errors were never properly corrected so far as the boundaries were concerned. The boundaries definitely overlapped into the Becerra grant unless the 1875, 1883, and 1896 maps were in error, which was doubtful. Placing the 1849 Becerra plat on the 1896 map produced astounding results. In addition to the Power grant, the following names appeared: D. M. O'Connor and I&GNRR Company with the same infernal numbers that were on the 1875 map; Edwin C. Sloan; John M. Swisher; J. M. Cross; and C.E.P.&I. Manufacturing Company. There were thirty-seven such numbers, and the name appearing upon each as having come into possession of the land that they encompassed was Thomas O'Connor of Refugio County. This information was found in the General Land Office and is a matter of public record.[3]

In 1842, Francisco de la Garza was near the Texas-Mexican border in what was later Cameron County.[4] He was a member of the landed and wealthy Becerra-de la Garza family of Goliad and Refugio settlements, as well as those de la Garzas from the border. The youngest of the de la Garza brothers was a headstrong and spirited young man. His motives for moving hundreds of miles from his family toward the troubled border area was a secret only he knew. It is certain that Francisco did not go to the Rio Grande for the purpose of seeking employment, as conditions in that part of Texas were wretched in 1842. However, along the border area the powerful de la Garza landowners were anything put poor. These same de la Garzas of the border were relatives to those from the La Bahía, Refugio, and Nueces settlements. Thus, Francisco was among his family.[5]

Despite vigorous opposition from his uncles, Francisco returned to the Refugio settlement about 1844 or 1845 where he remained for the rest of his life. By early 1850, he was in possession of half of the Becerra grant on the Alamito Ranch, until it was redivided to accommodate the Becerra-Koehler transaction. He controlled at least 1,107 acres of the grant from the 1850s until his death in March of 1870. Francisco was only about fifty-four years of age when he died.

In 1870, the full responsibility for protecting the Becerra land holdings fell on the young shoulders of Francisco's only son, Antonio de la Garza, then twenty-one years old. Antonio's mother,

Francisco's first wife, had died when Antonio was two years of age. María Josefa and her husband had become like second parents to the lad. All his life Antonio referred to this aunt as "Mother Josefa." She and José, being childless, had no direct heirs. Antonio came into their part of the Becerra property. On his range there browsed nearly 500 head of cattle, over a hundred head of horses, eight oxen acquired from his aunt, María Josefa, and uncle, José María de la Garza, including an abundance of chickens and turkeys and a few Mexican goats which he would give to his sister, Trinidad. Antonio and his wife, Ponposa, were happy and relatively well-off, except that he may have brooded over the untimely death of his father, Francisco.[6] Everything was apparently peaceful on the Alamito Ranch.

Antonio and Ponposa were in Goliad County on July 27, 1870; but in 1871 they were back on the Alamito Ranch in Refugio County. During the summer of 1870, there were over a hundred calves to be branded. The hardest task was separating the little creatures from their mothers and then making sure they did not escape into the thick brush or wooded areas. During branding season, Antonio was ably assisted by Trinidad, his brother-in-law, Juan Elias Lozano, and his two single sisters, Genoveva and Rosalia, both of whom would be married within two months. The work of branding was done by Antonio, Juan Elias, and Trinidad. Genoveva and Rosalia took care not to let the cattle — especially the calves — escape into the brush.

The de la Garza cattle ear markings and brands were a common sight in Refugio County. The more prominent that showed up in Refugio County records include:

Ponposa Bontan de la Garza, registered April 19, 1874. $\mathcal{I}$

Francisco de la Garza, registered March 28, 1854. $\mathcal{AG}$

José María de la Garza, registered April 17, 1855. $\mathcal{B}$

Carlos de la Garza, registered November 15, 1853. AC

Juan Elias Lozano, registered April 13, 1869. $\mathcal{H}$

And by the mid-1870s there was Antonio de la Garza, who registered his own on February 11, 1874. $\mathcal{HC}$

For several years, or at least until the latter part of 1873, Antonio continued to prosper by hard work and the sweat of his brow. The herds of cattle and horses had increased substantially since

1870, when he was ordered by the district judge to manage his father's estate. Even before Francisco's death, Antonio and Ponposa lived on the ranch and had their own stock and branding irons. When in need of money, he simply sold some of the cattle and horses. On December 8, 1869, he sold three mules, probably the last of these animals, because after this date there were no longer any mules in his inventory. Antonio and Ponposa never seemed in financial distress while living on the Alamito Ranch. In 1870, Ponposa inherited some cattle from her father, Benito Bontan of Goliad County, and these increased the herds on Rancho Alamito. They were not, however, meant to enjoy their happiness and success for very long; an ominous shadow of impending doom was now nearly upon them.

The unsuspecting Antonio and Ponposa could not have known that greedy land-grabbers had zeroed in on their domain. The beginning of the end for Antonio and Ponposa in Refugio County must have been sometime in January 1874. It was about that time that the young herdsman began to discover all or parts of approximately half his herd of cattle mysteriously dead on his range land. Around this time, the exact day is not known for certain, Antonio found one hundred head of cattle and thirteen horses evidently killed by human predators, the identity of which he could only guess at that time.[7] Several years before, in the winter of 1871–72, a "big freeze" had killed thousands of cattle in the region; but this tragedy in early 1874 was obviously unrelated.

Antonio later told his grandchildren that it was a time of great grief for him to have such a large portion of his stock killed. No doubt the vultures of the area feasted for days on these dead animals.

Deeply grieving at the horrible and senseless slaughter of his fine cattle, the de la Garza *ranchero* must have sat on his horse viewing with heavy and aching heart this ghoulish panorama perpetrated by evil men. Having a terrible temper, de la Garza may have tried in vain to chase the birds of prey away from what was left of his livestock.

Aunt Sálome Rubio de Lambardia related that her grandfather, Antonio, was hurt as a result of the cruel act. During the second week in February 1874, Antonio went into Refugio and, with the help of the district clerk, made an inventory showing the

deaths of all the livestock.[8] But the record of the occurrence he made in the county record was only a shadow of the effect which the death of all his livestock had on his mind and spirit. It was a story he would recount again and again, especially in his old age. It would soon, however, become evident to Antonio that it was his land, and not his livestock, that the fiends were after.[9]

On the same day the inventory was filed, the young herdsman did what he probably should have done when his father, Francisco, had died in 1870: he registered his own cattle brand with the county. This may have been his attempt to make his presence felt on the range even more than it already was. Had he then felt that he had taken it for granted that people knew of the de la Garza ownership of Rancho Alamito?

Antonio and the family believed that the destruction of the livestock was the first warning from an unidentified foe. Still, Antonio chose to remain on his land. He was virtually alone since all the old de la Garza *dons* had gone to their graves. His first cousin, Carlos de la Garza, Jr. — whose godmother was Jane P. O'Connor — was only a fourteen-year-old lad, and of little help. His youngest brother, Rufino de la Garza, by Francisco's second marriage to Gertrudis Garcia, was even younger than Carlos, Jr.

Antonio was not without friends in Refugio County. According to Uncle Tomás Rubio, one of his neighbors named Henry Scott did not want Antonio to leave Alamito Ranch.[10] Scott was a well-known rancher in the area who was known as a friend to everyone.

The rest of 1874 apparently passed without incident, but when the crucial moment came in early 1875, Antonio stood alone. Armed horsemen — all strangers — rode up to the house and threatened Antonio. Before departing, they solemnly warned him to vacate the ranch lands. Ponposa, thoroughly frightened, implored her husband to make immediate preparations to vacate the ranch, fearing for their lives if they stayed. Antonio was not one to be easily intimidated and, in spite of the threats, chose to remain on his ranch. Ponposa's forebodings proved unerringly accurate.

Around the time of Antonio's confrontation with the mounted men, the unfortunate Gregorio Esparza Bontan was caught by these same men and hanged on the outer town limits of Refugio. What Bontan did to deserve this terrible fate has never been known. His only fault may have been that he was Antonio's

brother-in-law and a Mexican resident of Refugio County. According to family tradition, Bontan was cruelly dragged through the
streets of Refugio by the mounted gunmen who finished their gruesome task under a mesquite tree.[11]

With the death of Gregorio, there remained only his sister,
Ponposa, to carry the family name; but for all practical purposes,
the Bontan name was now extinct. The grieving Ponposa, now
pregnant with daughter Petra, was nearly paralyzed with fear after
the death of her brother. She implored her husband to abandon the
ranch and land and seek safety in Goliad County, as they had numerous relatives there.

Finally, early in July of 1875, Antonio's barns and corrals were
deliberately burned to the ground by raiders.[12] Some days later,
mounted horsemen returned and gave him the ultimatum: *remain
and you will surely be killed; vacate the ranch and land and your life shall be
spared.* They gave the young Antonio twenty-four hours to remove
himself and family from the ranch and land.[13]

Ponposa Bontan knew that her worst fears had come true.
Their tormentors had struck, and Antonio was fighting for his life.
Ponposa was pregnant and already had two other small children,
José and Francisca. She feared for their safety.

Ponposa was ultimately responsible for Antonio's departure to
Goliad County during the latter part of July 1875. Antonio resisted
at first but finally agreed with his wife; by doing so, he very likely
saved their lives. Uncle Tomás Rubio told me that his grandfather
left the Alamito Ranch during the last days of July 1875 and arrived in Goliad County on the day their daughter, Petra, was born,
August 1, 1875.

The last of July 1875 must have been typically hot. It was the
time of year that *Tejanos* call *La Canicula* when the sun shows no
mercy to man or beast. The night was probably humid and sultry,
but the moon was bright and the stars shone magnificently except
when moving clouds partially obscured the moon. On this night,
probably July 29, 1875, a youthful and beautiful but terrified Ponposa and her husband Antonio fled Refugio for safety in Goliad
County. Ponposa was driving the family wagon, heavily loaded
with all their possessions and pulled by four sturdy horses. With
them were seven-year-old Francisca and five-year-old José.

The young mother anxiously glanced back to ascertain that

Antonio was not far behind the wagon. Antonio's cursing at the team of oxen, the crack of the bull whip, and the bellowing of the beasts was assurance enough to Ponposa that he was all right. These beasts were pulling the cabin, probably on skids. Antonio had acquired the oxen from his uncle José María de la Garza, and aunt, María Josefa Becerra.

Ponposa could clearly hear the foul language her husband was using; she knew he was in a raging mood. The recent murder of her brother Gregorio, the death of her father Benito and older brother José, and the loss of the land on Alamito Ranch caused Ponposa to weep. She believed that the gunmen were not too far behind, and feared they might come to La Bahía and kill her husband.[14]

Antonio was about five feet nine inches tall and weighed about 160 pounds — certainly not a big man, but what he lacked in size he more than made up in courage. He was handsome and sported a handle-bar mustache and neatly trimmed beard on his square chin.

During this night and until they reached Goliad County, Antonio was well armed with pistol, rifle, and shotgun on his saddle horse, which was tied behind the cabin being pulled by the bellowing oxen. Antonio was greatly concerned about the condition of his wife driving the team up ahead, too. There were gold coins aboard the wagon, and Antonio constantly kept looking over the back trail and hoping desperately he would not see the shapes of night riders.

These were evil times in Refugio County, especially for its Mexican residents. Subsequent research showed that Antonio and Ponposa were caught up in violence that was taking place against many local *Tejanos.*

In the summer of 1874, Thad Swift and Irene Barlow who owned a sheep ranch on Saus Creek were brutally murdered by unknown persons. Apparently, robbery was the motive. The Anglos of Refugio suspected Mexicans of the deed, although no one knew with certainty who the guilty parties were. Refugio Anglos were joined by hundreds of armed citizens from surrounding counties, including Goliad, and these riders divided into several vigilante groups. As one observer noted: "practically every Mexican of the laboring class in the surrounding country was regarded as a likely suspect." [15]

One group of about a hundred vigilantes proceeded to Goliad County where they captured and brutally murdered Marcelo and

Antonio Moya and their elderly father. Simultaneously, three un-
named Mexicans were arrested and jailed in Refugio. A mob of Anglos soon assembled, dragged them from the jail, and hanged them
behind the Swift house. Their bodies were left to dangle for a week
for all to see.

    Coinciding with the date and particulars of the death of Gre-
gorio Esparza Bontan, one of these unfortunates may well have
been Ponposa's younger brother.

    The purge of Refugio County of its Mexican residents pro-

ceeded apace. No less a historian than J. Frank Dobie notes that
soon after these bloody affairs, a Captain Coon Dunman of Refugio
and his "Regulators" made it "their business to check up on every
Mexican in the vicinity, and if he could not give a satisfactory account of activities to order him out of the county on the alternative
of being hung." [16] Hobart Huson in his history of Refugio relates
that hundreds of Anglo ranchers and cowboys considered "exter-
minating all Mexicans" in the area. They were talked out of it by
cooler heads; however, within a few weeks of the Swift murders

only a few Mexicans remained on their land, most pathetically having fled the county.

Apparently, Antonio had been able during that bloody summer to account for his time during the Swift affair and clung to Rancho Alamito. No doubt when he would not leave, those who wanted his land began their own timely intimidation of him and Ponposa.

By the spring of 1875, vigilante groups once again took to the countryside outraging and murdering peaceful Mexican farmers, this time in response to Mexican bandit activity in nearby Nueces County. Historian Arnoldo De Leon called this the "darkest hour" of border troubles for the local residents, and many innocent Texas Mexicans paid with their lives. In the midst of all this generalized violence, who was to note the particular plight of one *ranchero* family that held lands being coveted by others? There was nothing for Antonio and Ponposa to do but flee to Goliad.[17]

Tomás Rubio said that shortly after his grandfather arrived in Goliad County, strange horsemen came from Refugio County and informed Antonio that he could return to his lands, provided he gave them the original Becerra grant documents. Rubio said that the documents, which Antonio kept in a metal box, had once been stolen in Refugio County. His grandfather gave chase after the thief, an unknown *Tejano*, and literally lassoed the culprit like a wild horse. After severely beating the miscreant he intended to hang the terrified man, who fell on his knees pleading for his life. He told Antonio that he thought the metal box contained money and nothing else. This and only this saved his life. Antonio told his grandson, Tomás, that he was greatly tempted to kill the man because he suspected that he was working for those who had raided his ranch. Tomás said that his grandmother only knew that Antonio had retrieved the metal box, but that she never found out about her husband's dramatic episode in the woods with the thief. Antonio's daughter Petra was in possession of the metal box in 1939. These old papers have been the cause of several deaths in the family, not to mention terrible grief and hardship.

The de la Garzas arrived at La Bahía on July 31, and on August 1, Ponposa gave birth prematurely to a daughter, Petra. The reason for the infant's premature birth, the family claimed, was due to Ponposa's frightening experiences at the ranch in Refugio

County and the difficult trip to Goliad County. This type of unfortunate tragedy was not uncommon among landowning Mexicans in Texas before and after 1875.

In Goliad, Antonio purchased a small eighteen-acre tract of land and tried to establish a new life, but things were never the same.

According to Tomás Rubio, the cattleman named Henry Scott and others came to Goliad County in 1879 and implored Antonio to return to his land. However, Antonio feared that if he took Scott's advice, harm would come to him and his family.[18]

After Antonio and Ponposa had been dispossessed of the majority of the ancestral property, there yet remained other members of the de la Garza family on a portion of the Becerra lands. These included Antonio's sister, Trinidad, and her family. But in 1877 a series of events began that would, within a year, result in their complete dispossession. My first knowledge of this unfortunate episode had come in the early summer of 1973, when my cousin, Benito Martinez, sent me a copy of the letter written by his grandmother, Paula Lozano de Martinez.[19]

Trinidad de la Garza and her husband, Juan Elias Lozano, owned a small 300-acre ranch situated on the Manuel Becerra grant.[20] Antonio may have conveyed the acreage to his sister since he was the administrator of the estate of their father, Francisco de la Garza. The land-grabbers would soon be able to move in on this last piece of the de la Garza lands in Refugio County.

In May 1877, a land boundary dispute between the two brothers Severo and Valentin Castillo and John Welder resulted in the shooting death of Welder on the road between Refugio and the town of St. Mary's, apparently by accomplises of the Castillos.[21] Again, a great outcry was raised against the few remaining Mexicans who stayed on their land. Family tradition maintains that the Castillo brothers had actually stayed on the Rancho Alamito for a while and were related to the de la Garza and Lozano families. Around the time of the Welder killing, Juan Elias Lozano lost his life, and his wife Trinidad de la Garza had to flee. Severo and Valentin fled to Mexico where later they were shot and killed by paid Mexican *pistoleros*.

Juan Elias Lozano had been a Confederate soldier during the Civil War. He was tough, and by all family accounts, ill-tempered.

He apparently rode into Refugio and confronted one or several of the locals connected with the harassment of the de la Garzas and perhaps with the death of the youthful Bontan. Perhaps he was too closely associated with the Castillo brothers who had already fled Refugio County. On his way home later that day, he was murdered. Uncle Tomás said that Juan Elias was shot in the back, deep in the woods of Refugio County, on August 8, 1877.[22] When shot, Lozano fell off his mare and the frightened animal ran to the ranch house. Trinidad saw blood on the saddle and followed the trail to where her husband lay dying. Lozano told her that after he had been shot one of the gunmen dismounted and put a pistol to his head. Another of the culprits, however, ordered that Lozano not be shot again for he was already near death. Trinidad managed to get her husband to a doctor in Refugio, where he died the following day.[23]

With the murder of Juan Elias, Trinidad was subjected to intimidation and constant harassment day and night. She was cruelly subjected to terror by evil Anglo-Texan gunmen; no Mexicans were involved. The gruesome tactics employed by the gunmen against this woman and child for the mere sake of acquiring another piece of land leaves a dark page in the history of that county for the years 1877–78. The events and ordeals as experienced by Paula are outlined in this letter from family records:

> I, Paula Lozano de Martinez, remember that an American man [name omitted] used to come from a nearby town to tell my aunt [Trinidad de la Garza] to vacate the ranch and land because it was not theirs. He would not get down from the horse; he would just sit on his horse outside the fence and tell my aunt that they had already killed Uncle Juan Elias Lozano [on August 8, 1877] and that my aunt should leave the ranch in the year 1878. This man [name omitted] came to the ranch two or three times and repeated the message over and over again. The ranch and land was not theirs and to pack up and leave. My aunt had two nephews about eighteen years old to help her manage the ranch, but they were terrified and feared for their lives.
>
> The man [name omitted] and many others would return at night and began talking outside the house. Once we actually saw the American men mounted on horses. The two young boys were so terrified they had to sneak out of the house at night and go sleep in the brush. The American men meant to kill the young boys. The ranch was in a very desolate area; the cemetery was

about a hundred yards away from the ranch house of uncle Juan
Elias Lozano. These things I remember because I was born in the
year 1871.

Signed Paula Lozano de Martinez.[24]

Paula also told her children many stories of these tragic times.
She at first had been happy and content living with her aunt Trinidad and uncle Juan Elias. These two reared her as their own
daughter. Trinidad and Juan Elias never had children of their own,
but they had a daughter in Paula. Paula's mother, Genoveva, had
died and was buried next to the walls of Our Lady of Loreto
Church at La Bahía. Paula's father, Miguel Lozano, had also died
and was probably interred on Rancho Alamito.

Paula's youthful happiness and contentment was shattered
once again, however, in Refugio County on August 8, 1877, when
her uncle Juan Elias Lozano was killed by Texas gunmen. The men
continued their unmerciful harassment and persecution against the
grieving widow, but they did not reckon with the indomitable courage of Trinidad.

While the family was experiencing very difficult and turbulent times, local peace officers apparently did nothing to aid them. It is very possible, as well, that the officers knew nothing of the happenings on the isolated Rancho Alamito some fifteen miles from Refugio. Violence was erupting against Mexicans across Refugio, but the men who tormented Trinidad and her children wanted them off the land. Clearly, these tormentors were concerned with more than the death of John Welder.

If the land-grabber who sent the gunmen to intimidate and murder the family had had clear title to the land, the sheriff would have been enlisted to oust the Mexican land-squatters. Clearly, Trinidad had title to the 300-acre tract. The 1877–78 Refugio tax rolls show this acreage as deeded to her by her grandfather, Manuel Becerra.[25] There were no Mexican land-squatters in Texas. Certainly, the Becerra-de la Garza families were not. It was sheer suicide for the Mexican who possessed the audacity to settle on lands owned by Anglo-Americans.

Paula Lozano eventually grew into womanhood and married Polano Martinez. The marriage was blesed with four sturdy sons, the oldest being Don Plácido Martinez, to whom she related these stories.

Paula told her son, Plácido, that before her aunt Trinidad vacated the ranch in 1878, she used to hear many strange noises coming from the family cemetery at night. Paula knew this was no nightmare, for she was being held protectively in Trinidad's arms in the dark cabin. Trinidad had a loaded rifle pointed at the door, and she was determined to die to protect her child. The gunmen dared not shoot a woman and her child; they knew that such an act would not be tolerated, even by the Anglo-Texans.

Some of these eerie noises were moans of anguish and suffering. They would get very loud, and little by little would fade away only to resound closer to the cabin. At this time Trinidad would point the loaded rifle in the direction of the moans. The horses in the corral would neigh frightfully as if attempting to break down the fence; the cows also joined in on the commotion. To add to the frantic movement and noise in the corral came the terrified bleatings from six or seven nervous goats that Trinidad owned. The little creatures slipped out of the pen and fled for the heavy underbrush but not before one actually was killed by the family's tormentors. The night always brought on sinister happenings.

Trinidad dreaded the appearance of dawn for she knew that death had struck her livestock during the night. At first light she and her eldest nephew, who had emerged safely from the woods, were cautiously walking toward the corral. Just as she had expected, one of the milk cows had been killed during the night. The perpetrators had slit the throat of the poor animal. Quickly, she and the boy saddled their horses and just as quickly began dragging the cow far out into the brush. During these anxious moments Trinidad was desperately hoping Paula would not see the animal, but the curious girl later asked about the disappearance of the milk cow. The reply was simply that their tormentors had stolen the animal during the night or early dawn. After the dreadful chore with the cow, Trinidad returned to the corral to look for the goats. She dismounted and began to inspect the ground around the corral. Then she saw the blood. One or more of her goats had been killed or badly wounded.

Trinidad rounded up the remainder of the goats and herded them toward the corral. She became extremely angry at her tormentors and vowed to remain on her grandfather's land come what may. Trinidad desperately wished that she had two or three older brothers with the same temperament as her father, Francisco. Her youngest brother, Antonio, was like their father, but he had been driven off his land by these same cowardly gunmen on the Alamito Ranch. She had feared for her young brother's life as he was alone and, regardless of how brave he was, he certainly was no match for the gunmen. When her father Francisco and her uncles Paulino, José María and Carlos de la Garza were alive, none of these vermin dared intrude into the de la Garza lands. The reputation of the de la Garza *pistoleros* was well known from the Guadalupe River to the Rio Grande and beyond. Evildoers feared them and brave men respected the old *dons*.

But Trinidad's brave and gallant menfolk were all gone now; she and Antonio were the last holdouts on their ancestors' land. She could not endure the cruelty and injustice much longer. The only recourse was to vacate the land and the ranch house.

Trinidad packed their belongings in two wagons and departed the cabin never to return.[26] She, Paula, and the two nephews headed for La Bahía in 1878. Trinidad later acquired a small tract of land comprising 184 acres south of the San Antonio River. She conveyed fifty acres of land to her brother, Antonio, on January 9, 1893.[27]

Paula, as a grandmother, later remembered the tears of sadness when they loaded the wagons. She knew that after their departure, they would never see the cabin again. Indeed, they never did.

Such crimes were common in Texas in those days. Trinidad and her wards on that isolated ranch, deep in the brush country, were easy prey for the marauders. They held the power of life and death over her and the children. Their motive for this heinous crime was their craving for land. The people who now own the land have perhaps unknowingly profited from the deeds of evil men in the period 1875–78.

By July 1878, the final portion of the Becerra grant had fallen into the evil clutches of murderous perpetrators. The de la Garzas in their hour of need could turn to no one in Refugio County.

Antonio's grandchildren vigorously maintained that their grandfather kept a black book in which he had written an account of the events that had befallen his family in Refugio County from 1874 to 1878. Ponposa Bontan did in fact have an old black prayer book, and older family members may have confused the prayer book with the black book in their minds. Such a book would prove valuable, for it would reveal the names of those responsible for Antonio's downfall in Refugio County.

In old age, Antonio told his daughter-in-law, Julia Flores, that "the injustice of the times" was by no means restricted to Refugio County, though the county far surpassed all others in this regard. Antonio was not the only victim in Refugio County. Poor Anglo-Americans may have also been victims of these injustices, but it was generally always most common to persons of Mexican origin. Feeling that there was no justice for them, many of these unfortunate Texas Mexicans fled with their families south of the Rio Grande and safety — their cattle and lands abandoned to the great delight of the land-grabbers, who were their persecutors and murderers. Eventually, though, like *lobos* emerging from the woods, the grandsons of these old-time *Tejanos* crossed the Rio Grande with revenge in their hearts. The raids were especially directed at those whom they suspected had persecuted their grandfathers. The cattle, *las vacas de tata*, were driven into Mexico by the wily raiders. To the

Mexican raiders it simply meant that they had only reclaimed their grandfather's cattle which the Anglo-Americans had stolen first.

Antonio de la Garza lost all his in-laws, Benito, José, Gregorio Bontan and later Juan Elias Lozano in 1877 to Texas gunmen. Yet there is nothing in the record to indicate that Antonio sought revenge, which, according to the times, would have been the proper thing to do. There remained a great bitterness in the old man's heart until the day he died. De la Garza was well versed in the use of the pistol, rifle, and shotgun, and he was an excellent horseman. He could have easily ambushed and killed the murderers of his family. Doubtless, he knew who they were but failed to record their names on paper. Paula Lozano recorded on paper the name of the Refugio County killer, and Sálome Rubio de Lambardia told me the names of the two who killed Benito and José Bontan at La Bahía in 1870. Unfortunately, these names were not written by an eyewitness or other knowledgeable person such as Benito's wife, Jesúsa Esparza. Aunt Sálome said that the killers were from Blanco and were angry at Benito and José over a horse race that the murderers had lost.

In 1890, thirteen-year-old Eliza de la Garza happily accompanied her ailing mother, thirty-eight-year-old Ponposa Bontan, to Sunday services at Our Lady of Loreto Chapel. Young Eliza cast admiring glances at her mother's lovely dress, one her father, Antonio, had purchased for her. Sometimes Eliza became rather gloomy because she and the other children were very worried about the rapidly failing health of their mother.

The condition of Ponposa was worsening daily. Ponposa, with dark mantilla covering her head, still looked very lovely. The mantilla and the whiteness of her face made her green eyes larger by contrast. Her delicate face revealed the unmistakable signs of pain and suffering.

After the services, Ponposa took Eliza by the hand and showed her the location of the graves of her father, Benito, and brother José. Nearby were the graves of Carlos de la Garza and her sisters-in-law, Genoveva and Rosalia de la Garza. There is a sketch of all the graves in the museum at Presidio La Bahía.

Ponposa Bontan died on March 3, 1891; and with her death also ceased to exist the Bontan name in La Bahía-Refugio. Funeral services were held in the cabin she and Antonio had shared so happily for twenty-four years. (The cabin still stands, and at every opportunity I return to wonder about those who lived within its walls over a century ago.)

The funeral of Ponposa Bontan was attended by family members and friends from Goliad and Victoria counties. Sheriff George S. Petty and several of his deputies came to pay their respects, including a deputy, Juan Rubio, the son-in-law of Ponposa. The pallbearers were all family members and probably included Carlos de la Garza, Jr., Rufino de la Garza, Macario Cabrera, and Juan Rubio, Sr. It was generally contrary to Mexican custom to allow immediate family members to perform this sorrowful duty. After everyone had departed, Antonio remained alone by his wife's grave; he remained a widower for over forty-six years.[28]

In 1899, Sálome Rubio, then ten years old, was playing in front of the cabin belonging to her aunt, Petra de la Garza, and uncle, Juan Ybarbo, whom she had come to visit. Sálome was waiting for her grandfather, Antonio de la Garza, to come and take her home. The young girl always rode with her grandfather back to back, facing the horse's rump. The girl soon looked toward the trail leading to the cabin and saw a rider approaching. Sálome grew apprehensive, for the lone horseman was not her grandfather but instead was Anglo-American. She already knew that it had been Anglo-American gunmen who had killed her uncles, Juan Elias Lozano and Gregorio Bontan, in Refugio County. And it was Americans who had burned her grandfather's barns and corrals.

The horseman reined in his mount and stared down at the girl and then, smiling, spoke to her. She nodded her head, but refused to return his smile, for she was not yet sure of the purpose of his visit. Sálome Rubio stood her ground and continued to stare at the giant American whom she did not make welcome at her uncle Juan's cabin. *"Este era un hombre muy grande y fuerte.* (This was a big and powerful man),'' Sálome told me seventy-five years later. She wondered if the moment of truth had arrived for Uncle Juan Ybarbo.

The suspicious girl need not have worried, for the giant she spoke of was Dennis O'Connor. The son of Thomas O'Connor, he was one of the most influential South Texans of the time, having inherited an empire from his father. Juan Ybarbo came out of the cabin and made O'Connor welcome. Petra prepared hot coffee and sweet bread and other delicacies for their guest.

O'Connor had come to ask his former *vaquero* to return and work for him. Since his youth, Juan had worked as a *vaquero* for O'Connor. According to Sálome, Juan was highly esteemed by O'Connor and other members of that family. Everywhere O'Connor rode in his huge domain, Juan was by his side. Since the boy was too young to work cattle, he may have been employed by O'Connor as a messenger. Juan was an excellent horseman and could speak English fluently, a rarity for a young *Tejano* during that era.

When Juan Ybarbo married Petra de la Garza, he decided to start a ranch on his own. He prospered and learned the cattle business from Dennis O'Connor. Juan was a cattleman all his life; no one ever molested him and his wife, nor his property for as long as he lived. His prosperity may have been due to the fact that he was under the protective wing of O'Connor. Stevan Rubio (1892–1979), a nephew of Petra de la Garza, worked as a *vaquero* on the O'Connor ranch nearly all his life. I visited him in November 1953 on the ranch. None of the ranch employees questioned my presence. Perhaps they knew I was of the Rubio family.

Sálome said that Dennis O'Connor was about the same age as her grandfather Antonio. In this year (1899) Antonio was fifty-one years old. While the guest was inside the cabin, Sálome Rubio moved to the edge of the porch and began to sulk. The girl prayed that her grandfather Antonio would not yet put in an appearance, for she knew how her grandfather felt about the O'Connors. Both of these men had had words some years past in regard to the lands in Refugio County.

Several months later, Antonio de la Garza met Dennis O'Connor face to face in the town of Goliad. Sálome, as usual, was riding behind her grandfather facing the horse's rump. This time she stared down at him and she reckoned he did not appear so big from where she sat. Antonio, who spoke English, asked O'Connor about the land in Refugio County. Antonio believed that O'Connor possessed the lands of Rancho Alamito. O'Connor became extremely angry and told Antonio that he might compensate him for the land in question, but that he (de la Garza) would never get the land back. Both men were very angry.

Antonio was armed, and Sálome was certain that O'Connor

had a gun in his coat pocket. Neither of the men made a move toward his weapon. Sálome believes that her presence prevented
bloodshed. De la Garza sat on his horse and stared at O'Connor as
he walked away. Sálome said that her grandfather was so angry
that she could see him shaking with rage.[29] The two men never met
again.

Antonio's sons, José, thirty years old, Ismael, twenty-one, and
Guadalupe, seventeen, were quite capable of contesting O'Connor
for possession of the land, but the chances of success were slim indeed. Antonio and his sons were brave men, but in 1899 Texas was
still a frontier, and no Mexican dared harm an Anglo regardless of
how right the Mexican was. Antonio and his sons knew this and re-
frained from going to Refugio County on a personal vendetta.

By 1935, Antonio de la Garza was quite elderly. His once powerful physique was thin and frail, and he was stoop-shouldered and
used a cane for support while taking his slow walks around the back
roads of La Bahía. He was always accompanied by Tomás Rubio,
that curious and mischievous youth of earlier days. During the funeral of his daughter, Francisca, he walked from Goliad to the de la
Garza cemetery. A horseman all his life, the proud eighty-seven-
year-old refused all offers of transportation. The stubborn Antonio
never set foot in an automobile.

By 1937, Antonio was eighty-nine years old and beset with the
infirmities of old age. Antonio could walk, but only with the assistance of his grandchildren. He remained the favorite of these children, now themselves elderly, who remember their grandfather
with the deepest affection. He died on April 8, 1937, without ever
having the opportunity to redress the injustice done to him and his
family.

On many occasions, as Antonio grew old, his grandchildren
would accompany him to Ponposa's grave. He would kneel and
pray for her, and then stand and look in the direction of Refugio
County. His grandchildren, who were his constant companions,
knew that his thoughts were on his former tragedies, his lost land,
and the happier times as well before he and Ponposa had been dispossessed. He was a lonely old man.

Somewhere within the boundaries of the Becerra survey plat in
Refugio County lies the forgotten and lonely family cemetery; the

bones of Don Manuel Becerra and his wife, Juana María Cadena, are probably buried there. Don Manuel ranked among the earliest settlers of La Bahía, but there is no record that he was buried in Goliad. Their daughters, María Josefa, and her husband, José María de la Garza, and Gertrudis and her husband, Francisco de la Garza, and possibly Gregorio Esparza Bontan also are buried on the ranch. Sacred to the family, this land bore silent witness to the terrible violence committed against the brave woman, Trinidad de la Garza, and her daughter, Paula. A hundred yards away was the cabin which sheltered the terrified girl Paula who, on numerous occasions, heard the strange nocturnal sounds in 1877–78. The cemetery has been desecrated by wandering cattle, horses, wild beasts, and lastly by man, the most evil of these creatures.

[11]

A Lawsuit and Family Troubles

The trip to Texas had been fruitful, but it was time to return to California, meet with our attorney, and see how he thought the Becerra descendants should proceed. Soon we would confront the present owners of our ancestral land. Little did I suspect the trials and tribulations that we would encounter. However, between 1973 and 1975, the Becerra Family Association would formally organize and initiate its first lawsuit to regain our birthright. We would also learn more about our family's claim to the grant.

My wife and I arrived at Orange, California, on June 30, 1973. We met with Harris so he could examine our records. Harris was in a jubilant mood before leaving for Texas; however, his trip proved to be unsuccessful as he failed to find a Texas attorney who would agree to join in the lawsuit which was now a certainty.

He arrived at Goliad on July 12 and met with the Becerra family. He was impressed with these people who peppered him with a barrage of questions. They appreciated his simple and honest replies to their questions. He had gained a great deal of their trust and confidence; this was the most rewarding part of his trip.

After meeting the family, Harris returned to Refugio and went directly to the Refugio Mission Title Abstract Company to meet

Hobart Huson. These two had had previous communication by letter but had never met. Huson was more than eighty years old but appeared keen of mind and knowledgeable of his business. I found him to be one of the best land attorneys in Texas. Harris directed his conversation to old maps of Refugio County and the de la Garza family. Huson was most courteous and friendly, but he dropped a bombshell on Harris: he was an attorney for the Thomas O'Connor family. Our attorney had innocently walked into the old lion's den. Evidently, someone in Refugio was keeping O'Connor well informed as to the status of the search. Huson surely must have surmised as much when he received our first communication.

Huson told Harris that he had received instructions from Dennis O'Connor that if we had a valid claim he would be willing to give it serious consideration. Huson also told Harris that the O'Connor family had settled a claim for "some squatters" some years past. Harris reminded Huson that the de la Garza family were the earliest Mexican colonists to settle in Refugio County and that they were anything but land-squatters. In many respects, the confrontation between the O'Connor and Becerra families began on July 12, 1973. There was no turning back now, but to wrest land away from this powerful family seemed an impossible task.

Aunt Sálome claimed that Thomas O'Connor had been an adversary of her grandfather Antonio de la Garza in Refugio County, when Antonio was dispossessed of his property and retreated to Goliad County and safety. All of this was supposed to have occurred the year Antonio's daughter was born. Antonio made an entry in Ponposa Bontan's prayer book, which shows that their daughter, Petra de la Garza, was born in Goliad County on August 1, 1875. Romana de la Garza related that he paid the taxes on his land by mail for the years 1878 through 1881. These tax records were the last I found in Refugio during the recent search at that town. Romana was correct. Aunt Sálome claimed that Thomas O'Connor was occupying her grandfather's land and that none dared go against him as he was too powerful. However, there were no other eyewitnesses to support her statements which were based on what her grandfather told her and his other grandchildren. But the Thomas O'Connor family attorney had left a slight opening in the door for further communication. Huson's words to Harris indicated to me what I believed all along — that Señora Lambardia's account of our family's history was the truth.

Harris believed that the O'Connor family would not want to become involved in a land dispute to be settled by the courts. I believed the O'Conners would admit to no wrongdoing by their ancestor, and, under the circumstances, that Harris was in for a rude awakening.

After the successful search of the tax records, my next task was to locate an 1834 vintage Mexican map of Refugio County. The challenge was irresistible, for Don Manuel Becerra's name must surely be on the 1834 map.

I never knew that any such map existed. It was only an assumption because Refugio County was colonized from the early 1800s by settlers from Mexico until the latter part of 1834, then mostly with Irish, and land grants had to be surveyed and mapped. In spite of repeated failures in locating the 1834 map, I never relented. One day, somewhat dejected after so many failures (was God testing the endurance of his faithful creature?), I appeared again at the huge research center of the Los Angeles Public Library and found mention of the existence of an S. A. White map of 1834, of Refugio County. I never found the actual map itself. The North American colonist S. A. White was the owner of a Mexican land grant in Refugio County. Therefore, I concluded that indeed White lived in the Refugio settlement in 1834 and that such a map must exist. Otherwise, José Jesús Vidaurri could not have issued 201 land grants in 1834.[1]

I informed Harris an 1834 map was possibly at the General Land Office. He immediately wrote to Virginia Taylor, who replied promptly that she was unable to locate the 1834 map but found an 1841 map, which she sent. Anxiously looking for Becerra's name on the 1841 map and not finding him was a source of great disappointment — especially since Becerra was still alive on Rancho Alamito in 1841. Perhaps he had neglected to have his grant surveyed by Willard Richardson, the county surveyor. Such an oversight on the part of Becerra does not appear likely as the old man was methodical. Something else must have prevented Becerra from having his name on the map, but the reason may never be known.

Harris suggested that Becerra's name could surely be found on an 1849 map. This reasoning appeared sound since the Becerra tract was surveyed in 1849. He quickly wrote Taylor requesting maps of Refugio County for 1840–50. He again examined the 1841 map but found nothing. The map showed mostly Irish and Anglo names with a slight sprinkling of Mexicans. Why was the oldest settler in Refugio, Manuel Becerra, with his federal Mexican land grant, not on the map, and yet the recently arrived foreigners were now prominent? Highlights of the search for the Becerra grant thus far showed that it was flawless. The original petition was approved by the *ayuntamiento* of Goliad on May 14, 1832. It was approved by Governor Francisco Vidaurri on January 25, 1834. Manuel Becerra paid the taxes on the entire grant in 1847. W. M. McFarland, district clerk of Refugio, recorded it as a deed from the government of Mexico on September 6, 1848. The Becerra-Cadena conveyance to Henry Koehler of Cameron County was made on October 14, 1848; the David Snively survey of March 12 and 13, 1849, was recorded in Book A, page 26.

These transactions were performed by duly authorized officers of the sovereignty — in 1832 by *alcalde* Juan José Hernandez of Goliad, in 1834 by Governor Francisco Vidaurri of Coahuila and Texas, in 1848 by the district clerk of Refugio, W. M. McFarland, and in 1849 by the district surveyor of Refugio, David Snively. Furthermore, there were no defects noted in these transactions nor on the original Becerra grant paper now safely guarded by Don Manuel's descendants. Thus it could easily be seen that the transactions were made according to law and appeared flawless in every respect. These revelations proved conclusively to us that Manuel Becerra diligently complied with the laws of the land.

Had Becerra been involved in a land boundary dispute in Refugio County? I was certain that the Power grant overlapped by a substantial margin into the Becerra tract. The former grant had been conspicuously omitted from all Refugio County maps; but in 1875 it appeared ominously on that county's map. This monstrous parcel of real estate, with all the complexities in its boundaries, was beset with enormous problems. Research has not revealed that a proper survey had ever been made since its inception to the year 1875. That Becerra's name failed to appear on the maps, in spite of the David Snively survey, was most likely due to the erroneous boundaries of the Power tract. This intricate situation can only be resolved by a resurvey of the Becerra tract. A survey would prove even further that the original Snively survey was a good one.

When Harris finally received the package of maps from the General Land Office, he immediately and with great anxiety began to unwrap it. We examined both maps of 1841 and 1850 very carefully but failed to find Becerra's name. David Snively, the surveyor, made a note on the 1850 map indicating that all county surveys to that year were up-to-date. If this were true, what then happened to his survey of the Becerra tract? Even if Snively had plotted the Becerra plat on an 1849 map (if indeed such a map was made), then his name would most definitely have appeared on the 1850 map. It is certain that only David Snively knew the reasons for omitting Becerra's name from the county maps. As mentioned earlier, when the Power tract first appeared on the 1875 map, its boundary line was not specific, especially on Copano and Alamito creeks. The Power tract, as shown by the 1875 map, began on the west bank of Copano Creek and extended west across Alamito Creek. Also, simply placing the Becerra plat of 1849 on the 1875, 1883, and 1896 maps showed that the Power tract did indeed overlap into the former's tract. This was the root of the problem for the Becerra grant.

The persons ultimately responsible for ensuring that the Power tract be shown on the 1875 map, and those following, made certain that the Manuel Becerra tract was omitted from the maps. By doing so, it became possible that someone could claim the Becerra lands without chance of dispute or detection.

Omission of the Becerra plat from the maps was an oversight made by Refugio County surveyors and other interested parties. This seemingly unimportant oversight resulted in dire consequences to a poor Mexican-American family very soon. Whether the omission of Becerra's name from the maps was purposely contrived by one or more deceitful persons will probably never be known. But it is unmistakably clear now that an error was definitely made, and the effects of this error were devastating to Antonio de la Garza and his sister Trinidad de la Garza on the Alamito Ranch. Since the names of the rightful owners of the Becerra tract, the de la Garzas, were not shown on the 1875 map, this then could allow open intimidation of the family on all fronts. Remember, it was during 1875 that Antonio found himself in deadly peril.

From the inception of the present search, fate deemed it inevitable that one day a confrontation would materialize between the descendants of Manuel Becerra and those now wrongfully occupying our family land. Strangely, the inevitable happened on February 21, 1974, almost 100 years from the time Antonio de la Garza was confronted with the ghastly sight of his dead livestock in January 1874. On this fateful day, Harris prepared a letter of abstract of title together with a 1954 Vidaurri map of Refugio County, which showed the boundaries of the Becerra tract. Unofficially, this was a land claim for 4,428 acres belonging to María Josefa Becerra de la Garza and Francisco de la Garza, both of whom asserted title to the tract in question beginning in 1850. This somewhat unorthodox abstract prepared by Harris was sent to Hobart Huson, attorney of record for the Thomas O'Connor family of Refugio County. The reaction was possibly one of anger and frustration at the absurdity of poor Mexican-Americans asserting title to the acreage; but it is certain that this claim came as no real surprise to them. On March 2, 1974, the reply to Harris's letter came from two sources, one from Huson and the other of March 6, 1974, from V. B. Proctor of Victoria County. Huson's letter appears to have been prepared by a cool and level-headed man. Proctor's letter was the complete opposite of Huson's. The former's letter was very hostile and, when carefully analyzed, revealed certain information valuable to Harris.

Huson indicated that he had found a petition made by Manuel Becerra in 1832; however, he was unable to find a grant made by Governor Francisco Vidaurri nor approval of such a grant. Huson's apparent inability to locate the document might have been due in part to the recording of the Becerra deed by W. M. McFarland, district clerk of Refugio County in 1848. McFarland erred in that, during the translation of the deed, he failed to include the governor's first name. In 1834, there were two men named Vidaurri and both were officials of Coahuila and Texas. These two men were Governor Francisco Vidaurri and the Mexican land commissioner of the Power and Hewetson Refugio colony, José Jesús Vidaurri. Thus, McFarland simply wrote the name Vidaurri without making any distinction between the official capacity of the two men.

Huson did not deny that the O'Connors now possessed the land in question. Proctor, Dennis O'Connor (a direct descendant of the Dennis O'Connor whom Antonio confronted), and others no doubt felt at least some discomfort over a mere inquiry into the Becerra lands. Obviously, Harris had struck a sore spot. According to Proctor, Harris made an error on his drawings on the U.S. geological survey map which outlined the boundaries of the land in question. Harris's drawings on the map were parallel and very nearly adjacent to the Aransas County boundary line. These drawings did not overlap into the Aransas County line but appeared very close. Harris never made use of the 1875 and 1883 maps, and consequently made an error. His error merely served to stir a hornet's nest. Proctor insisted that nearly half of the drawings on the map mentioned overlapped into an area known locally as the Melon Creek Ranch; they asserted titles, statutes of limitations, and the doctrine of laches. He did not make mention of the lower half of the drawing submitted by Harris.

O'Connor let it be known that they were quite prepared to defend their titles against any adverse claims; however, it was not the intention of the Becerra family to claim any lands not owned by our ancestors. It was clear that the O'Connors would become adversaries of the Becerra family.

Harris told me that the cost of bringing the case to court would be at least $10,000. There would be court, attorney's and surveyor's fees. On April 30, 1974, Benito Martinez reported that the Plácido Martinez family had collected over $1,000. This branch of the Becerra family was particularly aggressive and closely united, while some folks from Goliad moved slowly and were still somewhat disorganized, in spite of strong efforts by Manuel Garcia to unite them. By September, the family had collected more than $7,000. It was time to act. On the recommendation of the Plácido Martinez family, Harris arranged with José F. Olivares, an attorney from San Antonio, to help represent the family. Olivares supposedly possessed some experience in Mexican land grants, otherwise nothing more was known about him other than he had been involved in a lawsuit in nearby Bee County.

Back in Texas, Harris and I met with Richard Delano, a son-in-law of Plácido Martinez, prior to a family meeting with the attorneys. I had interviewed Don Plácido on numerous occasions and had the greatest respect and admiration for him. I always called him *tío,* and he would call me *hijo.* On October 25, we met with Olivares, who was nearly a half day late. From the beginning, I was building a mistrust of our new attorney. My first impressions proved to be accurate. Olivares never wanted to meet in his office and was always late and making excuses. We were becoming quite irritated with his unorthodox and elusive ways. In the first meeting, absolutely nothing worthwhile was accomplished. That night, Olivares asked to meet at, of all places, a local Mexican bar. At Goliad the next day, Harris explained the various ways that could be used to regain the family land in Refugio County. He made it known that this would be an extremely difficult undertaking with very little chance of winning the case in Texas.

Olivares spoke in Spanish so that everyone, particularly the elder members, could understand what was being said. Most family members appeared satisfied with Olivares. However, Alfredo de la Garza of Bee County and his wife, Romana, were unimpressed with him. Romana said that there was something about the man that she did not trust.

It was decided that the civil trial would be entered into the records of the district court in Refugio County, possibly before the end of 1974. The attorneys said that they would be prepared to take the case to the United States Supreme Court should the issue become unresolved in Texas courts. Both seemed to doubt that the case could be won in a Texas court. Harris was actually preparing the Becerra family for a long struggle.

On November 8, 1974, Harris and I met to file the lawsuit in Refugio County. Olivares had prepared the necessary filing documents and included a copy of authorization for Harris to practice law in Texas. Harris suggested that the Martinez name be used as the original plaintiff in the lawsuit. But I reminded him that the family in Goliad should make this decision. To maintain peace among the various family branches, I recommended that it would be prudent to have one de la Garza, one Rubio, and one Martinez in the original complaint; to do otherwise could be a disaster. At my suggestion, approved by the family, the heirs appeared on the lawsuit in the following order: Alfredo de la Garza, Abel Rubio, and Benito Martinez. Alfredo de la Garza was the grandson of Antonio, who was my great-grandfather. Antonio was the great-uncle of Benito Martinez. Antonio's grandchildren should thus have been listed first. Genoveva de la Garza was the mother of Paula Lozano, although Paula was raised by Trinidad de la Garza. Genoveva was the great-grandmother of Benito Martinez. Such protocol in the lawsuit was perhaps symbolic, but very important to our family.

The family was not entirely united behind the lawsuit. Some heads of families had not seen fit to support the endeavor. On the other hand, the sons and daughters of Guadalupe de la Garza and Julia Flores were extremely active in support of the Becerra family. Their daughter, Ponposa, and her husband, Ernesto, rarely missed a family gathering in Goliad. The other branch of the family giving support was that of José María de la Garza and Regina Laso. Regina was born in 1875 in Goliad County. José María was born in Refugio County on August 10, 1870, to Ponposa and Antonio de la Garza. José María and Regina had thirteen children, according to their youngest daughter, Carmen. The eldest daughter was Trinidad, who was my godmother.

Of all the family members, Uncle Tomás Rubio was perhaps the most dear. He was a pillar of support and a fountain of family history for our pursuit. His presence, however, was soon to be denied to me. I returned to Texas in the spring of 1975, where on April 27, I visited him on his deathbed in Victoria. He again admonished that I return to live in Texas because it was the land of my forefathers for 200 years. Also, he told me, "*Hijo*, we will not meet again." I left for California, determined to relocate to Texas and follow my uncle's advice so that I could more intently pursue the trail of our lost grant. I returned to Houston to take up residence about May 27 or 28, 1975, but neglected to inform the relatives where I was. Around May 30, Uncle Tomás, that mischievous boy who had listened so well to his grandfather Antonio de la Garza, was taken by cancer. I will always regret not being at his bedside; but I think he knew that the knowledge he entrusted in me would be put to good use. I would pass the truth of our family's history, both its triumphs and its misfortunes, down to my descendants just as Uncle Tomás Rubio told them to me.

The three years of researching, gathering, and analyzing the Becerra-de la Garza land records in Refugio County was now complete. Neither Antonio de la Garza nor his sister, Trinidad de la Garza, had ever conveyed any lands to Thomas O'Connor in 1875 nor at any other time. The records of Refugio County did not show any such conveyance. Any Becerra lands claimed by O'Connor I knew must have come into his possession by means other than a conveyance from the original grantee, Manuel Becerra or Antonio de la Garza.

On June 20, 1975, Harris arrived from California and hired a legal secretary to complete the work. The ultimate responsibility for preparing the lawsuit belonged to Olivares. The lawsuit Harris prepared contained a number of technical errors due to his unfamiliarity with Texas rules and procedures. He was seething with anger, and the friction between the two lawyers would have adverse effects on the Becerra family. I felt Harris had neglected to furnish Olivares with adequate documents and maps to prepare the lawsuit, and I attributed this to his distrust of Olivares, who was not aggressive enough to demand of Harris the proper documentation. Had he done so, perhaps things would have ended differently.

On June 26, Harris and Olivares filed a lawsuit in the 24th Judicial District Court of Refugio County, against Dennis O'Connor, et al. The plaintiffs, Alfredo de la Garza, Abel Rubio, and Benito Martinez, in Case No. 4946, alleged that O'Connor and all other predecessors were in wrongful possession of the Becerra grant lands. The claim was for 8,856 acres plus damages for improper use of the land since the year 1878. The penalty sought against O'Connor and others was $1.62 billion. The Becerra family claimed title to the land, and at the same time alleged that the O'Connors had never possessed proper title to the lands.

We filed suit for the entire 8,856 acres for two reasons. Even though Becerra had conveyed the lower half of the tract, 4,428 acres, to Henry Koehler, it was stated in that conveyance that the descendants of Becerra were bound to defend that title. We thus owed an obligation to stand up for the sanctity of our ancestor's conveyance to Koehler. Also, by suing for all 8,856 acres those presently occupying the property would have to show title back to the Young and Koehler transactions and ownerships. If they did so they would fall right into our hands because Koehler had received his from Manuel Becerra. We reasoned that since Koehler legally owned the bottom half and had come by it from Becerra, then Becerra also had proper title to the upper 4,428 acres. They would thus be affirming our right to the part of the grant that our ancestors had never alienated from the family and was still rightfully ours.

A family meeting I called at Goliad on July 5 was attended by at least sixty of the Becerra heirs. Among topics discussed was the strong opposition we could expect from Dennis O'Connor's attorneys from Refugio and Goliad counties. On July 19, another large family meeting was held at San Antonio for a news release regarding the lawsuit in Refugio. Olivares was the speaker in releasing certain portions of the lawsuit to the public through the news media. At this meeting we discussed formation of a nonprofit family organization to be named the Manuel Becerra Association and to be chartered by the state of Texas. Heirs voted unanimously to name it in honor of our ancestor. On this historic day, we received the reply from defendant Dennis O'Connor. As everyone expected, O'Connor denied the plaintiffs' allegations in the lawsuit. He retaliated by claiming that a portion of the premises sued for by the plaintiffs were in direct conflict with the boundaries of the Becerra tract. It appeared that O'Connor did not deny possession of portions of the Becerra lands, but there was a problem with the method Harris used for our claim.

Unfortunately, Harris had resorted to the 1954 Vidaurri map of Refugio County to mark the Becerra tract boundaries. That particular map does not show Alamito Creek as it should have. O'Connor definitely claimed land that fell within these boundaries drawn by Harris. However, these included a tract described in a deed dated January 1, 1908, from Mary V. O'Connor, et al., to Thomas O'Connor, Jr. Harris's drawing of our plat also wrongly entered into the Melon Creek Ranch, another piece of land rightfully owned by the O'Connors.[2] Harris had drawn faulty boundaries for our claim because he had selected an improper map and had not precisely placed it on the right creeks. In doing so, he damaged our case. While it was certain the O'Connors could not claim proper title to the Becerra lands, Harris had not correctly outlined those lands. The mistake was crucial to our suit. The O'Connors could at best assert title by claiming squatters' rights and the various statutes of limitations.

Numerous young descendants of Manuel Becerra were bitter at the misfortune which struck the family on the wilderness ranch so long ago. They were angry and frustrated that someone else occupied their ancestor's land. These young men had come to realize the full impact of what they had lost, and some were possessed of violent tempers. These *bravos* talked of arming themselves, proceeding to Refugio County, cutting all the barbed wire fences, and awaiting those who would appear to oust them from their land. Fortunately, cooler heads prevailed.

The de la Garzas could never win outside the law. Violence was surely not the answer. Had these surly de la Garza descendants been living during the frontier era, they would have done what they now greatly desired to do. The town of Refugio, which they utterly despised, would not have escaped their vindictive wrath. But, such a venture proposed by some of these hot-bloods would have resulted in terrible consequences for the family. Such foolhardiness would not have been tolerated by the majority of the family. We believed one must trust in the law of the land. Any other attempts of repossessing land would have been futile.

A classic case of violence in a land dispute involving descendants of the early Spanish colonists was in New Mexico. Reyes Lopez Tijerina, a tough Mexican-American from Texas, had become the undisputed leader of a battle for repossession of all Spanish and Mexican land grants there. The dispute developed into violence, and before the dust cleared blood was shed and the *nuevo mexicanos* had to withdraw in humiliation. The cause was just, but, in my opinion, the means were wrong, tragic, and ill-conceived.

In the meantime, we made a last-minute search for a map prior to 1850 that would show Becerra's land grant. A search of the archives in Austin for the S. A. White map of Refugio County for 1834 was not successful nor were any others found.

However, a letter from Juan Martin de Veramendi was found indicating his desire to locate a part of his eleven-league grant in Refugio County. He did succeed in acquiring title to five leagues in Hays and Comal counties, but no survey in his name was found in Refugio County. The resurvey of 1849 specifically stated that some of the Becerra boundaries were adjacent to a survey made in the name of this Veramendi. The Becerra conveyance to Henry Koehler of Cameron County, recorded in Refugio County on June 5, 1849, showed Veramendi having his tract adjacent to that of Becerra. If Veramendi had wished to locate four leagues in the Refugio settlement, he was in for trouble. His petition would have had to been approved by the *empresarios* James Power and James Hewetson, which would have been highly unlikely. Worse yet, the petition was for 17,712 acres; the most a settler received at that time in Refugio was 4,605 acres.

Robert Hinojosa, a de la Garza descendant, did find the James Bray map of Refugio County for September 1834. I found no trace of either Becerra's name or that of Veramendi. The map was heavy with non-Hispanic names, all foreigners in Texas. Names of Mexican colonists were not to be found, though they had lived in the area for decades.[3]

On July 18, our attorneys received a request for an abstract of title for our land claims from the O'Connor attorneys. We felt it would be difficult to obtain the abstract since the owner of the only abstract company to our knowledge in Refugio was O'Connor's attorney, Huson. Previously, Huson had declined to perform an abstract of title for Harris on May 5, 1972. Considered one of the best attorneys in Texas, Huson was particularly so in his own domain, Refugio County. He had been the attorney of record for Thomas O'Connor in 1944, winning a lawsuit involving land titles. The plaintiff, a Robert G. Harris, had presented evidence that the James Power grant was declared invalid by the Supreme Court of Texas in *Smith v. Power*, 14 Texas 146 and *Smith v. Power*, 23 Texas 29, 30.

On July 5, I was unanimously voted co-chairman, with Manuel Garcia of Goliad, of the Becerra family association. By the end of 1975, I had attained the sole leadership in the association. Unhappily, the organization would be beset with strife among various branches of the family. On September 12, I appointed Gilberto Perez to prepare the articles of bylaws and constitution. This may well have been the first time in Texas that an organization of heirs was created to lay claim to a Mexican land grant. The association charter was approved on January 6, 1976, by the then secretary of state, Mark White, later to become governor.

This was indeed a good beginning for the family association, but the road ahead would be a rocky one.

On November 24, 1975, in district court in Refugio, we finally came face-to-face with Dennis O'Connor's three attorneys and with Hobart Huson, whom I saw for the first time. He was white-haired and slightly stoop-shouldered, of small frame, and appeared to be quite frail, possibly owing to his nearly eighty-five years. Despite the fact that Huson was helping represent those occupying our family land, I grew to respect him. I wished this man had somehow been on the side of the Becerra heirs.

The O'Connors were people of wealth, and their highly skilled attorneys had the almost unlimited O'Connor money behind them. In sharp contrast were our attorneys who sat at opposite ends of a long table without consulting each other. It became evident to the family as well as to the opposition that there was disunity between our attorneys. They were unprepared for the task now confronting them.

Hearings on O'Connor's objections were heard in the court of District Judge Frank Crane. All O'Connor attorneys were from Victoria, with the exception of Huson. Present for the hearing were about seventy members of the Becerra family. Neither O'Connor nor any member of his family made an appearance in court.

After the hearing, with Harris standing next to him on the courthouse steps, Olivares told family members that we "had lost or would lose the land claim." His remark nearly created a family panic. Ponposa de la Garza, namesake of her grandmother, Ponposa Bontan, severely censured him, and the entire family present lost all faith in his ability as our attorney. The disgruntled Becerra family that day left angry and frustrated. Olivares was definitely not the man for the task that lay ahead. To say that he conducted himself improperly in front of the family was a gross understatement. Harris interceded and attempted to make right the blunder committed by Olivares. Damage to our cause had not been created by the opposing attorneys; rather, it came from our own legal counsel!

All the years of research and hard work and the unity of the family was nearly ruined in two minutes by the San Antonio attorney. Harris left for California disheartened.

"From the time I had the misfortune of seeing that man, Olivares, I have never nor will I ever trust him," said Romana de la Garza. Her humble but precisely correct prediction was fervently shared by Ponposa de la Garza and others that day on the Refugio courthouse steps. Olivares seemed to possess a knack for saying the wrong thing. The ominous dark cloud threatening the young Becerra association now became a reality. We were gripped as if by a curse.

The first strike of this curse had actually happened in San Antonio on July 19. The family had been faithfully collecting funds for the Becerra trust since August 21, 1972. At a family meeting, Olivares approached Rose Martinez, the treasurer, and requested $750 to "pay news media for publicity in San Antonio about our lawsuit." Martinez innocently complied with the request, which to her seemed proper, not realizing the media does not charge for news broadcasts. As an afterthought, he also requested $5,000 to be held in a Becerra trust account of a San Antonio bank. He assured her that he would personally take care of establishing the account in the name of the association.

Now thoroughly suspicious and somewhat skeptical, she wavered at this critical instance. But when Olivares told her that he had Harris's approval, she, in conference with Manuel Garcia, consented to the request and gave him a check. Surprised and angry, Harris denied having given Olivares approval to acquire the funds.

His denial threw the Becerra family into an uproar. It was painfully apparent that Olivares alone had planned to misappropriate the hard-earned family funds. Harris advised us to use caution in attempting to regain at least a portion of the funds. He immediately requested $1,000 for expenses and Olivares sent him the money. However, when our treasurer sent Olivares registered letters demanding accountability of the funds, he ignored her pleas.

Later, in December, Olivares was in Houston for a thirty-minute televised news report regarding our lawsuit. I knew no charge was made to the family and suspected the $750 charge for "television coverage" in San Antonio was unnecessary. I confronted Olivares with his refusal to give us an accounting of the money he had received. When he replied that he did not consider such matters of much importance, I was aghast.

At the same time, I requested $1,500 for research and other expenses of the association. Instead of complying with the request, he contacted Harris, who reminded him that the funds belonged to the family and most certainly not to him. After this episode, I resolved as president of the association to have Olivares removed from our case. The board of directors acted swiftly and authorized Harris to fire Olivares, though it would be some time before that could be accomplished.

In the meantime, a hearing of our lawsuit had been scheduled in Refugio for February 1976, but was postponed by the judge at the request of O'Connor's attorneys. Later, Judge Crane became ill and the trial was postponed indefinitely. Later that year, I sought legal advice from Robert Hinojosa, who was very sympathetic with the cause and agreed to serve as an adviser to the family.

At this point, our real enemies seemed to have been among those we were depending upon for help, rather than the powerful O'Connor family.

To add to our problems, some of the family were becoming dissatisfied with our California attorney. A year before, a serious disagreement arose among several members of the family in Harris's presence. He appeared to have sided with the Martinez family and allowed himself to be drawn into the family feud. One of the disagreements arose over the issue of soliciting help from political officeholders. I strongly opposed it, as did others of the Goliad members of the family. The Martinez family was temporarily alienated and did not attend the next meeting.

While the association board voted to dismiss Olivares, there was a move to oust Harris as well. For a time, the association seemed to be splitting into two factions, one led by the Martinez family and the other by de la Garza descendants from the Goliad area. But serious problems relating to Olivares, and in a lesser degree with Harris, helped relegate family differences to the background.

On learning the board of the association had dismissed him, Olivares filed a complaint with the district judge, and ignored the dismissal letter. After about three months, the board authorized Harris to file a charge of unethical conduct with the grievance committee of the Tenth District of the State Bar of Texas. As 1976 came to a close, all was not well with the descendants of Manuel Becerra.

Early in 1977, the grievance committee acted swiftly and conducted a hearing on February 23 at which Olivares was required to answer the charges. The family was to be vindicated later in the year, but more pressing problems were at hand. The family was without proper counsel, and since Olivares's status had not been resolved, Robert Hinojosa could not legally help us. Fortunately, time was in our favor for a change.

On August 3, the grievance committee for the Tenth Bar District of Texas authorized disbarment proceedings against Olivares.

Meanwhile, the family faced what to some seemed a disaster. Harris was severely ill and in the intensive care unit of a California hospital. Due to his illness, the trial was postponed indefinitely. Thus our land claim was still hanging by a thread. By the end of 1977, the tension within our family was at a critical stage, threatening the very existence of the association. Conflicts over the election of president and board of directors continued to simmer, and members complained that no general membership meeting had been held in more than a year.

As the new year of 1978 opened, the future for the Becerra family seemed uncertain indeed.

Olivares, represented by Waggoner Carr, former attorney general of Texas, was found guilty of the ethics charge and on March 1 was disbarred from practicing law in Texas for two years. The judge first ordered that he account for and return funds he had received from the association. However, this order was reversed through what I considered a loophole in the law, and the association never received the money. Several years later, Olivares attempted to file a complaint against me and others that he had been deprived of his civil rights. Nothing came of it.

With the Olivares problem out of the way, the association board determined to deal with the growing movement in the family to dismiss our California attorney even in the face of a continuing lawsuit. In an emotional and traumatic meeting on March 4, the board voted in favor of retaining Harris. Antonio Flores Jr., who had served as president during a tempestous year of the association, favored the dismissal but could only vote in the case of a tie. Gilberto Perez and I cast the only dissenting votes. I had originally asked the board to employ Harris, but as time went on, I had lost faith in his ability to represent the Becerra family case in court. Not wanting to become embroiled in a family feud, Robert Hinojosa notified the board that he would no longer provide legal representation. Flores resigned in protest, and the first vice-president, Efrien Guerra, a patient and mature man of sound judgment, became president. He was to be one of our best leaders. He was firm and fair and was most considerate in his dealings with family members.

The board soon realized that Harris was no longer effective as our legal counsel. This was a perilous time for the family, for we were bereft of legal counsel. Fortunately, the O'Connor attorneys did not act quickly enough.

Our most pressing problem was to have an abstract of title for our claim prepared. In June, the board approved the expenditure of $1,800 for a Houston attorney, Fred A. Lange, Jr., to prepare the abstract. A trip to Austin was fruitless, but he did call the Refugio district clerk's office and made an inquiry regarding the status of the Becerra family land claim. That telephone call proved to be most fortunate for the family, because Lange had left his address and telephone number with the clerk.

When we learned that Lange had a longtime acquaintance with some of the O'Connor attorneys, he agreed to withdraw from the title search. The end seemed to be in sight, so the board decided to let the case be dismissed. When the October 24 hearing for trial or dismissal came up, no one appeared in behalf of the Becerra family.

Shortly after October 24, Dennis O'Connor's attorneys led by Conde Anderson of Victoria, apparently were not satisfied in allowing the Becerra family land claim to be dismissed for want of prosecution. Accordingly, Anderson and his associates began moving swiftly in defense of their client. All of Anderson's and the court's communications were mailed to Lange, who denied being our attorney of record. Nonetheless, Lange kept sending copies of the court's communications to me as soon as he received them. Harris finally sent copies of the last court communication, but he was rather late. It was Lange who had alerted us of the seriousness of the problems now facing us.

Indirectly, Lange became the savior of the Becerra family. Had it not been for him, the land claim would have been lost forever. He was not associated with the family nor was he compelled to inform me of the communications he received from the district clerk in Refugio or Conde Anderson. Had Lange not left his address with the clerk of the district court in Refugio County, the final episode would have spelled doom for the Becerra family. But it seemed that providence and a sympathetic Houston attorney intervened on behalf of the family in our darkest hour. With Lange's urgency and advice in mind, I sensed Anderson's furious activity within one week's time spelled real trouble for our family.

The deadline was November 18. By far the most difficult and trying time I experienced since the inception of the Becerra grant search was between October 24 and November 7, 1978. The awesome opposition of the O'Connor empire and their battery of attorneys was a nightmare.

On November 4, I contacted Benito Martinez and asked if he had been successful in obtaining legal counsel. Martinez replied that he had tried but to no avail. After explaining the seriousness of the situation to Martinez and urging him to continue the search, he moved quickly, perhaps more so than usual, because within two days the big man found another Houston attorney, Robert E. Hudson, who agreed to a conference on November 7.

Hudson was quickly brought up to date on the situation. He knew that Dennis O'Connor's attorneys and especially Conde Anderson were indeed manuevering for the ultimate demise of the Becerra family land claim. O'Connor's attorneys were determined to have the lawsuit dismissed *with prejudice*. Hudson patiently and thoroughly explained the nature and consequences of a lawsuit dismissed with prejudice. Once determined as such, there would never be a chance to refile again at a later date. If this should happen to the family, the land claim would be lost forever. Hudson immediately contacted the clerk of the Refugio Court and learned that the district judge was ill but planned to return to court the following week. This unexpected turn of events caused some anxious moments. Time was now crucial. On Wednesday, November 15, with but three days to beat the deadline, Hudson hurriedly departed for Refugio. Arriving on time, he handed Judge Stevenson the petition asking the court to dismiss the Becerra lawsuit against Dennis O'Connor *without* prejudice. The judge accepted the petition and caused it to be entered into court records. Hudson remained in court until he was certain that the petition had been properly recorded. The Houston attorney breathed a sigh of relief and knew the Becerra family would do likewise. Within a few days, perhaps even hours, Hudson had pulled the Becerra family from a bottomless dark pit.

Shortly, he was contacted by the O'Connor attorneys who wanted to know if the Becerra family intended to file again. Much surprised, Hudson did not commit himself nor the family. I wondered why such a powerful family and their attorneys were so concerned about whether the Becerra family intended to confront them again in a court of law. It seemed more incredible that the poor but proud Becerra family had caused some uneasiness. Conde Anderson told Hudson that they were pressing to have the lawsuit dismissed for good, meaning, of course, *with prejudice.* Hudson's fine legal strategy ended all their plans.

Thomas O'Connor descendants, it appeared, were curious as to what the descendants of Manuel Becerra and Antonio de la Garza would do next. Without any doubt, they believed that the Becerra family, sooner or later, would confront them again.

Benito Martinez accomplished his task of finding legal counsel in a creditable manner worthy of his name. Had it not been for his aggressive spirit, the family search could have ended on November 18, 1978. The Becerra family was becoming united again and the fight for repossession of the Manuel Becerra land grant was far from over. The setback was temporary. It was not due to lack of desire or fighting spirit on the part of the leaders or the family. Rather, incompetent attorneys, poor preparation and coordination, and, who knows, perhaps even the curse stood in our way. The search had become a financial drain on me and the family, but the end of the odyssey which had begun on March 30, 1972, was not yet in sight. New evidence would provide new hope to reinforce the validity of our land claim.

Si Dios quiere, Lord willing, one day we would share the fruits of Don Manuel Becerra's stolen heritage.

[12]

A Battle Lost;
the War Continues

Nothing in life is certain except death, but with every new piece of evidence I found, I became even more convinced that my family had been wrongfully dispossessed of land they owned in Refugio County. It was now evident to me that "proving" the illegality of what happened to my ancestors over 100 years ago was a difficult process.

By late 1978, two problems weighed upon my mind. The first of these was obtaining good legal counsel. This we accomplished, albeit with great difficulty, so that by early 1984 we stood on the brink of reinstituting our lawsuit to regain the land. The other task was to understand even further how others could have "legally" obtained title to property my ancestors had owned, occupied, and paid taxes on between 1834 and the 1880s and never conveyed to anyone. In 1979, I learned how O'Connor gained title to our land, and how our family's original ownership was obscured and deceptively covered up in the nineteenth century. I was convinced that neither the original Thomas O'Connor nor his son ever acquired proper title to the Becerra lands. I had found no evidence to indicate otherwise in public records.

In December 1978, sometime after Conde Anderson had communicated with Robert Hudson, Benito Martinez and I met with Hudson and implored him to take the case. He politely declined saying that it was now over 100 years since Antonio de la Garza and Ponposa Bontan had been dispossessed of their property in Refugio County. He cited the various statutes of limitations but agreed that a terrible injustice had been committed against Antonio de la Garza and his family in Refugio County. Hudson further stated that even if Antonio had brought a lawsuit in 1880 to recover the land, he would have lost. Antonio stood absolutely no chance of claiming the land even then because the composition of the jury in those frontier days was such that any Mexican was doomed to failure before he entered the courthouse. Worse yet, Antonio would have had to go against Thomas O'Connor, whose growing power in the county involved dispossessing Antonio of his property in 1875.

Hudson gave me numerous documents he had found in Refugio County on November 15, 1978, relating to the O'Connor family's land transactions. Glancing through the documents, I noticed the strange numbers that I had previously seen on the maps of 1875 and 1896. I was more determined than ever to discover their exact meaning.

About November 12, 1981, I met with our new attorney, Vincent Rodriguez, a man already known to the family, to review the records found during the long research. Rodriguez suggested we search the records in Aransas County. This was done; but nothing was discovered that we did not already possess. We then continued to Refugio and found records showing James Power had obtained in 1834 some 6,642 acres of land in the region of Alamito and Copano creeks. Rodriguez was convinced the Power claim erroneously overlapped onto the Becerra acreage from the time Power had tried to claim that land. This discovery about overlapping boundaries would later prove to be an integral part of the missing Becerra lands.[1]

This was to be our final trip in the attempt to locate additional information. As soon as we returned, we made a complete report to the family. The association president, Efrien Guerra, and I had made vigorous efforts to unite the Becerra family but to no avail. In 1982, Guerra suffered a serious injury and as a result could not continue as president. William Zermeno, the first vice-president, assumed the leadership and continued trying to rally the family. Only a few responded. At a meeting on December 4, I was elected president of the association.

The problems with our former attorney, José Olivares, were not yet over even though everyone had believed that the lawsuit to reclaim our funds from him had been completed. At the request of the family, the pending suit against Olivares, scheduled to go to trial in January 1983, was dismissed without prejudice. The association was free to reopen the suit at a future date.

In April 1983, Rodriguez suggested that we obtain an aerial photograph of the Becerra land. In July 1975, our opposition had asked for the exact location of the land we were claiming, and Harris and Olivares had blundered in using the 1954 Vidaurri map to show the location of the land. No attempt to properly locate the Becerra grant on the older map had been made. The junction of Alamito and Copano creeks would surely show up in an aerial photo. The 1896 map compared with the aerial survey photo would clearly define the exact location of the land in question, and no one could plead ignorance regarding lands we were claiming.

With family approval on May 18, 1983, I contacted the Adams Aerial Survey Company and learned that the costs for this project would be $1,385. A meeting of the Houston chapter on July 26, at the home of Benito Martinez, was attended by nearly the entire Martinez family. This was all a tremendous morale boost for me. The family unity was similar to that first gathering at Goliad on August 21, 1972. The assembled members gave us the go-ahead on the aerial survey photograph project regardless of the cost.

With this important meeting out of the way and having completed my documents research, I still had a hollow feeling inside. My mind was fixed upon the question of the cemetery mentioned by Paula Lozano in her letter. This sacred piece of ground had to be found, but I had absolutely no idea where to begin. I decided to contact the Catholic Archives in Austin.

On July 15, 1983, I spoke to Sister Dolores Kasner at the archives about my desire to locate the lost cemetery. Sister Dolores suggested that I contact the bishop in Victoria. After many futile attempts to locate the bishop, in near desperation I made contact with the secretary of Our Lady of Refugio Mission at Refugio.

The ministering *padre* at that mission was not in, so I told the secretary that my intent was to locate a lost cemetery in Refugio County. She said that the church would have to obtain permission from the local ranchers, which would doubtless take a long time, and suggested I contact Lucille Fagan Snider of Tivoli. Mrs. Snider, according to the secretary, had been active in locating old cemeteries in the Refugio-Goliad region.

A few days later I spoke with Mrs. Snider by phone and told her that I was descended from the old de la Garza *ranchero* families. She asked if these de la Garzas were those who had settled in the San Antonio River area. She seemed very pleased when I replied that this was true. Mrs. Snider then said she was a direct descendant of the Fagan family who had settled near the de la Garza *rancheros* in 1829. Quickly, I told Mrs. Snider of the Paula Lozano letter in which the little girl described the homestead and also the cemetery. Little Paula had mentioned the cemetery being on the Rancho Alamito in 1877. Mrs. Snider said there was a de la Garza cemetery near the San Antonio River and offered to take me there.

I was on the threshold of reestablishing a warm and long-standing friendship between the Fagan and de la Garza families which dated over a century and a half. These two early Texan families had lived on the Mexican frontier of Texas in the early nineteenth century; and as I was to discover with great delight, family friendship still remained strong to the present day. Lucille Fagan Snider was a direct descendant of the first Fagan colonist to arrive in the Mexican province of Texas so long ago. Now, 155 years later, a direct descendant of the de la Garza *rancheros* came seeking the assistance of the Fagan family. This assistance was given without hesitation.

According to Mrs. Snider, her great-grandfather, Nicholas Fagan, was in New York in 1817. Years later he moved to St. Louis and then to New Orleans. In early October of 1829, he arrived on the Texas coast at El Copano and made his way inland where he settled in the Power and Hewetson colony at Refugio. Nicholas received a Mexican land grant which he located on the south side of the San Antonio River. He finally received title to his grant from Commissioner José Jesús Vidaurri in late 1834.[2] The Fagan grant was located very near to that of Carlos de la Garza and other members of my family, who lost little time in welcoming him to the

Texas wilderness. The *rancheros* undoubtedly acquainted their new neighbor with the territory and locations of the various settlements and, of course, the Indian tribes of the coastal area, including the Karankawas and Cocos. Don Carlos and Nicholas Fagan became friends and the de la Garzas helped him establish his ranch, which in time became a settlement. Known as Fagan's settlement, it offered protection to colonists from Indian depredations.

The first cattle to graze on the Fagan grant were given to Nicholas by the Carlos de la Garza family. It is not known if Fagan spoke Spanish when he arrived on the San Antonio River; however, Nicholas and his son, John, soon learned to speak Spanish fluently.

When Stephen F. Austin's colonists and other North Americans revolted against the Mexican government in 1835–36, it became evident to the Irish colonists that they must support the Anglo-American cause. Surely, the Fagans and de la Garzas discussed the pros and cons of the war that was nearly upon them. When fighting broke out in 1836, Nicholas and John Fagan joined the command of Colonel James W. Fannin at La Bahía. Other Irish colonists joined Colonel Fannin's command or other units being organized in the settlements. Not only were his friends gone, but two of Don Carlos's own family, Paulino de la Garza and José María de la Garza, "went astray" and joined Lieutenant Plácido Benavides and later Captain Juan N. Seguin. To make matters worse for Don Carlos, Paulino and José had their own homes in his settlement. But in spite of this turn of events, the proud Mexican *ranchero* organized the de la Garzas into a small but potent guerrilla organization. Don Carlos and his small but daring band of mounted horsemen were active against the Anglo-Americans in the Goliad-Refugio regions in 1836. He and the family, remaining loyal to their *patria*, cast their lot with the losing side.

Nicholas and John Fagan fought gallantly against Mexico in the battle at Coleto, but Colonel Fannin surrendered his troops to the Mexican General José Urrea. The Fagans could not have known that with the surrender of Colonel Fannin, the entire command was doomed to execution on Palm Sunday, March 27, 1836.

The de la Garzas, through their own spies, learned that Fannin and his entire command were to be put to the sword. Don Carlos reacted swiftly and, probably urged on by his father and mother, Antonio and Rosalia, appeared before the Presidio La

Bahía with his horsemen. The de la Garza appearance at La Bahía must have been sometime around or on March 26, because the executions were scheduled for the next morning. There was little time to intervene for his friends' lives at that late hour.

Exactly what influence Carlos used with the Mexican officials to save the lives of his friends, Nicholas and John Fagan, has never been known. Whatever it was, it must have been powerful and likely posed danger for himself and his family. Although General Antonio Lopez de Santa Anna's orders were to execute all prisoners, General Urrea attempted to intervene on behalf of the doomed prisoners. Instead, he received a sharp reprimand.

Mrs. Snider related that on the day of the massacre, a young Mexican boy approached Nicholas Fagan and told him to take a quarter of beef to a certain place and wait until sent for, but he neglected the order. Fagan disregarded the order when the boy again repeated the instructions. When the boy repeated the order for a third time, Fagan obeyed. Soon he heard shooting and cries of his companions as they were being brutally murdered. He remained hidden until nightfall, at which time he escaped without further incident. John also escaped but how he managed to do so is not known. Others saved through the intercession of Carlos were James W. Byrne, Edward Perry, Anthony Sidick, and John B. Sidick. (Many years later, on May 13, 1860, Captain James W. Byrne became the sponsor for the baptism of Carlos de la Garza, Jr., the son of Don Carlos and Antonia.)

The de la Garzas and the Fagans, although fighting on different sides in 1836, remained steadfast friends for as long as they lived. Members of both families served as Indian fighters during the years of the Republic of Texas.[3] In August 1840, a large band of Comanche raiders struck the Texas coast leaving terrible destruction in their path. Soon a sizeable group of these raiders struck south of the San Antonio River, but the fierce warriors were immediately confronted by Don Carlos and his *rancheros* and colonists from Fagan's settlement. In the savage encounter with the Comanches, the de la Garzas and Fagans stood firm. It was probably during this engagement that Don Carlos was severely wounded by Indian arrows. The Comanches from this riding party had intruded into the domain long since occupied by the de la Garza *rancheros*, but the Indians were soon put to flight.

It was utterly fascinating to discover the great drama taking place at the Presidio La Bahía on March 27, 1836. At this ancient Spanish fortress, life and death hung in the balance for a few souls. Indeed, it was most gratifying for me to know that my ancestors performed a noble deed on that memorable day so long ago; and the principal actors in the drama enacted in and about the old *presidio* were the de la Garzas, Fagans, Byrnes, Perrys, and Sidicks. This poignant episode where human life was at stake truly ranks with other memorable moments in early Texas history.

Lucille Fagan Snider agreed to join me in a visit to the Fagan cemetery. At long last, I was but a few feet from the graveside of the famed old Irishman, Don Nicholas Fagan, prominent colonist of the San Antonio River area. Lucille, his great-granddaughter, and I stood silently viewing his grave and headstone, which was marked with a Texas centennial marker. Somehow I knew his old friends, the booted de la Garza *rancheros*, came to this same spot in 1850 to pay their last respects. Now I, a descendant of those ancient Mexicans, stood on this hallowed piece of the good earth. Some of the inscriptions on his headstone noted that he was saved from execution in 1836 through the intercession of Mexican colonial friends.

We next visited the old de la Garza cemetery, also near the San Antonio River. There was a road in this heavily wooded area known as de la Garza trail. Mrs. Snider almost immediately located the grave of Carlos de la Garza. We were surprised because it was generally believed he had been interred outside the walls of Our Lady of Loreto Chapel at La Bahía. However, recent research revealed that there were two young men named Carlos de la Garza residing at the old pueblo of La Bahía in 1825. One was listed in the household of Clemente de la Garza, and our subject was listed in the household of Antonio de la Garza. Based on the census of 1825 and additional information, it is certain that our subject was interred at La Bahía.[4]

Continuing on with the search of family names in this old cemetery, I came to the grave of my great-aunt, Petra de la Garza. She was born on August 1, 1875, and died January 17, 1940. Her husband, Juan Ybarbo, was buried next to her. While viewing her grave and noticing the year 1875, I remembered the flight of her father, Antonio de la Garza, and Ponposa Bontan, to Goliad County and safety in late July of 1875.

Mrs. Snider had thought this was the cemetery I had been seeking, but it was not; and again there was disappointment. We next went to the home of her brother, William Fagan, who told me, "Had it not been for your ancestors we would not be here today." He took me on a tour of his two-story home, built in 1868 by his grandfather, Peter H. Fagan.

Before departing, I showed Mrs. Snider a copy of the Manuel Becerra survey plat of 1849. She examined the plat and said that she had never heard mention of a cemetery being located in the region of Copano and Alamito creeks. The Fagans still occupied all of the Mexican land granted to Nicholas Fagan in 1834. It was a twist of history that here was a family still solidly in control of their ancestor's land while the de la Garzas, on the other hand, owned not a single acre of land of the many thousands once controlled with an iron hand. Instead of enjoying peace and happiness, the de la Garzas were stalked by bloody violence and death. Their lives had been marred by violence of one form or another. *El demonio,* the devil, surely must have dogged every footstep the de la Garza *rancheros* took until the final blow struck Antonio. However, as I stood there, for the first time in my many years of research, the interview with Mrs. Lucille Fagan Snider was by far the best and most enjoyable portion of this work. I had found new and solid friends in the Fagans.

On August 25, 1983, I again returned to the Fagans, for Mrs. Snider had contacted me about another cemetery. This time I met her brother, Frederick Fagan, a Refugio County commissioner. Mr. Fagan was as amiable as his sister, Lucille, and brother, William. He knew of an old cemetery in Refugio County and asked his old friend, Jesús Villarreal, to guide me.

Old Jesús and I immediately departed for the woods. We saw flocks of wild turkeys and many fine cattle before finally locating the cemetery, which was in the Salt Creek area. Later I calculated that this cemetery was located about five miles from the outer boundaries of the Becerra tract. When Jesús turned left off road 774, I knew that this was not the place. Indeed it was not. I had hoped he would continue ahead and turn right, but this was not to be. Mrs. Snider had told me that some cemeteries dating back to the frontier were not marked. Instead of headstones on the graves, the ranchers used wooden crosses. In time, these crosses fell down or else were trampled by cattle and horses; thus, this was probably the reason no one knew anything about the cemetery mentioned by Paula Lozano. I was still convinced that the cemetery was within the boundaries of the Becerra lands, but entering those lands was prohibited because that territory was claimed by someone else.

Mrs. Snider suggested that I interview her old friend, Rafael de la Garza, of Victoria County. Rafael, she said, was ninety-five years old and had been an old-time *vaquero* of Refugio County. De la Garza possessed great knowledge in regard to lands in Refugio County; and if there was indeed an old cemetery, he would know of it. He was one of the last surviving *vaqueros* of the South Texas brush country.

Don Rafael de la Garza, an amiable man, stood over six feet tall without his boots on. Standing straight and walking without the aid of a cane, he was a living symbol who continued to perpetuate a nearly forgotten page in Texas history. He was born on February 19, 1888, in Victoria County, the son of Jesús de la Garza and Beatrice Hernandez. In 1903, when he was fifteen years old, he began working cattle on the O'Connor brothers' river ranch in Refugio County. Rafael had been an employee of the O'Connor family his entire life, most of it as a *vaquero*. Now retired, he was well taken care of by the present-day Thomas O'Connor family. It appeared that taking care of lifelong faithful ranch employees was a tradition of the O'Connors.

As I talked with the old *vaquero*, I realized that this might be my final interview with a living piece of family history. In my long search for an almost forgotten heritage, this interview was yet another emotional moment.

Don Rafael told me he had spent much of his time herding cattle on Copano Creek and was thoroughly familiar with Refugio County. Rafael patrolled Copano and Alamito creeks, constantly pulling cows from the mud. He told me that in 1907 much of the lands in Refugio County were still open range, extending from the San Antonio River to the present town of Tivoli. By 1908, however, barbed wire fences began to appear. He never cared for barbed wire as it was the cause of many serious injuries to cattle and horses.

Don Rafael said he had never heard of a cemetery on Copano Creek. If there had been one, he would have known of it, as he knew the area like the back of his hand. He knew all the Rubios, including Francisca de la Garza. He and Guillermo Rubio, my father, while young *vaqueros*, used to ride the back trails to the nearest *cantina* in Goliad County. On numerous occasions, he saw a lone horse tethered outside the *cantina* and knew the rider was probably Guillermo, a rip-snorter and constant worry for my grandmother Francisca.

As a young boy, Rafael first met the gunman Ismael de la Garza in 1896. He said this man was wicked and lethal with a pistol. Ismael once shot a man twice simply because he didn't like his looks. Another time Ismael shot a man through the face; Ismael said he didn't know that the pistol was loaded! Once while riding through the woods at night, Ismael was challenged by a group of Mexicans camped on the trail. De la Garza boldly rode to their campfire and told them who he was. By morning they had vacated the premises. Don Rafael laughed as he recalled this incident.

In addition to his expertise with a pistol, Ismael was an excellent horseman and *vaquero*. Don Rafael said all of the de la Garzas, especially the elders, had been very tough men. The last and youngest of this breed had been Ismael. Another Don Rafael had known was Antonio de la Garza, the ill-tempered old man who had been chased out of Refugio County.

Don Rafael claimed the de la Garzas once owned about 9,000 acres of land on Copano Creek. I simply sat and listened and did not try to lead the old man on. What he merely mentioned made me more positive of what I already knew.

He went on to say that in 1904, while rounding up cattle, he came upon what appeared to be an ancient road. The surprised youth wheeled his horse around and galloped back to where he located an old *vaquero* whom he worked with named Macario Serrata. Rafael told him that he had found a road in the Copano area. The grumpy Serrata replied that he knew of no such road. Rafael insisted the elderly *vaquero* accompany him to the area so that he could verify his discovery. In ill humor, Serrata mounted his horse and reluctantly accompanied the excited boy to the alleged new find. Reaching their objective, Serrata, still in a sour mood, reined in his mount and stared at what young Rafael had thought was a road deep in the woods. The boy, however, was mistaken, and Serrata explained what had taken place here in the ancient days.

According to Serrata, these were the last traces of a long trench dug by early Mexican *vaqueros*. The trench, he said, was expertly dug to trap wild burros. When the trench was ready, the *vaqueros* scattered in all directions and began herding burros out of the woods. The wild little creatures were driven toward the trench. While still some distance from the trap, the *vaqueros* gave chase and the terrified animals always attempted to jump over the trench but were never successful. The hardy little beasts landed in the mud where they became stuck, and the *vaqueros* soon had the ropes around their necks. Despite heroic efforts to escape, the wild burros were doomed to a life of labor.

During the war between Mexico and Texas in 1835–36, Rafael said, Carlos de la Garza was the undisputed leader of nearly 200 *rancheros*. The source of this information was apparently Rafael's grandfather, Vicente de la Garza, who was old enough to know the particulars. Hobart Huson, in his *History of Refugio County*, mentioned that Don Carlos led seventy-five or more horsemen against the Texans in those troubled years. Though the exact number will probably never be known, this group of horsemen must have been sizeable.

Rafael said that Carlos paid $500 for a Negro slave whom he named Jimbo. When a Texas norther began to show even a slight appearance (undetected by others, it is said) Jimbo would run outside his cabin, utter hideous screams, and begin jumping up and down and pointing toward the direction of the norther. Finally, he would give a mighty leap high in the air, emit one last terrifying scream, and run headlong toward the woods. The de la Garzas could hear his screaming even while he was deep in the woods. After some time he would emerge from the woods and go inside the cabin. When the family reckoned he had regained his senses, he would repeat the same thing all over again. Jimbo's demonic behavior terrified the womenfolk, who thought him mad. Some of the de la Garzas considered the unusual slave a messenger of the devil. Others thought he was a bad omen and had cast an evil spell over them. The truth was that the pitiful man was innocent. His strange behavior was his only means of warning the family of an impending Texas norther, for which he was unerringly accurate.

I enjoyed the reminiscences of Don Rafael, the last living contact I had with the past. He was intelligent and still alert, and he was the best source in my quest to locate the cemetery. Regretfully, the quest was unsuccessful.

Someday someone is going to locate this *campo santo* — this piece of holy ground. The little Mexican-American girl, Paula Lozano, surely was not mistaken in what she saw in that remote frontier region in 1877.

Don Rafael's comments about the approximately 9,000 acres our family had once owned in that region compensated for the fact that the cemetery's whereabouts yet remained a mystery.

But I had had my moment of truth. The documents attorney Robert Hudson had given me in November 1978, and information Vincent Rodriguez and I found in Refugio in November 1981, led to the discovery of how O'Connor gained title to our land, and how and why our family's original ownership was obscured and deceptively covered up.

During his November 1978 trip to Refugio to dismiss our suit "without prejudice," Hudson had made a search of the records himself. Through a small, local title company he had obtained the available documents involved in all the land holdings of the O'Connors in Refugio and Aransas counties. I scrutinized the documents myself. No Becerra or de la Garza names appeared on these documents as grantors — that is, no Becerra or de la Garza conveyed land to them. They had therefore not obtained our land from us. Again, I remembered those strange numbers on the tracts of land that appeared inside and around the approximate boundaries of the Becerra grant.

Also, as I perused the nineteenth-century O'Connor land acquisition documents that Hudson had obtained, I wondered at the almost pathological desire old Thomas and his son Dennis must have had for land. What manner of desire must it have been? The documents listed town lots, large acreage, small acreage, everything from an acre here to 8,500 acres there. They virtually gobbled up the land. The documentation consisted of dozens upon dozens of pages that noted all the O'Connor transactions to acquire land, land, and more land.

I thought that no normal person could have been motivated to acquire so much land. It amounted to well over 390,000 acres by 1889 — more land than a dozen men could ride over in a week or perhaps a month, more land than was necessary for an honest man to earn an honest living for his family. What those documents had said to me was that these men were driven by greed. They had a desire for land and would not tolerate a Mexican family to stand in their way. A choice tract of land which lay on two flowing creeks like the Alamito and Copano provided water for thirsty herds of O'Connor cattle. Rancho Alamito in the 1870s was too choice a morsel for the expanding O'Connor empire to ignore.

A year after the conference with Hudson, I finally went to Austin, arriving on December 15, 1979, a very cold and dreary day. I was greeted by Lanell Aston of the records section of the General Land Office. I told her of the numbers appearing on the Refugio maps, and she immediately knew what I sought. She brought out Volume 108 of the General Land Office records for my inspection. Much of the material in this volume pertained to land located by virtue of land scrips.

The volume revealed that the commissioner of the General Land Office issued to the International and Great Northern Railroad Company numerous land scrips worth 640 acres each. These scrips were supposedly issued from vacant state lands; the condition was that the railroad company must physically complete ten miles of road in good order for each certificate issued. The railroad company had twelve years to comply with the terms of the charter. If they were unable to comply with the terms forthwith, the lands would again become a part of the public domain.[5]

The commissioner issued thirty-seven such land scrips to the International and Great Northern Railroad Company on May 18, 1875; by May 25, 1875, all of these land scrips had been transferred to Thomas O'Connor of Refugio County. Thomas O'Connor came into possession of the following land survey numbers: 38, 239, 233, 232, 205, 240, 237, 238, 244, 205 (on patent 552), 291, 245, 39, 250, 248, 247, 246, 249, 271, 266, 267, 272, 270, 268, 269, 273, 265, 277, 274, 286, 284, 283, 282, 285, all with patents. Survey number 205, patent 552, is found in Volume 28. These survey numbers appear on Refugio County maps beginning in 1875.

It mattered not how much land O'Connor located by virtue of

the land scrips; what definitely mattered was the fact that he claimed lands occupied by Antonio de la Garza in 1875. Those lands he claimed as being vacant came under land survey numbers 38, 248, 249, and 277 for a total of 2,560 acres. These survey numbers were located on the territory of the Becerra tract (Refugio County maps of 1875 and 1896). The I&GNRR initials and survey numbers were erased from the 1883 map but appeared again on the 1896 map. I had plotted the Becerra survey of 1849 on the 1896 map. The plat, as drawn by David Snively, fit on the junction of Copano and Alamito creeks. The numbers were no longer a mystery.

The acreage acquired by O'Connor and his land scrips in 1875 amounted to nearly 24,000 acres in Refugio County. M. D. O'Sullivan, the county surveyor, recorded the survey on the body of the land scrips between May 23, 1892, and June 4, 1892. These surveys were for Dennis O'Connor, a son of Thomas. I wondered how this surveyor recorded so much land in less than two weeks. It appeared very likely that he was copying the surveys from other survey reports belonging to different landowners. I thought it incredible that so many tracts were vacant in 1875, especially when I knew that at least two families, my own ancestors, were on part of this land.

On June 2, 1892, O'Sullivan had recorded four survey reports amounting to 2,560 acres — indeed an impossible task for a man on horseback in the woods. This surveyor never could have accomplished this horrendous task unless he was busily copying from other survey reports. After I saw the land scrips and survey reports, the acreage involved, and the time involved (May 18, 1875, to May 25, 1875), I departed the General Land Office in a daze.

Governor James Hogg of Texas was formally responsible for the issuance of land survey number 274, patent 617, dated April 14, 1893. The commissioner of the General Land Office wrote the survey on the body of the scrip. I could not help but wonder how the commissioner and officials of the International and Great Northern Railroad Company knew which tracts of land were vacant in Refugio County. They had to have been copying from a previous survey, or else someone in Refugio County was informing them of the exact location of the tracts. Since Thomas O'Connor laid claim to the land scrips already listed, it must have been he who supplied the information as to the vacant lands. Locating these "vacant lands" immediately caused great hardship on Antonio de la Garza and Ponposa Bontan. Names of Dennis O'Connor and others, as well as the International and Great Northern Railroad Company, also appeared within the Becerra tract but without land survey numbers. My research revealed that this railroad company was not without its problems. The company was in receivership in 1878–79, 1880–92, and again in 1908–14. It was chartered by the Texas legislature on August 5, 1870.[6]

Thomas O'Connor, armed with the four land scrips already mentioned, moved in on de la Garza, the rightful occupant. O'Connor must have felt a sense of security because the documents had been approved by one of the leading state authorities, the commissioner of the General Land Office himself. This commissioner, representing the state of Texas, whose responsibility was to protect the property of the citizens, by his very signature to the four land scrips actually helped to deprive one of these citizens of his property. Not only was there deprivation of property but death in the family as well. It is probable that the commissioner never knew what evil things were happening in Refugio County and that he acted on information passed on to him from someone in that county.

Antonio de la Garza never knew that the four devilish land scrips were a force behind the destruction of his family. He surely must have been a very astounded man because he alone held title to the land; yet there were those who were most determined to acquire his land at the point of a gun. The four land scrips and survey numbers acquired by O'Connor between May 18, 1875, and May 25, 1875, were promptly placed on the Refugio map of 1875. Thus, while Antonio and his family were actually living on the land and paying the property taxes, all of these things were being accomplished behind their backs. Thomas O'Connor would claim lands that were already physically occupied by a citizen of Texas. There is no doubt he knew that Antonio de la Garza was the rightful owner. Thomas O'Connor was one of the largest landowners in South Texas. By the year 1890, he had amassed some 390,267 acres of land, mostly in Refugio County.[7]

Unfortunately, the Becerra lands owned by the de la Garza heirs were not registered in the General Land Office where they could have been noted by the land commissioner. Francisco de la Garza was from a time when a high-priority Mexican land grant, properly issued by the governor of Coahuila-Texas, meant every-thing — such as the land he acquired from his father-in-law, Man-uel Becerra. A tradition of years of ownership and occupancy fur-ther solidified his claim to Rancho Alamito.

When Antonio took over the lands after 1870 upon the rela-tively early death of his father, Francisco, the last of the de la Garza horsemen, he was a young man, barely twenty-one years of age. He was the first of the heirs to have been born after the American take-over of Texas. But he too was a son of the soil in Refugio County, and was no doubt convinced that the tradition of ownership since the 1830s by his illustrious grandfather and father was enough. An-tonio had never been to Austin, the Anglo-American capital cre-ated years after Manuel Becerra had first risked his life for the Re-fugio lands; a city named for the man whom his grandfather had introduced to Texas! That Antonio had gotten his land from Be-cerra and Francisco, that he had the land grant documents in his possession, that he paid taxes on the land, and that he and the de la Garzas were well known in the area, surely was enough, in Anto-nio's mind, to make him believe that his right to the property was secure. Such tradition meant everything to him. Antonio and Pon-posa were busy on the ranch making a living and raising a family, not seeing to the fine points of vacant land questions as they existed in Austin. The only problem was that someone else was seeing to this issue.

It is unfortunate that the de la Garza land was not registered in Austin when railroad land scrips were being distributed in 1875. It is also unfortunate that others searched the General Land Office records and discovered the land was not registered. These same persons also might have understood that, after the death of Fran-cisco, only the younger people were left. The de la Garza horsemen were gone; only Antonio, Gregorio Esparza Bontan, and Juan Elias Lozano remained. They could be dealt with — as were most all the Refugio County Mexicans during the violent 1870s.

But the men who swept the younger de la Garza and his rela-tives aside made a serious blunder in 1875 that I believed was com-ing to light. The picture was made more complete with my discov-ery of a significant boundary dispute between Don Manuel Becerra and the Irish *empresario,* James Power.

On September 29, 1834, Power claimed one and one-quarter

leagues of land on the Copano and Alamito creek areas and also a
one-quarter league for his son of the same name. The one and one-
quarter leagues, according to him, were due to him for marrying a
citizen of Mexico.[8] The most land granted by the Mexican government to a foreigner for marrying a native Mexican was an extra
one-quarter league. Power was a foreigner regardless of his *empresario* status. How he managed to get an additional one league of
land is not known, but Power's petition amounted to one and one-
half leagues or 6,642 acres. This tract was subsequently acquired
by Dennis O'Connor.[9] More than one-third of the 6,642 acres of the
Power tract obtained *after* Becerra received his land fell within the
Manuel Becerra tract. Thus, there was a question of overlapping
boundaries between Power and Becerra.

The above boundary dispute evidently became known to
Texas officials because the Power grant was voided in 1841 or
thereafter. If Power could not have his name on the maps, then neither could Becerra. Hence, this was the probable reason why Becerra's name never appeared on the Refugio County maps. Neither
man could have his name on the maps while there was a boundary
dispute.

Power's name began to appear on the maps in 1872 and 1875,
when O'Connor acquired the land. The Power name appeared on
the maps of 1872, 1875, and later maps.

Vincent Rodriguez and I had discovered the documents revealing this overlapping boundary dispute during our November
1981 trip to Aransas and Refugio counties. How strange it was that
this boundary dispute which began in 1834 between Power and Becerra was not over yet! Rodriguez told me that indeed our lawsuit
would have its beginning with this dispute dating back so far.

It was again startling to discover that O'Connor had obtained
the land scrips claiming our ancestral lands in 1875, the year
grandfather Antonio had been forced off Rancho Alamito, according to family tradition. Again, documentary evidence intertwined
with oral tradition to lend undisputed credibility to the latter. No
doubt they waited until later to persecute Trinidad because she
owned only 300 acres. Antonio held the largest portion, so he had
been their first target.

While O'Connor had the formal backing of the land commissioner, he apparently did not have the support of the Refugio

County sheriff, who would have known the legal owner of the land. Had Antonio de la Garza and his family been land-squatters, O'Connor, with the sheriff, could have ousted them from the property in a matter of hours. This simply did not happen because the de la Garzas were anything but land-squatters, and O'Connor knew it.

Evidence showed clearly that Thomas O'Connor knew the de la Garzas. Between 1846 and 1860, Carlos, José María, and Francisco de la Garza served as jurors of Refugio County.[10] One of the prerequisites was that the jurors be free whites, upstanding citizens of the county, and lastly, landowners. During one such term of the jurors, Thomas O'Connor was the commissioner of the court and it was his responsibility to select the landowners for jury service. Under the circumstances, O'Connor was in the best position to know who were the landowners in the county. He personally knew Francisco de la Garza and his son, Antonio. Thus, in 1875, O'Connor had to know that the property in the region he acquired by virtue of the land survey numbers 38, 248, 249, and 277 belonged to Francisco de la Garza.

There was not a single man — Anglo or Mexican — in Refugio County who could have gone up against Antonio de la Garza and dispossessed him of his land. It took a powerful man with powerful friends to do this. Involved in this drama were "legal" documents issued by the land commissioner, as well as officials of the International and Great Northern Railroad Company and Thomas O'Connor of Refugio County.

In the violent period between the 1874 Thad Swift family murders and the killing of John Welder, there was ample opportunity to capitalize on the persecution of Refugio Mexican landowners. While there is not absolute proof that Thomas O'Connor was involved in the destruction of the de la Garzas, he did claim the land at the time when they had to flee their property in 1875–77.

Finally, also appearing on the maps within the Becerra tract were the names John M. Swisher, Edwin C. Sloan, J. M. Cross, and A. M. Berry, assignee of Antonio Carrera. Berry land was shown south of the Aransas County line, as a portion of the Becerra tract extended into that county. Dennis O'Connor eventually came into possession of these tracts, except Berry's, including the 6,642-acre tract of James Power.[11] So it was that the entire Becerra grant came into the possession of Thomas O'Connor.

It is my belief that the home of Antonio and Trinidad as well as the family cemetery were located within the area covered by the I&GNRR land survey numbers. That location was near running water yet not between the creeks and subject to possible flooding. The remaining tracts of Swisher, Sloan, and Cross covered much of the rest of the land owned by our family.

It would be most interesting to learn exactly how the Sloan, Swisher, and Cross land patents came to be located on the Becerra grant. I have reason to doubt these families were residents of Refugio County in those years when the survey numbers appeared on the maps. A thorough search of the census records of 1870 and 1880 for Refugio County failed to reveal their names.

These changes of land claims must surely have encompassed all the property held by Antonio and Trinidad, some 2,214 acres. Manuel Becerra had originally owned 8,856 acres, but had conveyed 4,428 acres to Henry Koehler. Antonio and Trinidad had come into possession of 2,214 acres of Becerra's remaining acreage in the upper half of the grant. The other 2,214 acres had been passed down to Antonia Cruz de la Garza, wife of Carlos de la Garza, for the sum of $500. In late 1979, my research confirmed further that even this last 2,214 acres also had a suspicious change of hands, from Mexican to Anglo.

In June and July of 1884, Antonia Cruz de la Garza leased for one-third interest 1,000 acres of land to a Mrs. M. K. Plummer. The attorney for Mrs. de la Garza was E. P. Upton. According to the document, the de la Garza widow gave Upton power of attorney to lease or sell all her lands deeded to her by Manuel Becerra in 1853. These transactions involved 2,214 acres of land. She was to receive one-third interest from the lease or sale.[12]

When Vincent Rodriguez and I looked for Upton in the deed records of Aransas and Refugio counties we found nothing.[13] He never appeared in them, nor did Mrs. M. K. Plummer. The document stated that *most* of the land was in Refugio County, meaning that a portion was perhaps located in Aransas County. When this transaction took place, Antonia Cruz de la Garza was residing in Goliad County. Also in this year of 1884 *another* Mrs. De la Garza was residing in Goliad County. This was Ponposa Bontan, wife of Antonio de la Garza. Ponposa, not to be confused with Antonia Cruz, did not convey any land to anyone. The de la Garzas likewise never received anything for this other 2,214 acres of Antonia Cruz. Thus, this other portion of half of the original tract that Becerra had owned changed hands in 1884, but the de la Garzas received nothing. My ancestors once again lost land, though violence was not employed in this case as it was to Antonio and Trinidad.

The legal authority of the state officials and the International and Great Northern Railroad Company, reinforced with the power of Thomas O'Connor, was all simply too great for Antonio de la Garza. There were also those "apostles of death" who applied the *coup de grace* to Antonio and Trinidad. The de la Garza families stood firm for as long as possible before retreating to Goliad County, where for the rest of their lives they reflected on the injustices committed against them in Refugio County. All they could do was to pass these stories down to succeeding generations.

This is a classic example of how innocent and unsuspecting Mexicans were cruelly raped of their land grants by greedy and unscrupulous land-grabbers. That it happened in Refugio County against *my* ancestors in this case only adds insult to injury for me.

My search which began on September 30, 1971, was nearing an end. I was convinced I knew how Antonio de la Garza and our family lost our lands. But the struggle for repossession of the land, even though the costs had amounted to thousands of dollars, would not end.

The Becerra and de la Garza descendants, with competent legal counsel, will continue to seek redress from the injustice committed against Antonio and Ponposa in 1875. We must reclaim our landed heritage which was so wrongly taken away from our ancestors. This endeavor is certain to gain strength in the future. As long as there is a single Becerra descendant alive, the smoldering fire will be able to burn brighter.

The major obstacle may well be the statute of limitations which regulates old land claims — especially complicated Spanish and Mexican land grants. That legal question, however, does not alter the truth of history, nor the cause of human rights and dignity.

Endnotes

Chapter 1. THE SEARCH BEGINS

1. Cause #23, Estate of Francisco de la Garza, deceased, Probate Court, Refugio County, Texas, April 25, 1870. Francisco de la Garza died without leaving a will, hence the appointment of Antonio as the administrator.

2. The Becerra family is in possession of the original inventories for the years 1874 through 1876. The Becerra family and de la Garza family are one and the same, Manuel Becerra being the grandfather of Antonio de la Garza.

3. *Ibid.*

4. Cause #23, Estate of Francisco de la Garza, deceased, Probate Records, Refugio County, Texas. On August 20, 1872, the county clerk, Hough Rea, ordered sheriff J. C. Billingsly to find Antonio who had not settled the estate of his father. On September 29, 1872, the sheriff located Antonio and served the papers; this would happen again in 1881 in Goliad County.

5. Eugene C. Barker, *The Life of Stephen F. Austin*, 121.

6. Father William H. Oberste, *Texas Irish Empresarios and Their Colonies*, 126.

7. H. P. N. Gammel, *Decrees and Laws of Coahuila and Texas*, obtained through the courtesy of Sutro Public Library, Sacramento, California.

Chapter 2. MOUNTING SUSPICIONS

1. Simply, the federal land grant required the signature or approval by the *alcalde* (mayor) and secretary of the *ayuntamiento* (town government). Final approval was made by the governor and secretary general of Coahuila and Texas. The other class of grant was that issued by the *empresarios* to the settlers in their colonies. Title was then issued by the land commissioner of the colony, a process which generally required only a few days. See also, Title Book 17, Spanish Archives, General Land Office, Austin, Texas.

2. Hubert Howe Bancroft, *History of the North Mexican States and Texas*, Vols. 1 and 2.

3. Estate of Francisco de la Garza, deceased, May term of 1881, Vol. E: 48, Probate Court, Refugio County, Texas.

4. *Ibid.*

5. Cause #23, Francisco de la Garza, deceased, and petition to transfer cause to Goliad County, Vol. E: 48, Probate Court, Refugio County, Texas.

6. Hobart Huson, *History of Refugio County, Texas, from Aboriginal Times to 1953*, Vols. 1 and 2.

7. Manuel Becerra survey reports and field notes, March 12 and 13, 1849, Book A: 26, Probate Court, Refugio County, Texas.

Chapter 3.   HOME TO SOUTH TEXAS

1. Uncle Jesús was born at La Bahía on June 13, 1901, the son of Juan Rubio and Francisca de la Garza. (Jesús Rubio interview with author, August 19, 1972, Cuero, Texas.)

2. Joseph M. Nance, *Attack and Counterattack, The Texas-Mexican Frontier*, 301, 302, 303.

3. *Ibid.;* Nance reveals that Rubio was murdered in cold blood by Texas Rangers.

4. Oberste, *Texas Irish Empresarios and Their Colonies*, 266.

Chapter 5.   A CENTURY OF BECERRAS

1. Hobart Huson, *History of Refugio County from Aboriginal Times to 1953* extensively mentions Don Carlos de la Garza, who appears to have been a resolute and tough Indian fighter. He was the eldest brother of Francisco de la Garza (see Census of Pueblo of La Bahía, April 25, 1825, Nacogdoches Archives, Texas State Archives, Austin Texas), who himself was an early colonist of Refugio County. Manuel Becerra and other officials of the Mexican government signed a peace treaty with the Karankawa and Coco Indian tribes at Goliad, Texas, on May 27, 1827. Becerra signed for the town of Goliad. See also Becerra, Manuel, Treaty with the Karankawas, The Austin Papers, Vol. I, 1639–41, Barker Collection, University of Texas, Austin.

2. Huson, *History of Refugio County from Aboriginal Times to 1953*.

3. Vol. A: 1, Probate Court, Refugio County, Texas.

4. There appeared to be conflicting dates as to the year Grandmother was born. Her death certificate indicated her birth date as March 3, 1871; but the grave marker showed March 1869–1935. The date should have been March 3, 1869. She was interred at the de la Garza cemetery at La Bahía on August 23, 1935. Her son, Juan Rubio, Jr., born in 1897, lay next to her.

5. Aunt Sálome said her parents, Francisca de la Garza and Juan Rubio, were married in Goliad County on January 29, 1887. She said that her mother was nearly eighteen years old and her father was twenty-seven years old when they were married. Subsequent research revealed that Francisca de la Garza and Juan Rubio were indeed married on January 29, 1887. Sálome Rubio de Lambardia remembered well. A copy of the marriage certificate is in the author's possession. Document from Probate Court, Goliad County, Texas.

6. U.S. Census for Cameron, Starr, and Webb counties, Texas, of November 15, 1860. The senior Rubio died on February 11, 1927. He was interred in the Rubio cemetery at La Bahía.

7. It is not known when Teresita died, but it was certain that Juan married a second time to María Eugenia Garcia from Goliad County on June 21, 1877. I was much gratified to locate the marriage certificate in good condition in Probate Court, Goliad County, Texas.

8. U.S. Census of Goliad County, Texas, of July 11, 1860. Bontan was actually born in 1808 in La Bahía.

9. Kathryn Stoner O'Connor, *The Presidio La Bahía,* 266–267.

10. Spanish Census of Pueblo La Bahía, April 24, 1825, Nacogdoches Archives, Texas State Archives, Austin, Texas.

11. Spanish Census of Royal Presidio La Bahía, December 31, 1804, Nacogdoches Archives, Texas State Archives, Austin, Texas.

12. Governor Manuel Munoz report of May 21, 1792, Nacogdoches Archives, Texas State Archives, Austin, Texas. This report concerning foreigners residing in the towns and settlements of the province of Texas was actually a census. There appeared no Englishmen in this report.

13. Spanish Census of Pueblo La Bahía, April 24, 1825, Nacogdoches Archives, Texas State Archives, Austin, Texas.

14. Author's interview with Aunt Sálome Rubio de Lambardia, at San Antonio, Texas, October 7, 1972. Aunt Sálome may have been in error as to the Bontans being residents of San Antonio. My research has shown the Bontans as being inhabitants of the Pueblo of La Bahía in 1825.

Chapter 6. NEW LIGHT ON AN OLD GRANT

1. Vol. 2: 750, Spanish Archives, General Land Office, Austin, Texas.

2. Vol. K: 398, 399a, 400a, Deed records of Refugio County, Texas.

3. Manuel Becerra survey of March 11 and 12, 1849; copy of such survey is in possession of the Becerra family.

4. Becerra's diary of the trip, Vol. 54: 71, Spanish Archives, General Land Office, Austin, Texas.

5. Cause #23, Estate of Francisco de la Garza, deceased, May 1881 term. District Court, Refugio County, Texas. Cause #23 also shows that the land and animals belonging to José María de la Garza and wife María Josefa Becerra were included in the estate of Francisco.

6. Antonia Cruz became the wife of the famed Indian fighter, Don Carlos de la Garza, on September 23, 1840, in Refugio County. Marriage Records, Probate Court, Refugio, Texas.

7. Deed Records, Vol. O: 152, Lease #77 to L. E. Upton, Probate Court, Refugio County, Texas.

8. Deed Records, Book E: 21–22, Probate Court, Refugio County, Texas, April 27, 1855, from Manuel Becerra deed (by María Josefa) of March 17, 1853.

9. Deed Records, Vol. O: 129, Lease #66 to E. P. Upton, Probate Court, Refugio County, Texas.

10. Manuel Becerra original petition, Vol. C: 430–431, Transcribed Deed Records, Probate Court, Refugio County, Texas.

11. Juana María Cadena was probably born at La Bahía around 1790. U.S. Census, Refugio County, Texas, June 17, 1860. The Refugio Mission was not actually completed until 1795. See also Census of Pueblo of La Bahía del Espíritu Santo of April 24, 1825, Nacogdoches Archives, Texas State Archives, Austin, Texas. According to this census Juana María Cadena was born in 1786. This same census shows Manuel Becerra as having been born in 1765; he was a carpenter by trade. Their daughter María Josefa Becerra was born in 1811, although she was

listed in a different house, and Gertrudis Becerra in 1819. María Josefa was listed in the household of Diego Cadena, age sixty, and wife María Josefa Hernandez, age fifty-eight. Gertrudis was listed in the household of Carlos Becerra, age sixty, and wife Francisca Galan, age fifty-six. Diego Cadena was very likely the father of Juana María Cadena and the grandfather of María Josefa and Gertrudis Becerra. The baptismals are in Vol. 2, Baptismal Registery, Catholic Archives, Austin Texas.

   12. Title Book 17, Spanish Archives, General Land Office, Austin, Texas.

   13. Oberste, *Texas Irish Empresarios and Their Colonies*, 64–66.

   14. The Power and Hewetson Collection, 1824–35, Bexar Archives (origi-nals in the Barker Collection, University of Texas, Austin, Texas); Bexar Archives 1822–36, Rolls 162–163, Activities of Manuel Becerra (originals in the Barker Collection, University of Texas, Austin, Texas). In one of the Spanish documents dated October 8, 1830 (Power and Hewetson Collection, 1824–35) Becerra and the *ayuntamiento*, in their bitter disputes with *empresarios*, reported to the Coahuila authorities that the worst disgrace of all was that the Mexican settlers were being made to feel as foreigners in their own country. These same Spanish documents show the elderly Becerra became *alcalde* of Goliad in 1834, and the confrontations with the foreigners over land boundaries continued.

   15. Most of the titles issued by José Jesús Vidaurri and approved by James Power indicate that the petitioner professed the Catholic religion, Title Book 17, Spanish Archives, General Land Office, Austin, Texas.

   16. The grants to the *empresarios* were declared invalid by the Supreme Court, *Smith v. Power*, 14 Texas 146; *Smith v. Power*, 23 Texas 29–30.

   17. Oberste, *Texas Irish Empresarios and Their Colonies*, 96.

   18. *Ibid.*, 138. For the acreage acquired by both *empresarios* see Title Book 17, Spanish Archives, General Land Office, Austin, Texas.

   19. J. P. Kimball, *Laws and Decrees of the State of Coahuila and Texas*, Decree 246.

   20. Deed Records, Book C: 189–190, Probate Court, Refugio County, Texas.

Chapter 7.   THE ORIGINAL TEJANOS: A FRESH LOOK

   1. Stephen F. Austin Journal of his first trip to Texas, Barker Collection, University of Texas, Austin, Texas; *Southwestern Historical Quarterly*, Vol. 3: 286, 298.

   2. Becerra's diary of the trip, Vol. 54: 71, Spanish Archives, General Land Office, Austin, Texas.

   3. Stephen F. Austin Journal of his first trip to Texas, Barker Collection, University of Texas, Austin, Texas.

   4. *Ibid.*

   5. Becerra diary of the trip, Vol. 54: 71, Spanish Archives, General Land Office, Austin, Texas.

   6. *Ibid.*

   7. Map drawing by Stephen F. Austin in 1821, as asserted by Manuel Be-cerra, appears in *History of the Refugio Mission*, 397, by Father Oberste.

   8. Becerra diary of the trip, Vol. 54: 71, Spanish Archives, General Land Office, Austin, Texas.

   9. Alcalde Tomás Buentello to Governor Antonio Martinez, Vol. 54: 71,

Spanish Archives, General Land Office, Austin, Texas. To make his claim more vigorous, he included a copy of the Becerra report.

10. The Austin Papers, Vol. 1: 1639–1641, Barker Collection, University of Texas, Austin, Texas.

11. *Ibid.*

12. Romana de la Garza to Alvin L. Harris, 1974. Copy of letter in author's possession. Francisco Vidaurri became governor of Coahuila y Tejas on January 8, 1834.

13. Title Book 17, Abstract of Original Titles, 68–75, Spanish Archives, General Land Office, Austin, Texas.

14. *Ibid.*

15. *Ibid.*

16. H. P. N. Gammel, *Decrees and Laws of Coahuila and Texas,* courtesy of Sutro Public Library, Sacramento, California.

17. Baptismal Registry, Vol. 2, Catholic Archives of Texas, Austin, Texas.

18. José María de la Garza to Commissioners Court of Refugio County, November 19, 1861, and District Court of Bexar County, April 19, 1861. See file C-3062, Court of Land Claims, Records Section, General Land Office, Austin, Texas. This file contains the names of famous Texans including S. A. Maverick, Judge T. J. Devine of Bexar, and many others.

19. Paulino de la Garza to clerk of county court of Bexar, file C-3070, to Commissioners Court of Refugio County; file C-3072, for his bounty of land (320 acres); Bexar-B-1330; Bexar-B-1393, Court of Land Claims, Records Section, General Land Office, Austin, Texas. One of the witnesses for Paulino de la Garza was Juan Seguin. Paulino stated in his petition that in 1835–36 he was residing at the *rancho* of Carlos de la Garza; he was in Bexar in 1821, got married and then returned to La Bahía. Commissioners Minutes 1, November 1860; Minutes County Clerk, Refugio, 1861. It is not recorded where the additional 80 acres of the 320 granted were located.

20. U.S. Census of Refugio County, Texas, September 30, 1850.

21. Refugio County Tax Rolls for 1858, State Comptroller's Office, Austin, Texas.

22. Title Book 17, Abstract of Original Titles, 98. Spanish Archives, General Land Office, Austin, Texas.

23. Uncle Daniel Rubio interviews with author, summer 1972, at Goliad, Texas.

24. Adrian Flores was from Victoria County, and at the time was twenty-three years old (born on November 21, 1892). In a few years he would marry Teresita Rubio, my aunt, of Goliad County. On the fateful day of the gunfight Aunt Teresita was seventeen years old. It was her uncle, Ismael, who had shot her soon-to-be husband and left him crippled for life. I last saw Uncle Adrian on July 2, 1975; he was nearly eighty-four years old and still limping badly as he walked. He knew about the Becerra land grant investigation and urged me never to stop in my quest. He recalled how poor our family had been all their lives while the descendants of the non-Hispanics responsible for taking our ancestors' lands lived in Victoria and Refugio in great splendor. I could see the tears coming down between the

wrinkles of Uncle Adrian's thin face, and I shuddered on seeing the proud old man in such a pitiful condition.

Chapter 8.   PAY DIRT IN TEXAS SOIL

   1. 1850 Tax Rolls, Refugio County, Texas, State Comptroller's Office, Austin, Texas.
   2. Deed Records, Book E: 14–15, Probate Court, Refugio County, Texas, Conveyance to Francisco de la Garza from María Josefa Becerra and José María de la Garza. Deed Records, Book E: 21–22, Probate Court, Refugio County, Texas, Conveyance from Manuel Becerra Deed (by María Josefa) on March 17, 1853.
   3. Vol. G: 315–317, Probate Court, Refugio County, Texas.
   4. Baptismal Records, Our Lady of Refugio Parish, Refugio, Texas.
   5. Marriage Records, Probate Court, Goliad, Texas. Marriage certificates in author's possession. Trinidad married Juan Elias Lozano on June 7, 1867; Genoveva de la Garza married Miguel Lozano; and Rosalia married Santos Valdez.
   6. Deed Records, Book C: 189–190, Probate Court, Refugio County, Texas.
   7. Vidaurri to Musquiz, August 28, 1834, SA/BA, 286–289.
   8. Title Book 17, Power and Hewetson Colony, Spanish Archives, General Land Office, Austin, Texas.
   9. Essy Reed petition to Matagorda County Land Commissioners, Vol. 2: 750, Spanish Archives, General Land Office, Austin, Texas.
   10. Vol R: 398–400, Deed Records, Probate Court, Refugio County, Texas.
   11. It appears that James Power was indeed a ruthless *empresario* as he was in constant dispute with other *empresarios* such as John McMullen, James McGloin, Martin DeLeon, Fernando De Leon (of Victoria Colony), and the settlers of the Pueblo of La Bahía. Father Oberste in his work sheds a great deal of light on the character of Power in this regard.

Chapter 9.   THE SEARCH BEARS FRUIT

   1. H. P. N. Gammel, *Decrees and Laws of Coahuila and Texas* courtesy of Sutro Public Library, Sacramento, California.
   2. Texas State Comptroller's Office, Microfilm Department, Tax Records 1847–1877.
   3. Refugio County Tax Rolls, 1878, 1879–80, 1881, Clerk's Office, Refugio County Probate Court.

Chapter 10.   NIGHT RIDERS AND MURDER

   1. This land grant was issued under Decree 253, Article 1, and approved by Governor Francisco Vidaurri on February 11, 1834, at Monclova, Coahuila, Mexico; J. P. Kimball, *Laws and Decrees of Coahuila and Texas*, Sutro Public Library; Sacramento, California.
   2. J. P. Kimball, *Laws and Decrees of Coahuila and Texas*. As an afterthought, the governor added that the grant should not be on lands disputed by the town of Goliad.
   3. Vol. 108, Spanish Archives, General Land Office, Austin, Texas.

4. Starr, Webb, and Cameron counties appear in the census of 1850; however, the inhabitants listed are not shown by specific county in which they domiciled.

5. Tomás Rubio to author, January 28, 1973. Interview in Goliad, Texas.

6. Cause #23, Estate of Francisco de la Garza, Probate Court, Refugio County, Texas. This estate was finalized by Antonio on May 16, 1881. Francisco de la Garza was born at La Bahía in 1818, Refugio County Census, Lamar Precinct, June 17, 1860. See also Census of Pueblo of La Bahía, April 24, 1825, Nacogdoches Archives, Texas State Archives, Austin, Texas.

7. R. P. Clarkson, district clerk of Refugio County, certified as to the loss of the livestock on February 11, 1874. The original report is in the possession of the Becerra family.

8. *Ibid.*

9. Antonio de la Garza to his grandson's wife, Romana de la Garza, on December 24, 1931; also on March 21, 1974, eighty-six-year-old Julia F. de la Garza (Antonio's daughter-in-law) repeated the same story in a letter addressed to attorney Alvin L. Harris.

10. Tomás Rubio to author in interview, August 21, 1972, at Goliad, Texas.

11. Antonio de la Garza to Romana de la Garza, December 24, 1931; also Julia F. de la Garza to attorney Alvin L. Harris, March 21, 1974.

12. *Ibid.*

13. Aunt Sálome Rubio de Lambardia, in my interview with her on October 10, 1972, named the leader of the horsemen. She was positive of his identity because her grandfather Antonio told her. The leader was a prominent landowner in Refugio County. I cannot reveal his name here because there is no other documentary evidence to support her statement. Aunt Sálome also related that after Antonio and Ponposa vacated the land, their persecutor immediately fenced the property.

14. Tomás Rubio to author, January 28, 1973. Interview in Goliad, Texas.

15. Hobart Huson, *Refugio, A Comprehensive History of Refugio County from Aboriginal Times to 1953* (Woodsboro, 1955), Vol. II: 206–212.

16. *Ibid.*, 210; J. Frank Dobie, *A Vaquero of the Brush Country* (Dallas, 1929), 74–79.

17. Arnoldo De Leon, *They Called Them Greasers: Anglo Attitudes Toward Mexicans in Texas, 1821–1900* (Austin, 1983), 98–99.

18. Tomás Rubio to author, January 28, 1973. Interview, in Goliad, Texas.

19. Paula Lozano was the only child of Genoveva de la Garza and Miguel Lozano (married on May 30, 1870; license in author's possession). The girl became an orphan and was raised by Trinidad (the elder sister of Genoveva) and Juan Elias Lozano. Paula Lozano de Martinez was born in Refugio County on March 21, 1871.

20. Refugio County Tax Rolls for 1877–1878, State Comptroller's Office, Austin, Texas.

21. Huson, *Refugio*, Vol. II: 212-214.

22. Tomás Rubio to author, January 28, 1973. Interview in Goliad, Texas. Antonio de la Garza told his grandson Tomás that Juan Elias Lozano's bad temper and confrontations with the Texas Anglo gunmen was a major cause of the de-

struction of the de la Garzas in Refugio County. It appears that Antonio de la
Garza was more level-headed when in danger, while Lozano was reckless.

23. Paul Martinez to author, November 1981. Interview in Houston, Texas.
Paul as a youngster overheard this story twice between Paula Lozano de Martinez
and Ismael de la Garza in Goliad.

24. A copy of this letter written in Spanish is in the author's possession. The
original is kept by her grandson.

25. Refugio County Tax Rolls, 1877–1878, State Comptroller's Office, Austin, Texas.

26. The story narrated regarding Trinidad de la Garza and her child Paula
Lozano was based on an interview the author had with Paula's son, Plácido Martinez, at Houston, Texas, on January 27, 1973. Don Plácido said that what happened to the family in Refugio County in 1877–1878 was a terrible injustice.

27. Deed of Trinidad Garza de Lozano to Antonio de la Garza, Vol. 5: 243,
Deed Records, Goliad County, Texas.

28. Tomás Rubio to author, January 28, 1973, in Goliad, Texas.

29. The subject of the O'Connor-de la Garza confrontation was based on the
author's interview with his aunt Sálome Rubio de Lambardia on April 7, 1977.
This was the second and last interview with the eighty-eight-year-old matriarch of
the Rubio family.

Chapter 11.   A LAWSUIT AND FAMILY TROUBLES

1. Title Book 17, Power and Hewetson, Refugio Colony, Spanish Archives,
General Land Office, Austin, Texas.

2. Mary V. O'Connor, et al., to Thomas O'Connor, Jr., Vol. U: 174 et. seq.
of Deed Records of Refugio County, Texas.

3. The James Bray map of 1834 may be found in Report of Applees' Brief in
Robert G. Harris, et al., v. Thomas O'Connor, et al., #4355, in the Court of Civil Ap-
peals in El Paso, Texas, filed March 6, 1944.

Chapter 12.   A BATTLE LOST; THE WAR CONTINUES

1. Thomas O'Connor Estate of July 11, 1890, Vol. P: 253–257, District
Court, Victoria County, Texas.

2. Title Book 17, Spanish Archives, General Land Office, Austin, Texas.

3. Oberste, *Texas Irish Empresrios and Their Colonies,* 235.

4. Spanish Census of Pueblo La Bahía, April 24, 1825, Nacogdoches Archives, Texas State Archives, Austin, Texas. The young Carlos shown in the home
of Clemente de la Garza was born in 1807, and the headstone on his grave confirmed that year. He was buried on March 5, 1882, in the de la Garza cemetery.
The Carlos de la Garza of this narrative was born probably in 1802, though there
are doubts because his birth certificate has never been found.

If Carlos de la Garza had been alive in 1874 through 1878 when his nephew
Antonio and niece Trinidad were being brutalized by the gunmen, the old de la
Garza *pistolero* would have protected them. Such gunmen would not have had the
upper hand in the affair as they did. And Thomas O'Connor would never have put
his land scrips on the de la Garza land in 1875 if Carlos had been living. Thus, the

Carlos de la Garza in our story must have been interred at La Bahía. My great-aunt, Eliza de la Garza, told historian Kathryn Stoner O'Connor the names of those buried along the walls of Our Lady of Loreto Chapel. Eliza got the names from her mother, Ponposa Bontan. Ponposa, a niece of Don Carlos by her marriage to Antonio de la Garza, was certainly the best qualified authority in regard to who had been buried along the walls of the old chapel.

5. State Constitution of Texas, 1876, as amended in 1954, Section #3, Notes 1 and 2.

6. *Handbook of Texas*, Vol. 1: 889–890.

7. Thomas O'Connor Estate of July 11, 1890, Vol. P: 253–257, District Court, Victoria County, Texas.

8. *Ibid.;* Regarding the Power petition, this Spanish instrument is found in Volume A: 128–130, Probate Court, Refugio County, Texas. Power mentions that it was recorded in the *Libro Becerra;* it is a transcribed record from the original and was recorded on May 12, 1840.

9. Estate of Dennis O'Connor, Volume V: 174–180, District Court, Victoria County, Texas.

10. De la Garza on jury duty, 1846–1860, Commissioner's Minutes, County Clerk's Office, Refugio County, Texas.

11. See Vol. 108, Records Division, Spanish Archives, General Land Office for the land scrips of Swisher, Sloan, and Cross and their final disposition.

12. Vol. O: 129, 152, #66, Probate Court, Refugio County, Texas.

13. After Antonia Cruz de la Garza leased her 2,214 acres to E. P. Upton, there was never any further mention of these two individuals in the records in regard to those lands. How Upton disposed of the land (if indeed he did) remains a mystery. The 1870 Census of Refugio County revels that E. P. Upton was Refugio County judge, truly of the powerful elite in the area.

Bibliography

Books

Bancroft, Hubert Howe. *History of the North Mexican States and Texas*. 2 vols. San Francisco: A. L. Bancroft and Co., 1883; and The History Company, 1889.

Barker, Eugene C. Ed. *The Austin Papers*. Vol. 2. Washington, D. C.: 1924.

————. *The Life of Stephen F. Austin*. Nashville and Dallas: Cokesbury Press, 1925.

Brown, John Henry. *History of Texas from 1685 to 1892*. St. Louis: L. E. Daniell, 1892.

De Leon, Arnoldo. *They Called Them Greasers: Anglo Attitudes Towards Mexicans in Texas, 1821–1900*. Austin: University of Texas Press, 1983.

Dobie, J. Frank. *A Vaquero of the Brush Country*. Dallas: The Southwest Press, 1929.

Huson, Hobart. *Refugio: A Comprehensive History of Refugio County From Aboriginal Times to 1953*. 2 vols. Woodsboro, Texas: Rooke Foundation, 1953–1955.

————. *Captain Phillip Dimmitt's Commandancy of Goliad, 1835–1836*. Austin: Von Boeckmann-Jones Co., 1974.

Gammel, H. P. N. *Laws and Decrees of the State of Coahuila and Texas*. Austin: Gammel Book Company, 1898.

Kimball, J. P. *Laws and Decrees of the State of Coahuila and Texas in Spanish and English*. Houston: Telegraph Power Press, 1839.

Nance, Joseph Milton. *Attack and Counterattack: The Texas-Mexican Frontier, 1842*. Austin: University of Texas Press, 1964.

Oberste, Father William H. *History of Refugio Mission*. Refugio: Timely Remarks, 1942.

————. *Texas-Irish Empresarios and Their Colonies*. Austin: Von Boeckmann-Jones Co., 1953.

O'Connor, Kathyrn Stoner. *Presidio La Bahía Del Espíritu Santo, De Zuniga, 1721–1846*. Austin: Von Boeckmann-Jones Co., 1966.

Webb, Walter Prescott. Ed. *The Handbook of Texas*. 2 vols. Austin: Texas State Historical Association, 1952.

————. *The Texas Rangers: A Century of Frontier Defense*. Boston and New York: Houghton Mifflin Co., The Riverside Press, Cambridge, 1935. Reprint. Austin: University of Texas Press, 1982.

Yoakum, Henderson. *History of Texas From its First Settlement in 1685 to its Annexation to the United States in 1846*. New York: Redfield, 1856.

Manuscript Collections

Baptismal Records. Our Lady of Refugio Parish. Refugio, Texas.

Baptismal Registry. Vol. 2. Catholic Archives of Texas. Catholic Diocese, Austin, Texas.

Becerra, Manuel. Diary. Spanish Collection. General Land Office, Austin, Texas.

Deed Records. Probate Court. Goliad County, Texas.

Deed Records. Probate Court. Refugio County, Texas.

Deed Records. Probate Court. Victoria County, Texas.

Maps of Refugio County, Texas. Records Section. Spanish Collection. General Land Office, Austin, Texas.

Munoz, Governor Manuel. Report of Foreigners Residing in the Towns and Settlements in the Province of Texas, May 21, 1792. Nacogdoches Archives. Archives Division, Texas State Library, Austin, Texas.

Power and Hewetson Collection, 1824–1835. Bexar Archives. Originals in the Barker Texas History Center, University of Texas, Austin, Texas.

Rolls 162–163. Activities of Manuel Becerra. Bexar Archives, 1822–1836. Originals in the Barker Texas History Center, University of Texas, Austin, Texas.

Tax Records. State Comptroller of Public Accounts. Tax Section. Austin, Texas.

Periodical Articles

"The Austin Journal." *Southwestern Historical Quarterly* (quarterly of Texas State Historical Association) 7: 296–298.

Unpublished Spanish and Mexican Censuses

Mexican Census of Pueblo La Bahía, April 24, 1825. Nacogdoches Archives. Archives Division, Texas State Library, Austin, Texas.

Spanish Census of La Bahía Del Espíritu Santo. December 31, 1804. Nacogdoches Archives. Archives Division, Texas State Library, Austin, Texas.

Spanish Census of La Bahía and Refugio Missions, 1809, dated January 4, 1810. Bexar County Archives. Roll #43 Microfilm. Spanish Archives. Bexar County Courthouse, San Antonio, Texas.

Spanish Census of La Bahía Del Espíritu Santo, June 10, 1815. Saltillo Archives. State of Coahuila, Mexico. Copy in author's possession but not used in this narrative.

Ponposa Bontan de la Garza — Wife of the crusty ranchero, *Antonio de la Garza.*

Antonio de la Garza, ca. 1920 — The last male heir of Manuel Becerra to occupy Rancho Alamito lands. He insisted until his death that he had rightful ownership to over 8,000 acres in Refugio County.

*Francisca de la Garza, ca. 1910 —
Wife of Juan Rubio and grandmother of
the author.*

*Paula Lozano de Martinez, 1871–
1955 — Mother of Don Plácido Martinez. As a little girl she witnessed the
dispossession of the de la Garzas in Refugio County in 1877–78.*

Ismael de la Garza, the pistolero, *as a young man, ca. 1901.*

Daniel Rubio — A grandson of Antonio. With his brother, Tomás, he helped to guide the author to a discovery of their family's fateful past.

Tomás Rubio — A grandson of Antonio. Tomás related many stories about the family's dispossession of land as told him by his grandfather.

State of Texas
County of Refugio } Resurvey for the Heir
of Emanuel Becerral two leagues of land.
Situated on Copano Creek. About 12 Miles
East of the Mission of Refugio being the qua-
ntity of land to which he is entitled, by virtue
of a Deed from the Government of Mexico,
Begining at four Cotton wood trees in
the bed of Cottonwood branch, a tributary
of Copano Creek

at Set post in Mound for the S.W.
Thence S 81½ E at 2100 vrs. Cross
Copano Creek runing S 39° W. at 10000 vrs
Set post in Mound from which a bunch
of Musquite beans S 83° W 420 vrs also a
Mot beans N 20 E 2000 vrs, a
Thence N 9° E at 5000 vrs. Set-
post in Mound for the N.E. Corner
Thence N 10 W at 7150 vrs Cross
runing S 10 E at 10000 vrs to place of
begining. Record Book A page 26
Surveyed on the 12th & 13th March
1849
John De La Garza a
William Reid } c   } and Snively
District Surveyor
District of Refugio

1849 resurvey of Manuel Becerra grant. Note the plat at the juncture of the creeks.

I David Snively do Solmnly declare
under the oath of my office that the limits
Boundaries and Corners, of this Survey with
the marks Natural, and Artificial are truly
Discribed; in the foregoing plot and a field notes
And furthermore do Certify that I have
Examined Said field notes And find them
Correct, And the Surveys made according
to law Given at Refugio this 14th day of
March 1849

David Snively
District Surveyor
District of Refugio

Second page of 1849 resurvey of the Manuel Becerra grant.

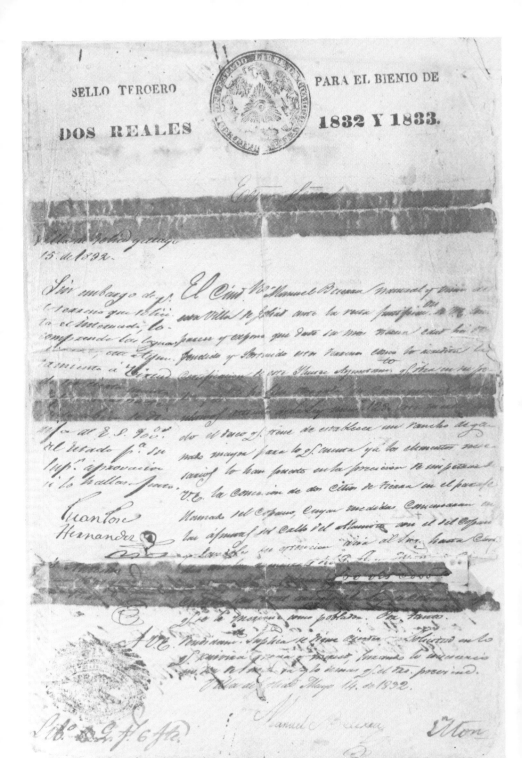

Land grant petition of Manuel Becerra, 1832.

Second page of Manuel Becerra land grant petition with signature of Governor Francisco Vidaurri, 1834, and certification of W. McFarland, 1853.

SELLO TERCERO

PARA EL BIENIO DE

DOS REALES

1832 Y 1833.

Back page of Becerra petition with recording fee.

Refugio County map, August 1896, with location of grant outlined.

The author as a young Marine.

INDEX

217

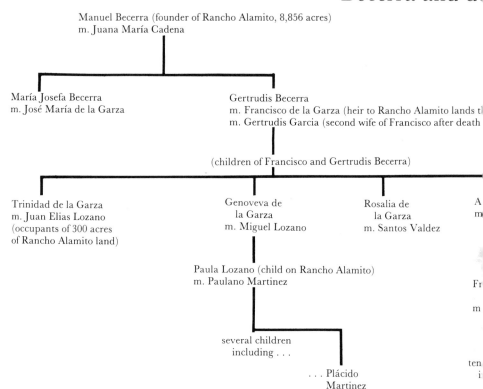

Genealo
Becerra and d

Manuel Becerra (founder of Rancho Alamito, 8,856 acres)
m. Juana María Cadena

María Josefa Becerra
m. José María de la Garza

Gertrudis Becerra
m. Francisco de la Garza (heir to Rancho Alamito lands t
m. Gertrudis Garcia (second wife of Francisco after death

(children of Francisco and Gertrudis Becerra)

Trinidad de la Garza
m. Juan Elias Lozano
(occupants of 300 acres
of Rancho Alamito land)

Genoveva de
la Garza
m. Miguel Lozano

Rosalia de
la Garza
m. Santos Valdez

A
m

Paula Lozano (child on Rancho Alamito)
m. Paulano Martinez

Fr

m

several children
including . . .

. . . Plácido
Martinez

ten
i

Guill
m. Es